WHY THE LEAFS SUCK AND HOW THEY CAN BE FIXED

AL STRACHAN

Collins

First edition

Published by Collins, an imprint of HarperCollins Publishers Ltd

All photos © Toronto Sun Media Inc.

HarperCollins books may be purchased for educational, business, or sales promotional
use through our Special Markets Department.

HarperCollins Publishers Ltd
2 Bloor Street East, 20th Floor
Toronto, Ontario, Canada
M4W 1A8

www.harpercollins.ca

Library and Archives Canada Cataloguing in Publication
Strachan, Al
Why the Leafs suck and how can they be fixed / Al Strachan.

ISBN 978-1-55468-546-2

1. Toronto Maple Leafs (Hockey team)–History. I. Title.
GV848.T6S73 2009   796.962'6409713541   C2009-903160-4

Printed and bound in Canada
9 8 7 6 5 4 3 2 1

For Andrew and Ian

Contents

Foreword

The gap between us, I would always have thought, was at least the distance between Lenin and Genghis Khan, Willie and Ozzie Nelson, Donald Brashear and Pavel Datsyuk.

If Al Strachan and I ever ended up playing for the same hockey team—and a couple of times we sort of did, as I dressed for the Canadian media in the annual Canada–U.S.A. slaughter during All-Star weekends, while Al variously baited opposition players from behind the bench and exhorted us Canadian players to "run up the score"—I'd be left wing, he'd be right, I'd be floating up near the blue line waiting to cherry pick, he'd be catching someone with his head down and parking him somewhere into next week.

Friends? Not very likely . . .

I first encountered "Strach," as everyone calls him, in print—as a sports reporter for the Montreal *Gazette,* then a sports reporter and columnist with *The Globe and Mail* out of Toronto. On the page, he was sharp, tough, accurate and challenging. If he had a bone to pick, he used a lance to pick it. No shying away; no backing down; no apologies. And he knew the game, something that cannot always be said about those who make their living explaining sports events to those who can read.

Getting to know him as a person took some time, as I was in magazines when he was first in newspapers and then in Ottawa when he was in Toronto. I covered the Ottawa Senators when he was covering the Maple Leafs, which was a bit like being imbedded with the Lancasters and the Yorks during the Wars of the Roses—a bitter conflict Strach, I could not possibly know then, could likely have discoursed knowingly about while those about him scratched their heads in wonder. How does he know these things?

When I did get to know him well was, much to my shock, during the modern NHL's first lockout, the shutting down of the league for the start of the 1994–95 season. I knew, as everyone did, that Strach had long had a friendly relationship with the game's biggest star, Wayne Gretzky, and when word began spreading that Gretzky and some of his hockey pals were planning a barnstorming tour of Europe to put in the time, Strach called to suggest I come along. It was both a generous suggestion and a welcome one, as I was desperate myself for something to write about in the *Ottawa Citizen* sports pages. The paper agreed and off we all went, flying out of Detroit, on one of the greatest sports jaunts in hockey history.

I got to know an entirely new Al Strachan on that trip. Not just that he's eccentric enough to pour his beer from one glass to another endlessly—"Gets rid of the gas," he claims, patting back a burp—but that he is erudite, widely read, bright and extremely funny. Thanks to Strach and his long-time pal Tony Gallagher of the Vancouver *Province,* I found myself daily in stitches. Strach has one of the most irreverent, wicked—and totally politically incorrect—senses of humour that law currently permits. I found myself laughing, uproariously, at things in other years I might have marched against.

Take this wicked sense of humour, and this astounding under-standing of the game, and you have the perfect author for *Why the Leafs Suck*. Strach was there during the Monty Pythonesque Ballard years, there during the dreary decades that followed—and is still there for the "New Age" Leafs of general manager Brian Burke and coach Ron Wilson. They won't like what they read. But then, Strach has always written for his readers, not his sub-jects—again, something that separates him from the pack.

If you've ever been to a circus, think of Strach as the guy in the black top hat and red tailcoats, smiling deviously as he snaps his whip from centre stage.

And take this book for what it is: a three-ring delight, certain to thrill, guaranteed to amuse, sure to infuriate and impossible to put down.

While it may drive some Leaf fans to drink who aren't already there, I predict sales through the roof in Ottawa.

And embraced, as well, in every other place where the true joys of the great game are appreciated—from loving the manner of play to laughing at the main players.

—Roy MacGregor

Introduction

"Are you trying to get me to totally disown you?" asked my son Andrew.

Andrew is thirty-one, and for as many of those thirty-one years as he has been capable of forming a comprehensive thought, he has been a fan of the Toronto Maple Leafs.

When the Leafs lost the seventh game of the Western Conference semifinal to the Los Angeles Kings in 1993, he locked himself in his room and refused to talk to me, as if I deserved the blame. After all, I counted Wayne Gretzky among my friends, and Gretzky had single-handedly eviscerated the Leafs, so who else's fault could it be? Surely the Leafs themselves couldn't be responsible for the loss.

Over the years, I managed to convince Andrew that I neither liked nor disliked the Leafs. Most of their players were good guys, but the closer you got to the top of the organization, the less enjoyable the experience of dealing with them tended to be.

I pointed out that I had pretty much the same relationship with all the other teams in the National Hockey League. NHL players are, for the most part, articulate, accessible and accommodating. I had an affinity for certain players, but not for any specific team.

Even so, when Andrew learned that I was writing a book entitled *Why the Leafs Suck,* the revelation did not go over particularly well.

He's like millions of Leafs fans. To him—and to them—there is only one team that matters. They are the members of Leafs Nation. They bleed blue and white. They wear the gear. They get the tattoos. Leafs fans they were born, Leafs fans they will die.

You have to admire their devotion to their team and their dedication to the cause. If you suggest to them that maybe the tattoo wasn't such a good idea because affinities to sports teams can change over the years, they look at you with undisguised horror. "I'll *always* be a Leafs fan," they say.

And really, it is for them that I wrote this book. They deserve better and perhaps, if they're aware of some of the history of this team and are given clear evidence of the shoddy manner in which they've been treated by this organization, they might be able to see through the corporate misinformation that is routinely shovelled onto them, and thereby be better positioned to demand improvement.

When I was writing newspaper columns in Toronto, people would often suggest that because I ridiculed the way the Leafs operated, or because I berated the organization for yet another ill-advised decision, I was biased against the team. That wasn't the case. It is the job of columnists to point out the foibles, and when you get right down to it, that puts us on the side of the fans.

We don't do it because we're for or against a specific team, but because it is our duty to use the special access we are given and the inside information we acquire to apprise the fans of a situation that might otherwise be kept from their view.

The word *media* is Latin in origin. It means "in the middle." The media are in the middle, between the fans and the organization. It's not reasonable to expect a team to grant dressing-room access to every fan, or for the players to answer every fan's questions. Instead, a middleman is used—a media person.

And if you've been accorded that responsibility, is it fair to the fans that you're supposed to represent to then mislead them? Should the media join the team's attempts to paint everything it does in a favourable light? Should they become an extension of the team's public-relations department?

It was always my belief that you should be as honest as possible. It gets you respect from a lot of people, but it gets you disliked by many others. It must be admitted that by being honest, you can lose some contacts, and in the long run, that makes the job more difficult.

But at least you can feel confident that you've done your duty to the fans and that if they then think you're somehow biased against their team, you can absorb their abuse with a clear conscience, secure in the knowledge that you've told the truth as you know it. If that is then interpreted by some to be a bias, so be it.

This book follows those principles. It will no doubt infuriate a lot of people. It will confirm the suspicions of many others. I certainly hope that it doesn't get me disowned by my elder son. Instead, I hope that it shows Leafs fans how they have been mistreated by this team over the years—and more importantly, how it can all be changed.

1

Still Hazy After All These Years

If the coach can't hire good assistants, fill out a lineup sheet properly or even make sure he has enough players available to ice a full roster, what are the team's chances? Yet the man who was guilty in each case was probably the best coach the Leafs had put behind the bench in thirty years.

It was early in the 2000–01 season when the coach of the day, Pat Quinn, decided that, much as it went against the grain of his hockey philosophy, his team would have to learn how to employ a trap.

In its basic form, the trap is easily established. You just line up your three forwards like a picket fence, so that an opponent trying to carry the puck out of his own end is forced to head towards the boards. Once he gets there, he's trapped, hence the name. The defenders swoop in on him and take the puck.

Quinn was an old-line coach, a fact that in many ways was to his credit. But the Leafs were already thirty-three years into their Stanley Cup drought and by this time, coaches in the National Hockey League had evolved into a sub-species that bore no resemblance whatsoever to the type of coaches who had populated the game when Quinn first went behind the bench.

Unfortunately, the trap, a strategy used to force turnovers in the neutral zone, was a favourite ploy of new-line coaches. And if both teams have as their primary aim the creation of a turnover in the neutral zone, you can imagine how much excitement the game produced: virtually none.

Nevertheless, Quinn figured that if his team managed to get a lead—which it occasionally did—it could use the trap to prevent the other team from catching up.

Since twenty-eight of the other twenty-nine teams in the league were employing this tactic, this was not an unreasonable stance. Even the Edmonton Oilers, the one other team that had rigidly held out against any concession to the skill-killing trap strategy, had started using a diluted version.

So Quinn sent out his assistant coach, Rick Ley, to teach the boys in blue how to set up a trap.

A bit of background here: Ley and Quinn were the closest of friends, and their wives were every bit as close, having been sorority sisters. Wherever Quinn got a job, Ley, like Mary's little lamb, followed close behind. Unfortunately for Toronto fans of the day, the lamb would probably have done a better job than Ley.

The players had no respect for Ley whatsoever, and when they found out that Quinn had taken the day off and that Ley would actually be trying to pretend that he had a clue about the modern-day game, it was time for some fun.

So Ley told the forwards to set up a simple trap formation and they'd practise it. According to the players on the ice at the time, it was goaltender Glenn Healy, one of those irrepressible imps who loves nothing better than to stir up trouble, who gave Ley his first problem.

"What if they go hard D to D?" he asked. Translation to English: What if the defenceman who is carrying the puck fires a hard pass across the ice to the other defenceman? Now you've got your picket fence set up in the wrong direction.

Ley paused for thought. This was an unforeseen complication.

Gary Roberts, another agitator of the first order, quickly realized what was happening. He suggested that in the case of the counter-strategy Healy had suggested, the off-side winger has to go over. "Right, Rick?" he added.

Ley was still trying to form a response when another player—no one can remember who—joined the chorus.

"No, no," he said. "It has to be the centre. He has to go and then the winger goes over to cover for him."

This was the cue for everyone else to join in. Most of the players on the ice were arguing about the suitable strategy—not necessarily in English—and demanding that Ley settle the matter with some sort of definitive pronouncement. True to form, Ley issued the final word.

"Pat will be back tomorrow," he said. "He'll teach you the trap then."

This kind of ineptitude from the Quinn–Ley tandem was certainly not an isolated incident. Take, for instance, the 2002 playoff series against the New York Islanders.

In game five, with the series tied, the referee headed for the Leafs' bench at the first stoppage. The lineup sheet submitted by the Leafs showed the name of Mikael Renberg. But Renberg was injured at the time. It did not show the name of Robert Reichel, who was sitting on the bench.

As a result, Reichel was tossed from the game and the Leafs had to play with only nineteen men.

Oh well. They're both Europeans. Both their surnames begin with R. What the heck?

The reaction on the Leafs bench was mixed. Interestingly, none of the players exhibited any shock. Why should they? They knew Quinn and Ley very well.

A couple of players lowered their heads so that the TV cameras wouldn't see them giggling. Alex Mogilny rolled his eyes. A couple gave fist pumps below the sight line because Reichel was universally despised. More than one said something along the lines of, "Great. That's the best thing that could have happened."

They felt that way because with Mats Sundin already out of the lineup with an injury, Quinn would now have to use Alyn McCauley as his top-line centre—which was where his peers felt he should be, even though Quinn had been using him on the third or fourth line.

After all, if Quinn had used McCauley, with his fourth-line salary, on the second line, then he'd have to put Reichel—with his exorbitant and unjustified second-line salary—on the fourth line. That would be an embarrassment to the GM, and since Quinn was the GM, coach Quinn wasn't about to do that. Saving face is more important than winning games.

There wasn't much face to be saved about the submission of the incorrect lineup sheet, however. On teams run by capable people, there's a clear process for creating a lineup sheet. An initial list is drawn up. Then another list is written on a separate sheet and the two are checked against each other. An assistant coach then checks the official sheet for accuracy, and on many teams, the trainer also checks it just to make sure that the sweater numbers are correct.

The sweater numbers are irrelevant—it's the names that count. But if there's a wrong number, it might indicate a mistake elsewhere.

In the Leafs' case, it was Ley's job to draw up the sheet, and Quinn then checked it. So here we have two professional hockey coaches who can't tell the difference between an injured Swede and a healthy Czech. On their own roster. In the playoffs.

But as if that gaffe weren't bad enough in itself, this was the second successive game that the Leafs had been forced to play with nineteen men. On the previous occasion, both Renberg and Sundin had to be scratched not long before game time, leaving the team a player short. Quinn begrudgingly accepted the blame—not that anyone else could possibly be at fault—although he did suggest that the people who drew up the NHL's collective bargaining agreement were at least partly responsible. He explained that he had no reserves in place because he thought he'd have an extra player.

Why he would think that is not clear. Ever since the opening game of the series, there had been speculation that Sundin had a broken bone in his wrist—for the very logical reason that he had a broken bone in his wrist. Renberg had been in and out of the lineup for weeks.

In fact, Quinn was lucky he wasn't down *three* men. Both Gary Roberts and Shayne Corson were playing despite nagging injuries. And yet Quinn had no one extra available, he said, because he didn't want to use up his quota of call-ups from the St. John's farm team. Damn those CBA guys.

Those are only two stories from the Quinn–Ley era, but they typify what went on during those years and, to a large part, what also went on before and after. People in key positions in the Maple Leafs organization were rarely hired for their competence. They were hired because they were someone's friend, because they happened to be hanging around at the right time, because their services could be acquired cheaply, or sometimes, just because of a passing whim that crossed the mind of someone who owned a share of the team.

And when it comes to assuming the blame, it was fairly clear that Quinn wouldn't be rushing to the front of the line. When he was fired from the Vancouver Canucks, a reporter caught up to him at the airport and asked him about the fact that he was leaving behind a ravaged organization. "Surely you're not blaming that on me?" responded Quinn.

Let's see now: Quinn had not only been the coach, he had been the general manager and president. Just who did he expect people to blame? It must be those damned trainers who can't get anything right.

The Toronto Maple Leafs are an iconic organization. They are one of the National Hockey League's original six teams, and for almost a century, rabid fans from coast to coast in Canada—and even around the world—have supported them slavishly.

But from the time they won their last Stanley Cup in 1967, they have never been operated in a manner that any impartial observer would consider to be suitable for such a high-profile organization. Had the people at the top been anywhere near as professional as the people on the ice, this team would not be looking at such a lengthy Stanley Cup drought. The Leafs wouldn't have won the Cup every year, but at least there would have been the occasional parade down Yonge Street.

Look at the Leafs' traditional rivals, the Montreal Canadiens. Since that watershed year of 1967, the Canadiens have won no fewer than ten Stanley Cups. As Montreal mayor Jean Drapeau once famously announced after yet another Canadiens triumph, "The Stanley Cup parade will follow its usual route."

In Toronto, meanwhile, fans could only hang their heads and, if they were old enough, remember that when that 1967 Stanley Cup was hoisted, it represented a sharing of the honours by the game's two greatest franchises. At that point, both of Canada's franchises had won the Cup thirteen times since the NHL's inception.

But after that, the Leafs degenerated into a laughingstock, while the Canadiens went on to forge yet another dynasty and create what many observers feel was the most dominant team of all time, the 1976–77 Stanley Cup winners. Naturally, a team from that era could not hold its own against one of today's top teams, but using the not-unreasonable comparison of that team to the others in the league at the time, it may have been the best ever. It lost eight games in an eighty-game season, and only one at home.

Why were the Canadiens able to maintain their dominance while the Leafs sank into virtual oblivion? It all starts at the top.

It's no great mystery. Look at the companies that dominated American industry in its glory days of the early twentieth century, and look at the men who ran them: John D. Rockefeller, Henry Ford, Andrew Carnegie, J. P. Morgan. Look at the great military victories that changed the course of world history; all were commanded by men with strong personalities who were great leaders. Each had a vision and acted upon it. At no point in the Leafs' post-1967 evolution has there ever been anyone at the top who could be described as either a strong leader or a man of vision.

No wonder the team has never found success. Other than some vague notion of filling their pockets, the people who were running the team didn't have the slightest idea what they wanted from it. And if there's no guidance from the top, you'd have to be awfully lucky to end up with employees who know what they're doing.

At one point, the Leafs almost did get that lucky. They almost did manage to stumble onto the pot of gold. For a while, they had Cliff Fletcher as general manager, and had he been allowed to go his own way, it is not at all unlikely that Fletcher would have ended the Stanley Cup drought.

But again, it came down to ineptitude at the top. The owner of the day, Steve Stavro, searching for a scapegoat to cover his own shortcomings, fired Fletcher, and the team returned to its usual state, drifting along without direction.

The post-1967 Canadiens, on the other hand, were initially run by experienced businessmen who insisted on excellence throughout the organization. The Leafs were run by a penny-pinching curmudgeon who had no experience as an administrator and had become wealthy not by his own expertise but by winning the gene pool. His father had been a wealthy industrialist who had made much of his money by manufacturing and sharpening tube skates, the state-of-the-art model in those days.

In any competitive situation, leadership makes the difference. In the Canadiens' case—and in the case of most of the other teams that have won Stanley Cups while the Leafs and their fans looked on enviously—the guidance came from above. The executives at the top selected the next level of executives carefully, demanding dedication, devotion, experience and a long list of qualifications. Those people in turn imposed the same standards in making their own selections, and so it went down the line.

In Toronto, Harold Ballard, a convicted felon who served time in the penitentiary after being found guilty of forty-seven counts of fraud, hired and fired general managers on a whim. Not that it mattered an awful lot. Most of those general managers were emasculated by Ballard anyway. Whereas a competent organization would allow its GM to hire and fire coaches, in Toronto, as often as not, it was Ballard himself who did the job.

So through the years, the rot set into the Toronto organization and it permeated the structure so completely that it was far too ingrained to disappear when Ballard died. In theory, there were procedures in place that would execute the transition of ownership from Ballard to his successors. But like everything else to which Ballard had put his hand over the years, it was a flawed system that led only to more turmoil.

From Ballard, to a committee of short-term caretakers, to Steve Stavro, to Maple Leafs Sports and Entertainment Ltd., this team has never had a single strong personality at the top.

Major Conn Smythe left the board of directors in 1966. From that time forward, the Leafs have never been run by a single chief executive who was both capable of operating a multimillion-dollar enterprise in a professional fashion and at the same time keeping in mind that this is a sports franchise. It is not an accounting firm or a law office or a supermarket or an appliance store or a pension plan. It is, above all, an entity that, without its passionate fans, its unique heritage and its highly unusual product, would have disappeared into the depths of bankruptcy decades ago.

But it has never been run by hockey people, and as we chronologically follow the course of the Leafs in the post-1967 era, we'll see it again and again. The blame always belongs at the top.

If you don't know what you're doing, yet you're running the organization, how can you possibly expect to hire people who do know what they're doing? If you yourself don't have any expertise, how can you evaluate the abilities of those you bring into the organization?

When you get right down to it, that's why the Leafs have, in the vernacular of the day, sucked. They've never been properly run.

The Man at the Top of the Team at the Bottom

Harold Ballard was a vindictive, despotic curmudgeon. And those were his good points. And he ran the Leafs like a banana republic for eighteen years. No wonder the Stanley Cup drought was underway.

Even though the Leafs are—and have been for decades—an iconic team in Canada, the era that began with Harold Ballard taking control in 1972 and ended with his death in 1990 was never anything more than a travesty.

There can be no success on the ice if the man at the top does not have the intelligence, the commitment, the foresight or the fortitude to build the kind of organization that surpasses those other organizations that do exhibit all those qualities.

For much of his tenure, Ballard was identified in the Leafs' official publications as both the president and managing director. What does a managing director do? Good question. But the only other one in the league at the time was Irving Grundman of Montreal, and he acted in the capacity of general manager.

So it's fairly clear that as far as Ballard was concerned, he was the GM, even if other pawns—like Gerry McNamara, Jim Gregory and Gord Stellick—held the title.

When John Brophy was fired as coach of the Leafs in 1988, for example, Stellick held the title of general manager. But in reality, it was Ballard who did the firing, and it was Ballard who appointed George Armstrong as the replacement.

Armstrong made no secret of that fact. He walked into the dressing room to address the team before his first night behind the bench and said, "Well guys, I don't want to be doing this, but the old man says I have to. You know what it's like around here. When the old man says you have to do something, you have to do it. I don't know what else to say about it. Just go out and have some fun."

It was clear that the fifty-eight-year-old Armstrong was not referring to the thirty-one-year-old Stellick as "the old man." He meant Ballard.

The Ballard era was nothing short of a fiasco. It cheated the fans. It made a mockery of their loyalty and was a relentless embarrassment to the entire National Hockey League. Even NHL president John Ziegler, not a man known for criticizing the league's governors, was once moved to respond to one of Ballard's many outrageous statements by saying, "As is often the case, I would prefer—and I think it's better for our business—if Harold does not speak. But Harold does that."

The single most significant reason for the Leafs not having won a Stanley Cup in more than forty years is that there wasn't a hope of winning under Ballard's stewardship. No trade could be made without Ballard's involvement, and in many cases, trades were made at Ballard's insistence.

The Leafs were, for example, a team that had perennial problems on defence, problems that would have been much more acute
had the team not been in the forefront of the Swedish invasion.
The Leafs stumbled into that development when Gerry McNamara,
who was a Leafs scout at the time, went to Sweden in December
1972 to look at a goaltender. As it happened, Börje Salming was
one of the defencemen who were playing, and it was he who most
impressed McNamara. On his return to Toronto, McNamara rec-
ommended that the Leafs sign him.

The Leafs paid the Swedish Ice Hockey Federation $100,000
for the rights to both Salming and forward Inge Hammarström and
then signed them, a move that marked the real beginning of the
European invasion of the NHL.

But Ballard didn't like foreigners, so he ridiculed Hammarström, saying, "That kid could go in the corners with six eggs in his
pocket and not break one of them." Despite having stumbled in on
the ground floor, the Leafs, at Ballard's direction, stopped exploring
Swedish options.

Salming shrugged off Ballard's bombast, and even Ballard recognized his talent, but after five years of being underappreciated,
Hammarström was shipped off to St. Louis. There, he had a couple
of decent but not spectacular seasons and, never having been totally
enamoured with North American life, then went back to Sweden.
But he still loved the game and he had a good hockey mind, so he
became a scout, first for the NHL's Central Scouting Bureau, then
for the Philadelphia Flyers.

Perhaps Hammarström might have remained with the Leafs in
a scouting capacity after his playing career ended had Ballard not
made his stay in Toronto so unpleasant. Instead, during his tenure
with the Flyers, he was the guy who insisted that they draft Peter
Forsberg with the sixth-overall pick, even though Forsberg was
rated by most scouts as deserving of selection only in the late first

or early second round. Forsberg went on to win the Hart Trophy as the league's most valuable player.

It's also fair to say that the Leafs' defensive problems might not have been so pronounced had they not packaged a young defence-man along with useful forward George Ferguson and traded them to Pittsburgh for journeyman defenceman Dave Burrows in 1978.

Burrows played a little more than two seasons for the Leafs, scoring five goals, before he was traded back to the Penguins, along with high-scoring forward Paul Gardner, for Kim Davis and Paul Marshall.

Combined, Davis and Marshall played twenty-five games for the Leafs and notched all of two goals.

The young defenceman? It was Randy Carlyle, who went on to win the Norris Trophy. No Leafs player has ever won the Norris Trophy.

Let's recap this series of deals. The Leafs gave up a Norris Tro-phy winner (Carlyle) and two high-scoring forwards (Gardner and Ferguson) in return for seven goals. And you wonder why they were so bad for so long?

There is another important reason for the Leafs' lengthy drought. The effects of an extended reign of error such as the one inflicted by Ballard cannot be eradicated overnight. The Ballard era lasted eighteen years, but its impact was still being felt well past his death and in some ways is still being felt today.

The situation is not unlike that of a country that has suffered under a despotic regime for decades. When democracy finally arrives, it takes many years before all the ingrained ills that were once a part of that society are expelled.

If we were to go through every mistake that Ballard made, every impropriety that he committed, every insult to the long-suffering fans that he inflicted, this book would make *War and Peace* look like a Post-It note.

When I first met Ballard, I was living in Montreal and covering the Canadiens, so he didn't despise me as much as he did all the younger Toronto-based writers—or as much as he came to despise me once I moved to Toronto and started working for *The Globe and Mail*.

In a roundabout way, it was because of Ballard that I got that job. Two *Globe and Mail* hockey writers, Lawrence Martin and Don Ramsay, had already angered Ballard to the point that they were not allowed anywhere near the team.

The Globe and Mail asked me to fly to Toronto for an interview and to bring along some clippings of stories I'd done for the Montreal *Gazette*. I got offered the job of Leafs beat writer but turned it down because I took the same general tack as Martin and Ramsay. That being the case, it seemed it would only be a matter of a couple of weeks until I too was banned. Then what?

But not long before that, Scott Young, one of *The Globe and Mail*'s two general sports columnists, had resigned as a protest against an evolving type of sports journalism—now the norm—which put the fans' concerns ahead of those of the teams. Because *The Globe and Mail*'s people liked what they saw in the clippings, they offered me Young's former job as a columnist, and I took it.

One of those clippings had to do with an evening out with Ballard at a posh resort in Key Largo, Florida. This occurred during the merger negotiations between the National Hockey League and the upstart World Hockey Association that dragged on through the second half of the 1970s.

Ballard was the most outspoken critic of any merger negotiations. "The idea is ridiculous," he said at one point. "If you run an appliance store and somebody comes along and steals all your washing machines, would you buy them back off him? That's what this thing boils down to."

One of the prime proponents of the opposite point of view was

Ed Snider, owner of the Philadelphia Flyers. It was his contention that the bidding war for players was costing the NHL much more than the cost of a settlement. While a merger might be distasteful, it was a sound course of action from an economic point of view.

When the merger finally was effected, Snider talked about the battle he had endured. "We've had people resist things for strange reasons," he said, in a clear reference to Ballard. "I didn't think anybody would resist a merger of the NHL and WHA because it was costing us a bloody fortune and everybody was losing. I led that fight, but it took me seven years.

"I thought it would be like a cakewalk when we had them wanting to come in in the very first year. We could have walked away with $5 million to $6 million a club and no losses. I don't know how other people's minds work."

It was this eminently sensible stance that earned him Ballard's enmity. At one of the merger meetings in 1977, a small fire had broken out in Ballard's hotel. "I wish Snider had been with me," he said. "I could have thrown gasoline on him."

During the dinner in Key Largo, Ballard elevated the level of vitriol considerably. As we sat at our table, Snider, who is Jewish, walked in with friends. Looking in the general direction of the kitchen, Ballard shouted to no one in particular, "Warm up an oven back there for Snider, will you?"

Snider ignored Ballard and sat down a few tables away. It wasn't far enough. One by one, Ballard took the rolls out of the bread basket and threw them at Snider.

Just in case anyone thinks this was a one-time incident, it should be made clear that Ballard also banned player agent Norman Kaplan from Maple Leafs Gardens because he, too, was Jewish. "I don't want any goddam Indians in my building," said Ballard, using one of his favourite euphemisms. The security people were called to usher Kaplan off the premises.

When we refer to security people, we should clarify that no one in Maple Leaf Gardens was hired to provide security. Ballard was far too cheap for that. But there were a few maintenance workers in the building, and as far as Ballard was concerned, it was their duty to respond to his whims. In fact, in later years, it also became their duty to take his dog for a walk and to clean up after it.

Ballard had other targets. Just prior to leaving for that Key Largo dinner, he received a written message from the hotel switchboard. The producers of *As It Happens,* a daily public-affairs radio show hosted by Barbara Frum for the Canadian Broadcasting Corporation, were offering Ballard $50 to go on the air. He crumpled up the message slip and threw it away. "It's worth $50 to me to stay away from that woman," he grumbled.

During an earlier telephone interview on *As It Happens,* Frum had interrupted Ballard, and that had angered him. He told her that people like her were good only when they were "on their back" and hung up the telephone. Frum had subsequently written an open letter to the *Toronto Star* suggesting that perhaps Ballard was under too much pressure because he was running both the Leafs and the Hamilton Tiger-Cats of the Canadian Football League.

"The Maple Leafs don't bother me," responded Ballard. "The Tiger-Cats don't bother me. Only ugly broads bother me, and if she looks in a mirror, she'll know what I mean."

Ballard didn't like John Ziegler, either.

Ziegler was the president of the NHL at the time, and Ballard took great delight in making his life miserable. He routinely referred to him as "that little shrimp" in media interviews and steadfastly refused to follow any league directive that he didn't like.

In 1978, for instance, when he was told that he had to put the players' names on the backs of their sweaters, he refused. Despite being the recipient of a torrent of abuse delivered by Ballard to the Toronto media, Ziegler insisted that Ballard conform to the directive.

Eventually, Ballard did. The requisite letters were sewn onto the jerseys. But they were blue letters on a blue background.

Ballard's apologists have painted him as a fun-loving imp whose only sin was that he enjoyed deflating a few egos. That description falls far short of the mark. He was, in fact, a miserable, vindictive man who routinely trampled roughshod over the sensibilities of those unfortunate enough to have to deal with him.

Coach Roger Neilson, for instance, was so dedicated to his work that when the team was on the road, he would spend the non-game evenings in his hotel room watching videotapes of the Leafs' previous performances. On one occasion, Ballard hired a prostitute and sent her up to Neilson's hotel room to see if she could distract him. She couldn't. Then Ballard told all his media pals about it and implied Neilson was a homosexual. He wasn't.

Ballard insisted on evening departures when the team had to play a road game the next day. That way, he didn't have to pay the daily meal allowance that was mandated by the league. As far as he was concerned, the team's road results were secondary to his profit margin.

He rarely had the courage to fire anyone face to face. They knew they had lost their job when they arrived at Maple Leaf Gardens to find that their parking spot no longer existed.

In 1985, Stan Obodiac, the Leafs media-relations man for twenty-six years (twenty-six extremely underpaid years) died. The day after the funeral, Obodiac's wife was awakened by a Ballard emissary who had been sent to pick up the company car. In his defence, Ballard pointed out that he had given Obodiac a plane ticket to Hawaii when he was dying. Indeed he had, but the ticket was almost certainly part of a contra deal and therefore free. Furthermore, it was for Obodiac only, and since Ballard paid him so poorly, he couldn't afford to go with his wife.

3

If a Good Idea Doesn't Bear Fruit, Never Have Another One

In his eighteen years at the helm, Ballard had one good idea. If he had two, it's hard to think what the second might have been. But because of his penny-pinching, his duplicity and his firm belief that everyone was as much of a cheat as he was, that one good idea came to naught.

In the summer of 1979, it finally dawned on Ballard that there was a common thread binding together the better teams of the National Hockey League.

There's more to building a team than building a team. You have to build an entire organization. You have to have a good coach and a good general manager, good scouts and good administrators. You also have to have good ownership, but Ballard conveniently neglected to bring that point into the equation. In his typically delusional fashion, he convinced himself that he was a good owner.

But at least, for one brief period, he saw the light concerning the rest of the organization and tried to impose what would have been a significant upgrade on the two men then in place—general manager Jim Gregory and coach Roger Neilson.

In May 1979, the Montreal Canadiens had just won their fourth consecutive Stanley Cup under coach Scott Bowman. The team that had come closest to ending that streak was Boston. The Bruins, with Don Cherry behind the bench, had pushed the Canadiens to a seventh game in the semifinal, then lost when a too-many-men penalty in the dying minutes gave the Canadiens a power play upon which they capitalized. The Canadiens tied the game at 18:46 of the third period and won in overtime.

So Ballard decided that he would hire both Bowman and Cherry to run his Leafs. By an unlikely but fortuitous circumstance, both were available.

Bowman wanted to get out of Montreal because, a year earlier, his close friend and mentor Sam Pollock had turned over the managerial reins to Irving Grundman, a man Bowman did not respect. A clause in Bowman's existing four-year contract gave him a twenty-day window at the conclusion of the season in which he could opt out of the remaining years.

Cherry was in the process of being fired by Bruins general manager Harry Sinden. Their relationship had been deteriorating steadily, and when the Bruins were eliminated because of what appeared to be a coaching mistake, that was the final straw. At that point, no one had yet told Cherry he would be axed, but everyone knew it was inevitable.

Ballard was waging his usual war with many members of the Toronto media, but I was working in Montreal at the time, so he was on good terms with me.

"I'd like to get Scotty as GM and Cherry as coach," he told me. "They'd be a great combination."

The problem, of course, was that if he were to hire the two, they could probably do quite well if left to their own devices. But these were the Toronto Maple Leafs, and it was therefore inevitable that the owner would be sticking his nose into matters he didn't understand.

Ballard denied that. "I never interfere as long as they win," he insisted. "There's one way to keep me out of it and that's to put a few wins together."

This was a purely hypothetical observation on Ballard's part. Under his tenure, no team had ever won anything of note, so his purported reaction to such an occurrence was guesswork at best.

Unbeknownst to Ballard, the groundwork for the creation of this elite tandem had already been laid. At one point during the season, Bowman had approached Cherry in the Montreal Forum and sounded him out on just such an arrangement—Bowman as GM and Cherry as coach.

At the time, Bowman had Buffalo in mind as the team that would hire them, but that could be amended. Cherry was enthusiastic about the proposed arrangement. The two had great respect for one another. They had done battle as NHL coaches, but they had also worked together on the coaching staff of Team Canada during the 1976 Canada Cup tournament. Cherry told Bowman that if a deal of that nature could be worked out, he'd gladly go along.

Ballard, a notorious cheapskate, did not seem to be a likely candidate to hire these two. The bill would have been high—over $175,000 annually for Bowman and at least $100,000 for Cherry. Those were upper-level salaries at the time.

In fact, Alan Eagleson, who was Cherry's agent at the time and a constant thorn in Ballard's side, suggested that either's price would be too high for Ballard to stomach.

"Who's he to say what's too high for me?" snorted Ballard.

Like most people, Eagleson ignored Ballard's remarks, followed his own conscience and offered Cherry's services elsewhere. While Ballard dithered, the Colorado Rockies made Cherry an offer. Given Ballard's reputation, Cherry knew that no matter what kind of promises were being made, there was a distinct possibility that a change of heart was just around the corner.

"I guess I should have made him a firm offer," Ballard said. "I told Eagleson we would make Cherry a good offer and that we were interested, but I didn't give him an exact figure because I didn't want him taking it around to all the other clubs and using it as a lever."

Given the choice of a firm offer from the Rockies and a promise of interest from Ballard, Cherry took the firm offer. Ballard's habit of doing things on the cheap cost him once again.

But it was a close-run thing. Cherry had agreed to terms with general manager Ray Miron of the Rockies, but had signed nothing when Ballard finally got around to putting a number to his promise. Under those circumstances, many people, including Ballard himself, would have pulled out of the Colorado deal. But Cherry prides himself on being a man of his word. He had promised the Rockies he would take their job and that's what he would do, signature or no signature.

"I had shook hands with Ray Miron and I gave him my word," says Cherry. "Alan Eagleson called me and said he'd got a three-year contract for me with the Leafs and it was $20,000 a year more than what Colorado was offering. I said to Eagle, 'I can't do it. I shook hands on it. I can't go back on my word.'

"Then I got fired at the end of the year and everybody laughed at me."

As if admitting his own stupidity weren't enough, Ballard then decided to ridicule the Rockies and their decision to sign Cherry. "If anybody can do anything for them, he can," he said. "But I have my doubts if anybody can do anything for that team. It's a lost cause."

There was certainly a lost cause in the equation. But it wasn't the Rockies. In 1982, they moved east and became the New Jersey Devils, a franchise that subsequently won three Stanley Cups.

Now, Ballard was left with only Bowman on his wish list. "I've been working hard on this for a long time," Ballard said, "and it would be very disappointing to me if he didn't accept the offer. I had hoped to get Don Cherry as coach, and if he hadn't been so quick to go to Colorado, I think I could have worked something out there. I don't want to lose Bowman as well."

Note that the person at fault for Ballard being too cheap and indecisive to sign Cherry had now become Cherry himself.

On May 31, a Wednesday, Ballard insisted he was very much in the Bowman sweepstakes even though Buffalo, Philadelphia and Washington were also interested.

"He's going to make the decision on Monday [June 4] and let me know then," said Ballard.

That sounded good. Unfortunately, it wasn't true.

"No way," said Bowman when presented with this information. "I'm going to take all the time I can. The season ended on the twenty-first, so under my contract, I've got fourteen days from the twenty-second. That's June 4. After that, I've still got six more days. I'm not going to hurry it."

By June 5, Bowman was still thinking—as he had said he would be.

Ballard, meanwhile, was getting pensive. "He could turn this team around," he said. "We haven't won a Stanley Cup here for years."

At that point, it was only eleven years. But already, the fans were something less than contented.

"I see the way they look at me sometimes when I'm walking out of the building after a bad game," said Ballard. "They're thinking,

'Look at that crook. He should be back in Millhaven.' And the way the team plays some nights, maybe they're right."

In fact, as one fan wrote to one of the local papers when Ballard refused to acknowledge Gordie Howe's record-setting 1,000th goal as a pro, "Harold Ballard gives us ex-cons a bad name. Whose record would you rather have? Harold Ballard's or Gordie Howe's?"

As for Bowman, Ballard was not to get his wish. Bowman narrowed his list down to Montreal and Buffalo, then, as the contractual window was about to close, opted for Buffalo.

"Harold was not a businessman," explained Bowman. "He wouldn't make an offer. I was making $90,000 in Montreal and Buffalo came with an offer of $200,000 a year for five years."

As for Ballard's assertion that he had made a good offer, Bowman said, "He never talked about a new contract. He just said, 'We'll take over your old contract.'"

So another opportunity for the Leafs to join the ranks of the respectable was lost. Bowman and Cherry would have made a first-rate tandem. Instead, having lost the people who might have pointed his team in the right direction, Ballard countered by making a move that could hardly have been worse. He brought back George "Punch" Imlach, the man he had fired in 1969.

And who got the blame for Ballard's inability to sign Bowman? Bowman, of course.

"He just took my offer and played it off against everybody else," said Ballard—even though there had never been an offer.

The Leafs
Take a Giant Step
—Backwards, of Course

In the 1960s, the world underwent radical changes. But time apparently stood still in Maple Leaf Gardens. Because Punch Imlach won four Stanley Cups in the '60s, Ballard thought he could do it again in the '70s. It was a foolish decision with disastrous consequences.

With Scott Bowman having refused to take the job of general manager, it's hard to imagine a worse second choice than Punch Imlach, unless it was Ballard himself.

Theoretically, Imlach was replacing Jim Gregory as general manager, but in that organization, nothing got done without Ballard's approval. And most of it got done at Ballard's instigation.

After all, it wasn't Gregory who had spent the first part of the summer trying to acquire Cherry and Bowman. It was Ballard. And as Imlach was to find out, it wasn't Gregory who had tied his hands with a load of contracts that put the team at a disadvantage.

But in an attempt to clean up the mess he had made, Ballard called upon Imlach, who had been behind the bench when the Leafs won their last Stanley Cup in 1967. He had also won three in a row starting in 1962.

But like the rest of the world, hockey had changed a lot by 1979, and in the long list of reasons for the Leafs not having won a Stanley Cup in more than forty years, this decision and its subsequent repercussions rank right near the top of the list. It's not that Imlach's tenure was a lengthy one. It wasn't. But instead of revitalizing the team by making some key changes, Imlach laid waste to it. He didn't improve the team; he destroyed it.

Had he stopped there, the damage might not have been so bad; but Imlach also destroyed any sense of unity between the players and the management. There was no longer any mutual sense of purpose. There was only a will on Imlach's part to smash everything in his path, and an equally strong will on the part of the players to prevent him from doing so.

A battle of such magnitude doesn't end when one side claims victory. The ill will, the mistrust, the bunker mentality, the misplaced objectives all live on. Eventually, Imlach disappeared from the scene, but the animosity he had created between the two factions of the organization lasted for years and years and poisoned player–management relations for decades.

If we look closely at one year, 1979–80, his first year back, it's easy to see why his impact had such a devastating effect on the organization and why those effects did not quickly fade.

When Ballard made his desperate move after being thwarted in his attempts to sign Bowman and Cherry, he had no idea what he was about to unleash on the team.

Since Ballard tended to live in the past, his decision seemed to him to make sense. Imlach had won the Cup before. He would come back now and do it again. It was a seductive fantasy, but it fell far short of reality.

Imlach started off his despotic reign by boasting that he was about to show the players who was boss. There was a new top gun in town, he said, and anyone who didn't like it would get his head shot off.

Then he couldn't understand why the players didn't take to him.

Anyone who gets to the National Hockey League has to fight the odds all his life. At every step of the way, from the first time he wobbles along the ice, he has to prove that the players he plays against—and the players he plays with—are not as good as he is. He accepts every challenge and he wins. If he doesn't, he doesn't get to the NHL.

So when a general manager comes in and, in his first press conference, aggressively issues a challenge and basically says, "It's me against the players and I'm going to win," it should be fairly obvious what the response of the players is going to be.

Imlach made it abundantly clear that he had not the slightest intention of working with the players. He was going to clean house. He was going to crack down. He was going to impose new rules. He was going to enforce those rules. He was going to take charge. He was going to get rid of the dead wood.

The players' response was, "Oh yeah? We'll see."

Darryl Sittler told the media that he thought Imlach came in with his mind made up before he had even talked to the players. Imlach agreed. He said he didn't need to talk to the players. He had seen them in action and they weren't up to his standards.

But when he started examining the contracts, Imlach found that, despite all his bravado, the previous efforts of Gregory and Ballard—especially Ballard—had significantly reduced his options.

Imlach loathed Sittler and would have loved to have started the rebuilding process by getting rid of him. For one thing, it would create a leadership vacuum among the players, a vacuum he was hoping to fill himself. For another, it would establish Imlach as the boss. He would have exercised his power by taking the team's most popular player and shipping him out. Therefore, no one else would be safe.

But you can't trade a guy who has a no-trade clause in his contract, and that's exactly what Sittler had.

Maybe there was another way for Imlach to send a message. What about Ron Ellis? He was slowing down and near the end of his career. He had been in the league for fifteen years, and in those days, that was pretty much the maximum tenure. He was well liked by the fans as well. If Ellis were released, that might get Imlach's point across.

No dice. Ellis had a no cut clause in his contract.

And so it went.

Imlach couldn't even hope that some of the Leafs' prospects would emerge and force the veterans to play better. By this time, Ballard had cut corners so much that the entire farm system consisted of half an American Hockey League team based in Moncton, New Brunswick. And it wasn't a very good team. Had there been any NHL players there, Gregory would already have promoted them to the NHL.

Drafting a few good players was out of the question as well. The draft was later than usual that year because the NHL had just expanded to take in four teams from the World Hockey Association—Edmonton, Hartford, Quebec and Winnipeg. Most of the players on those WHA teams were available to the NHL teams, and to give the NHL general managers more time to evaluate the possibilities, the draft was pushed back a few days.

It didn't matter much to the Leafs, of course. As usual, they'd traded away picks for stiffs. And as it turned out, what picks they had left, they squandered.

Unfortunately for Imlach, this was one of the best draft crops in NHL history, but he had only one pick in the first two rounds—ninth overall. Youngsters like Rob Ramage, Ray Bourque, Rick Vaive, Mike Gartner and other future stars had already been selected by the time the Leafs' turn came.

But the powerhouse team in junior hockey that year was the Brandon Wheat Kings, and its entire top line was available. Imlach and the scouts decided they didn't like Ray Allison and narrowed their choice to either Brian Propp or Laurie Boschman.

Imlach took Boschman.

Propp got 34 goals for Philadelphia the next season. Boschman got 16 for the Leafs. In his NHL career, Boschman accumulated 577 points. Propp got 1,004.

The Leafs didn't have a second-round pick and were slated to go fifty-first overall with their third-rounder. At one point, Imlach had mused about making a deal to move up a bit and asked his scouts about Mark Messier. He was told that under the rules of the NHL–WHA merger, Messier was not available, so there was no need for the Leafs to try to select any higher.

The Edmonton Oilers, picking forty-eighth, took Messier. The scouts had got it wrong. Messier was indeed eligible. Two years later, Messier had a fifty-goal season. By that time, Imlach was no longer with the Leafs.

Before the 1979–80 season even started, Imlach showed that he was going to be true to his word. He had rightly identified Sittler as the players' leader and the fans' favourite. So if Imlach was going to establish himself as top dog, he had to take down the guy who already held the position.

The first battle was waged over a between-periods TV show, of all things. At the time, "Coach's Corner" and "The Hotstove" had not become a part of the standard *Hockey Night in Canada* telecast. Instead, a series of rather inane shows were served up, the more inoffensive the better. The Peter Puck series was one. "Showdown" was another. The latter pitted the league's stars against each other in a series of penalty shots and skating drills, and naturally enough, the players liked to take part in it. More importantly, the teams were legally committed to provide players for it. "Showdown" participation was part of the rights contract that the NHL sold to *Hockey Night in Canada*.

But Ballard didn't like "Showdown," and neither did Imlach. Ballard concocted the rather curious reasoning that he owned each player's rights and could therefore prevent him from playing for any other club. He apparently considered *Hockey Night in Canada* to be a club.

Imlach and Ballard also trotted out the theory that players could get hurt. While that was true, it was also highly unlikely. They could also get hurt flying in the decrepit Convair 640 planes that Ballard used to charter because they were cheap, but that didn't seem to worry anybody.

Naturally enough, the people who ran "Showdown" asked for Sittler's participation. He was the Leafs' most identifiable star and the Leafs were the mainstay of *Hockey Night in Canada*. Imlach called Sittler into his office and told him to turn down the invitation.

Sittler refused. That infuriated Imlach. To him, Sittler was defying management. The possibility that he himself was defying the negotiated and binding contract between the NHL and *Hockey Night in Canada* apparently never entered his mind.

Never one to take defeat gracefully, Imlach proposed to Ballard that he seek a court injunction to prevent Sittler from taking part in the show. Needless to say, the court refused to grant an injunction.

Imlach sought the injunction, he said, not to get his own way, but to give Sittler a means of saving face. Had the court forced

Sittler to stay out of "Showdown," the players couldn't see their captain as a turncoat.

It was nothing more than convoluted Imlach logic. He forced the "Showdown" showdown, so to speak. He even went to court, not a move calculated to help repair the already ruptured relationship between himself and his team.

When all his machinations collapsed around him, Imlach expressed surprise that the media took Sittler's side. But at least he now had another group to which he could allocate the blame. The media had twisted the story, he said. And his next step, of course, was to blame Sittler for poisoning their relationship.

This whole episode was typical of the Imlach approach. First, he created a scenario in which he pitted himself against the team. He drew the battle lines, putting the team on one side and himself on the other. Then he decided that Sittler was taking his stand on the other side of the line because he would lose face if he gave in to Imlach's demands.

In short order, Imlach precipitated another battle that did nothing but make an already bad situation still worse.

Prior to the opening of training camp, he drew up a list of player-conduct rules. Then he told coach Floyd Smith to post the list in the dressing room and get every player to sign it. Having the normal quota of common sense, Smith simply ignored the edict. Imlach, however, was adamant. The list had to be posted, he said, and the players had to sign it.

Most of the rules were innocuous. They required players to be on time for practice, dress appropriately and so on. Then, right at the end—as if Imlach were hoping that the players would stop reading halfway through and sign the sheet out of boredom—was one that gave the team the right to suspend or fine any player who did "anything contrary to good hockey discipline."

And who was to decide whether an act was contrary to good

hockey discipline? Curiously enough, it would be Imlach. And who was to determine the punishment? You got it. Same guy.

Not one player signed the list. What player would?

Here was a general manager who had arrived on the scene and declared war upon the players and announced he wanted to get rid of most of them. Yet they are to give him the right to determine when they've broken an unwritten rule and let him mete out the sentence?

Again, in his typical fashion, Imlach placed the blame on his players. His players in Buffalo had signed just such a list he said. And really, it was for their own good.

Does this sound familiar? It was for Sittler's good that Imlach tried for an injunction. Now it was for the players' good that they were to make Imlach legislator, judge and jury. He didn't want to spell out the rules, he said, because then if a player broke one, he'd have to say which one it was and that could embarrass the player.

The season hadn't even started, and already, there had been two major conflagrations in the player-relations area.

Once the 1979–80 season did start, the Leafs were their usual atrocious selves, so much so that Smith identified the difficulty and took a courageous stand. He found out that some of his players were playing Ping-Pong in the dressing room before going out to play hockey. Clearly, this was the reason why the Leafs were being outscored on a roughly 2–1 basis. Clearly, this was the reason that they had earned only one point in the last six games. It's an insidious affliction, that Ping-Pong.

With the kind of fortitude that has rarely been seen in the annals of professional coaching, Smith bravely banned Ping-Pong from the Leafs' dressing room.

Ironically, this was the year that the Edmonton Oilers entered the league. Within a couple of years, the Oilers were to take the NHL by storm with guys like Mark Messier, Wayne Gretzky, Paul

Coffey and a host of other future Hall of Famers. And what did the Oilers do before every game? They played Ping-Pong.

Well, not all of them. Some of them bunched up hockey tape into a ball and, in their stocking feet, played road hockey outside the dressing room. This light-hearted approach to pre-game preparations was good enough for the youngsters who were forming a dynasty, but it wasn't good enough for the sad-sack Leafs.

And so it went, with Imlach conspiring to make the rift between players and management wider and wider at every turn. In his view, it was all the players' fault. He was trying to shape them into a better team and they were resisting. He, George Imlach, knew it all, and it was his cross to bear that the players were just lazy incompetents.

Imlach had the experience of a lifetime in hockey. Compared to him, these young whippersnappers were hardly out of diapers.

Which was probably at the root of the problem. Imlach had indeed spent a lifetime in hockey, but that lifetime encompassed an era in which the coach was a dictator. It encompassed an era in which the National Hockey League had six teams. It encompassed an era in which player salaries were no higher than those of workers in other professions and were allocated without negotiation. It encompassed an era in which there was no players' union.

By 1979, that hockey world was gone. But to Imlach, who was notoriously stubborn and averse to any change in the established order, and to Ballard, who had turned to Imlach as a means of trying to hold back the tide, the old ways were the only ways.

In the old order, the players kept quiet and let their bosses do the talking. That's what Ballard and Imlach expected. But this was the new hockey order. The players had earned themselves some rights and they exercised them.

For instance, when *Hockey Night in Canada* asked for Leafs players for between-period interviews, the request wasn't always well received. After all, this was a team that was invariably in the middle of a losing streak, and players who are getting hammered night after night are often not eager to be interviewed. So over the years, the job of talking these players into coming out for an interview had fallen to the captain. That was Sittler, and in this role, he had performed admirably.

Then Imlach arrived on the scene and decided that *he* would be the one who determined which players would be interviewed. Not only that, his first act as designated interview-arranger was to strike Sittler's name off the list of potential interviewees. Permanently.

Imlach made many mistakes, but picking a fight with Sittler was one of his worst. Not only did it align the team against him and make him universally loathed by Leafs fans, it also put him into conflict with one of the most powerful people in hockey at the time—Sittler's agent, Alan Eagleson.

Eagleson had his hat in so many rings that he was constantly in a conflict of interest, but he cheerfully admitted it and insisted that he was able to shift his loyalties as the circumstances required.

He was the guy behind all the international matches that were so popular at the time. He was an agent for individual players and he was the head of the National Hockey League Players' Association. He was also the driving force within Hockey Canada.

Because Ballard would never allow Eagleson to stage any games involving teams from the Soviet Union in Maple Leaf Gardens, the two were already at each other's throats. So when Imlach decided to use Sittler as his favourite whipping boy, Eagleson was doubly motivated to strike back at the Toronto organization.

On December 19, 1979, Ballard held a press conference to announce his plans to raise money for Ronald McDonald House by staging a February exhibition game between the Leafs and the Canadian Olympic team. The 1980 Olympics were to be held in Lake Placid, and with the exhibition game being played only a few days before the Olympic tournament, interest would be fairly high.

The venue for the press conference was Ballard's own Maple Leaf Gardens, and since Eagleson was a patron of Ronald McDonald House, no one suspected anything untoward when he showed up.

Not having the slightest suspicion of the impending ambush, Ballard stood up and proudly announced his plan. He had barely finished when Lanny McDonald, an Eagleson client and the Leafs' player representative on the NHL Players' Association, walked up and took over the microphone.

"I'm sorry," McDonald said. "We're not playing this game."

The media descended on Eagleson, who supported McDonald's stance but offered a compromise. If Ballard wanted the Leafs to play an exhibition game, Eagleson said, then he would also have to give his approval to a game between the Leafs and a touring Soviet team.

To rub the salt in a little bit more, Eagleson made it clear that the game would have to be played in Maple Leaf Gardens. If Ballard acceded to that demand, then the game against the Olympians could go forward, but only if it were played in a non-competitive format with some of the players switching teams.

The Leafs could play the Soviets head to head, said Eagleson, but they weren't going to go head to head against the Olympians, the game Ballard had envisioned.

For once, Ballard was humiliated. He had been hoping to salvage some of his tarnished reputation by holding a charity game, and now he had been upstaged right in his own building. Eagleson had made him look like a fool who planned an event without even getting the approval of the people who were to participate in it. Which, of course, is what he was.

Imlach was infuriated by this turn of events and decided that the only way to get back at Sittler was to trade his closest friend on the team, his second-in-command in the dressing room. Imlach would have much preferred to trade Sittler, but the no-trade clause prevented that. So Sittler's buddy, McDonald, the second most popular Leaf at the time, was shipped to Colorado along with Joel Quenneville in exchange for Wilf Paiement and Pat Hickey.

From a hockey point of view, the deal was a clear win for Colorado. Paiement was a power forward who couldn't shoot like McDonald but was a little more physical and a better skater. However, the Rockies also picked up a quality, serviceable defenceman in Quenneville. Hickey, by contrast, was a floater of the first order, a likeable guy who had some skill but generally preferred not to get any more involved than was absolutely necessary. For him to string together a series of shifts in which he never touched the puck was not at all unusual.

But Toronto fans didn't judge the deal only from a hockey perspective. They were furious that the much-hated Imlach had shipped out one of their favourites. The city was in an uproar. The Leafs were the biggest attraction in town, and now Imlach had traded away one of the leading lights.

Seizing the opportunity to get in another shot at the Toronto organization, Eagleson threw gas on the flames. He pointed out that the wives of McDonald and Paiement were both in the late stages of pregnancy, and he held up the entire episode as another example of Imlach's vindictiveness.

But Imlach had scored some points in the battle as well. McDonald was gone, and even though Eagleson did suggest that Paiement, another one of his clients, might not report to the Leafs, it was a half-hearted threat.

Perhaps Imlach thought that, after the initial uproar, he would simply have to hang tough for a while and the fire would burn itself out. If he thought that, he underestimated Eagleson. Prior to the next game, Sittler cut the captain's C off his sweater.

Over the years, there have been occasional suggestions that this was just a spur-of-the-moment decision on Sittler's part. Not a chance. The sports editors of the local newspapers had been alerted to Sittler's intentions and had sent extra staff. It was another broadside fired by Eagleson at the Toronto organization, especially Imlach.

Sittler even handed out copies of a prepared statement to the press corps. He certainly wouldn't have been allowed to use the Leafs' facilities to make copies, so he had to have brought them to the rink with him. Here is the statement:

I told my teammates and my coach before the game that I was resigning as captain of the Toronto Maple Leafs. When I was made captain, it was the happiest day of my life. I have tried to handle my duties as captain in a fair and honest manner. I took player complaints to management and discussed management ideas with players.

At the start of the season, I was personally sued by my own hockey team management. I was told it was nothing personal. I explained my position to Mr. Imlach and Mr. Ballard at the time. I told them I felt a captain's role was to work with players and management, not just management.

Mr. Ballard and Mr. Imlach made some negative comments about me and my teammates some weeks ago and I met with them to discuss it. I was told I was being too sensitive.

I have had little or no contact with Mr. Imlach and it is clear to me that he and I have different ideas about player and management communication.

I have recently been told that management has prevented me from appearing on *Hockey Night in Canada* telecasts.

I am spending more and more time on player-management problems and I don't feel I am accomplishing enough for my teammates.

The war between Mr. Imlach and Mr. Eagleson should not overshadow the main issue—the Toronto Maple Leafs.

I am totally loyal to the Toronto Maple Leafs. I don't want to let my teammates down. But I have to be honest with myself. I will continue to fight for players' rights but not as captain of the team.

All I want to do is give all my energy and all my ability to my team as a player.

As if the anti-Imlach sentiment hadn't been high enough already, it now reached epic proportions. It's hard to quantify it by today's standards. In that era, there were no twenty-four-hour sports radio stations, no Internet, and only scant television coverage. Nevertheless, anyone who lived through the great Imlach–Leafs confrontation knows that it dominated the discussions of the day and that it raged on relentlessly without any resolution in sight.

This was what the Leafs had been reduced to as 1979 drew to a close. The on-ice performance was abysmal, and no one seemed to be the least bit interested in improving the situation. The organization was reduced to two factions with opposing agendas. Management's primary aim was to force the players into submission, and the players' primary aim was to find any means of undermining the general manager.

At one point, Imlach ordered the team to stay after practice to watch game films. Ian Turnbull managed to procure a pornographic film and swapped it for the game film, which he then hid. When Floyd Smith started the projector, the players burst out laughing, and since the game film could not be found, the session was cancelled. Needless to say, Imlach was not amused.

Still, he persevered with his attempts to revamp the team.

He had the Gardens ice-making staff draw lines fifteen feet from the boards and parallel to them. At practice, the wingers were to stay between those lines and the boards. This was the age-old concept of wingers going up and down their wings. Apparently, Imlach had not noticed that hockey had undergone a revolution and that the swirling, creative European game had taken hold. The players shook their heads in amazement.

He had the phone taken out of the dressing room for no apparent reason other than to show he was the boss.

He brought in forty-one-year-old Carl Brewer after watching him play in an old-timers' game, a move that forced another defenceman, Dave Hutchison, to the sidelines.

Hutchison was also a friend of Sittler's, and the fans liked him because he was big and tough. When he started sitting out, he delivered his big body checks in practice—and most of them were directed at Brewer. Rightly or wrongly—almost certainly wrongly, knowing Brewer—the Leafs players looked upon Brewer as an Imlach spy who had been brought in only to keep the GM up to date on what was going on in the dressing room.

Before a road trip, the players noticed that Imlach had left his car parked with its lights on at the airport. Not one player cared enough to warn him of his oversight. When they returned, they gleefully watched him turn the ignition key to find that his car would not start. Hutchison drove his car alongside Imlach's, waved a set of booster cables and drove off. Little wonder that he was one of Imlach's targets. On January 10, Imlach traded Hutchison to Chicago.

That afternoon, as a sort of going-away party, some of the Toronto players went to Delaney's, one of their favourite watering holes. So did Jim Kernaghan, a hockey writer for the *Toronto Star*. One of the players tore a picture of Imlach out of the *Toronto Sun* and stuck it on the dartboard. Then the players took turns throwing darts at it.

The players knew that Kernaghan was there, and they knew that he would report what was being done. They also offered up their

opinions of Imlach, with the proviso that the quotes not be attrib-
uted—they could be used, but their source could not be identified.

One player said that Imlach was "responsible for the destruction
of a franchise." He went on to say, "We don't quite know what he is
doing except that he is proving one thing. He is the boss. There is
only one way this team can go under the circumstances—down."

Another player offered up a couple of rhetorical questions:
"Does anyone in his right mind think these trades were good? Does
anyone think that adding a forty-one-year-old guy to the team
and getting rid of a guy that will be playing for years on defence
[Quenneville] is smart?"

Once again, Imlach was in the middle of a furor, but in a curious turn of events, a large portion of the uproar was directed elsewhere.

In those days, when it came to sports media, the newspapers
ruled the roost. They covered the sports news, and they determined
the issues. But in 1980, the nature of newspaper sports coverage was
in the throes of a significant change.

For years, the beat writers had been little more than cheerlead-
ers for the teams. They would make all the road trips, and the teams
picked up the tab. Christmas gifts from the teams to the beat writers were sometimes extravagant—cases of liquor, all-expenses-paid
vacations, colour televisions (most people had black-and-white
back then), dozens of cases of beer and so on. And there was always
an understanding that no matter what he saw or heard, the beat
writer never produced anything that might embarrass the team.

Unfortunately for Imlach, his tenure coincided with a change
in attitude. Younger guys like Kernaghan saw their responsibility as
being to their readers, not to the people they were supposed to be
covering. They reported what they saw and what they heard. And
if they could get good quotes only by promising anonymity, they
would do it.

But Toronto was the top of the heap in the media business, so a lot of old-line, superannuated veterans were also on the scene. They liked the old ways, and they had known Imlach for a long time. Imlach had always been smart enough to feed them enough stories to keep them contented and to buy them enough drinks to keep them mellow. Many of them revelled in the glow that they felt accrued to them by being on a first-name basis with a famous sports figure.

So when Kernaghan produced his story about the dartboard, they were outraged. To them, what Kernaghan had committed was a combination of treason and blasphemy. Instead of ridiculing Imlach for creating a level of tumult that led the players to act in such a fashion, they attacked Kernaghan for using unattributed quotes.

But Kernaghan was not alone. At *The Globe and Mail,* there was a whole stable of young writers who didn't feel the need to grovel at the feet of people like Ballard and Imlach. The late Don Ramsay was one. Lawrence Martin, now in the *Globe's* Ottawa bureau, was another. Even the *Globe's* Canadian Football League writer, Jeffrey Goodman, was under attack from the old-line stalwarts for using unattributed quotes in a piece about the Toronto Argonauts.

In a 2009 interview, Martin, who broke the story regarding Ballard's disdain for Hammarström, recalled his days covering the Leafs.

"If you were a reporter in those days, it was heady stuff, so long as you could stay on the beat," he said. "Once, in Montreal, I was thrown off the Leafs' bus outside the Forum. Then they appointed the biggest guy on the team, a defenceman named Dave Dunn, to bar me from their dressing room.

"Later, on a flight out to Los Angeles, Dave Keon sauntered down the aisle. Keon was a beautiful hockey player, but by this time he had become one of the biggest pricks you could possibly imagine. 'I think you need a fucking haircut,' he said. 'When we get to L.A., we're going to give you one.'

"Some of the other Leafs on board heard about it and told me not to worry—they'd keep the scissors-wielders at bay. One offered me an invitation to a drug party he was going to attend the night before they played the Kings.

"On one of the next flights, in order to cover my hair, I wore a hat—an ugly brown corduroy cap of Bob Dylan vintage. The fun-loving Eddie Shack stopped me in the airport lounge. 'I wouldn't wear that thing to a shit-fight,' he roared.

"'You might want to take stock of your own headgear, Eddie,' I replied. We had a good laugh."

At the *Toronto Sun,* sports editor George Gross, whose kowtowing to Imlach was so shameless that it was still going on in 2008, long after Imlach had died, refused to allow any unattributed criticisms of his coveted friend. But that attitude merely put the *Sun* farther out of the loop. The writers from *The Globe and Mail* and the *Star* developed their sources within the team and passed along the nuggets to the reading public on an almost-daily basis.

As a result, the continuing tag-team warfare pitting the Sittler-Eagleson combo against the Ballard-Imlach duo played out in front of Toronto hockey fans for the rest of that dismal season.

Of all the bad seasons that contributed to the Leafs' long-standing malaise, this was truly the worst. It's easy for fans to think that once a season is over, it's forgotten and that the team can make a few changes and bounce back the following year. But that's not the case.

When you have a season like this, where the animosity and the vitriol are so prevalent, it's akin to a nuclear explosion. An incalculable amount of damage occurs at the time, but the debilitating effects stay around for years to come.

The mistrust between the players and the management was in existence for the entire time that Ballard owned the team, but it never reached the same level that was created during Imlach's second term. Both sides were out not only to win the battle but also to inflict as much pain and suffering as possible on the other side.

Ballard said that he was never as angry in his life as he was when Sittler cut the captain's C off his sweater. Imlach and Sittler engaged in venomous attacks on each other, and in Sittler's case, most of them were immediately made public. Imlach's public attacks came later, after he had left the team.

Eagleson and Ballard never patched up their feud. Some of the greatest games in Canadian hockey history were played in the various Canada Cup series organized by Eagleson, but not one of them was staged in Toronto. Ballard allowed training camps to be held in Maple Leaf Gardens, as well as some games against teams other than the Soviet Union. After all, exorbitant rent could be charged for that privilege.

But the USSR games were the ones that captured the fans' imagination, and if Eagleson wanted to capitalize on the Toronto hockey market for those games—and he did—the games had to be played down the Queen Elizabeth Way in Copps Coliseum in Hamilton.

After the Imlach years, Leafs coaches would come and go, and so would general managers. But the rancour that was created during his tenure festered on. The us-against-them attitude was evident until Ken Dryden came on the scene in 1997, but Dryden made so many other mistakes that, even though he healed some of the long-standing rifts, he created others.

Throughout that 1979–80 season, the battle raged in full force. Imlach made it clear that he would do everything he could to get rid of Sittler, but Eagleson was more than a match for him, thwarting every attempt.

Still, when the general manager is constantly and openly expressing his disdain for the guy who is the team leader and ex-captain, any chance of on-ice success is remote at best.

In his relentless attempt to strip the team of all its fan favourites and Sittler allies, Imlach next shipped out Dave "Tiger" Williams.

Williams was outgoing, outspoken and outrageous. On one occasion, after scoring a winning goal in a playoff game, he rode his stick down the ice like a hobby horse. He fought anyone who showed the slightest interest in combat—and some who didn't— and he said whatever came into his mind. In many ways, he was like a younger Ballard. And Ballard, fully aware of this, made no secret of the fact that he had a great admiration for Williams.

Williams promised Ballard that he would make him a present of the hide from the first bear he killed with his bow and arrow, and he was true to his word. Williams said he felt bad because it wasn't a large bear, but it was his first kill, and a promise is a promise.

So if Imlach were to trade Williams, it had better be a good deal. And it was. He got Bill Derlago and Rick Vaive from the Vancouver Canucks for Williams and Jerry Butler. Even so, Imlach was criticized in some quarters because he spent so long talking to Williams about the trade that Butler had to learn his fate from Williams and the media.

To make the overall Toronto situation even worse, coach Floyd Smith, something of a moderating force between the players and Imlach, had to be relieved of his duties.

On the afternoon of March 14, 1980, he decided to drive to his home in Buffalo, and when he got to St. Catharines, stopped for what was subsequently described as "a couple of beers." Shortly after he got back behind the wheel, he lost control, crossed the median and hit another car. Two people in that car were killed. Smith was not badly injured, but he was charged with impaired driving and criminal negligence causing death. He was eventually acquitted, but given the circumstances, someone else had to take over the coaching duties at least until the matter was resolved.

Imlach came up with the rather intriguing concept of naming

himself coach, while turning over the behind-the-bench duties to Joe Crozier, who had been running the Moncton farm team.

Neither this nor the acquisition of Jiří Crha to help out with the goaltending duties could save that team. It finished with a record of 35–40–5, and even though such a dismal performance was good enough to get into the playoffs, it wasn't good enough to win a game. They were swept in the best-of-five opening round by the Minnesota North Stars by a combined score of 17–8.

There were more battles to come between Imlach and Sittler. And, of course, there were more dismal seasons to come. The damage had been done. The team was as dysfunctional as any in hockey—perhaps as dysfunctional as any in professional sports.

5

The Circus Gets Rolling
for a Decade-Long Run

When it seemed that, thanks to Punch Imlach, the Maple Leafs had no-
where to go but up, they somehow managed to go farther down, exhibiting
astonishing incompetence at every level. In so many areas, in so many
ways, on so many occasions, the Leafs just got worse and worse.

Although it seemed that the Leafs had no choice but to stabilize
or perhaps even improve after their fateful 1979–80 season, in
fact they did neither. That point marked the beginning of the
full-scale circus that would be the Toronto operation until Harold
Ballard died. And the circus didn't disappear with Ballard; a few of
the acts just changed rings.

Increasingly, Ballard, who had always been the biggest problem,
insisted on running the team himself. He undermined the people
he hired. He made outrageous statements without ever considering

the consequences. He put his own personal peccadilloes and prejudices ahead of the well-being of the hockey team. He got involved in matters that should have been left to capable hockey people— had there been any in the Leafs organization at that time, which is a dubious assumption.

During the summer of 1980, Punch Imlach worked hard to get rid of Darryl Sittler. He and Ballard had agreed on a plan. They would trade Sittler and worry about the consequences later. Sittler's no-trade clause could easily be ignored. After all, it was only part of a legally binding contract. Why would an organization as omnipotent as the Leafs have to worry about the laws of the land?

Either way, insisted Ballard, Sittler would not be invited back to training camp. He was nothing more than an ex-captain. Just to make the point clear, he repeatedly referred to Sittler as "a cancer on the team."

In August, Imlach suffered his second heart attack and went into hospital for what would be a six-week recuperation. That meant there was no longer anyone available to point out to Ballard how colossally stupid his latest whim might be.

One can only imagine Imlach's response when, recovering from a heart attack, he read in the newspapers that Ballard had not only welcomed Sittler back but had offered to make him the captain. It's a wonder Imlach didn't fall off his perch right then.

At the press conference held to announce this happy little reconciliation, copies of the official 1980–81 Maple Leafs training camp guide were handed out to the media. Under the S, there was no Sittler, Darryl. And under the C there was no Cancer, Team.

Ballard and Sittler professed a willingness to try to love each other and to let bygones be bygones. But after the official announcement, despite all the surface warmth, there was still a chilly undercurrent. "Maybe now they'll put my name back in this thing," muttered Sittler, looking at the training camp guide.

"If he had come to me and said he didn't want to be captain, I could have accepted that," explained Ballard when asked about his earlier actions, "but the way he did it, that's what I could never accept. If he had been in the army and done that, they'd have shot him."

Short honeymoon.

As if he hadn't stirred up enough trouble for Imlach with his Sittler decisions, Ballard also let it be known that he would like to get McDonald back from Colorado as well. That prompted an accusation of tampering from the Rockies, and Ballard had to say that he hadn't really meant it. As if he ever really meant anything he said.

★   ★   ★

Throughout the 1980s, the Leafs developed a reputation for being an embarrassment to the National Hockey League.

An entire book could be written about the failures of the Leafs throughout that decade and for the entire duration of the Ballard regime. But it would become repetitive. More of the same stupidity and bluster. More of the same ill-advised, spur-of-the-moment decisions based upon whims rather than research.

There have been a number of books that record the history of the Leafs during the Ballard era, but a few examples, like those that follow, illustrate only too well the nature of that highly flawed regime as it wallowed along from year to year through the 1980s.

In those ten years, they won three playoff rounds. Not once did they finish over .500. They were even ridiculed in the syndicated "Tank McNamara" cartoon strip.

Yet still Ballard blustered on, changing the coaches, changing the general managers, but never once giving any thought to the possibility that his best course of action for the good of the team would be to hand over realistic power to someone who knew what he was doing.

With Imlach still recuperating when the 1980–81 season began, coach Joe Crozier had assumed a good deal of authority—as much as anyone not named Harold Ballard could have in that organization. But Crozier couldn't get the team to win, any more than any of his predecessors could, so in typical fashion, Ballard spared no expense and looked in every corner of the world to find a replacement.

Okay, some expense was spared. And maybe it wasn't every corner of the world. But it was an extensive search of Maple Leaf Gardens. And sure enough, who should be in the radio booth doing colour on the Leafs' broadcasts? Why, it was Mike Nykoluk, who had once been an assistant coach in the NHL.

Following his normal modus operandi, Ballard mused to some of his media pals that Nykoluk might replace Crozier. Of course, he also mused to some of his media pals that Crozier was going nowhere.

During the second intermission of a Wednesday game, Ballard was asked if Crozier was going to be fired that night. Ballard said he wasn't.

Would he be fired tomorrow?

"No. Not tomorrow, or the next day or the next."

Would he last the season?

"Sure. Why not?"

There was a pretty easy answer to that last one. He would not be around because Imlach and Ballard had already decided the firing was imminent and were trying to decide whether the replacement would be Nykoluk or Doug Carpenter.

The sequence of events went like this: On Wednesday, Ballard denied that Crozier would be fired. On Thursday, he told a local wire-service reporter that Crozier would be fired. On Friday, Crozier was fired and Nykoluk hired.

By Ballard's standards, that was a fairly direct approach. Nothing so clear-cut happened when it came time to fire Imlach, who, as it turned out, was also in his last year with the Leafs.

He finished the season, but the following September, he had another heart attack. While Imlach was away this time, Ballard ignored him. He didn't even send him a get-well card, and he told Leafs employees not to visit him.

Eventually, Imlach read in one of the papers that he wouldn't be back. Ballard, the ever-noble humanitarian that he was, explained that he had taken this course of action because he didn't want to be responsible for Imlach's death. Just to make Imlach's status crystal-clear, his nameplate was removed from his Maple Leaf Gardens parking spot.

* * *

Imlach's successor, Gerry McNamara, was not the worst general manager the National Hockey League had ever seen, but he was close. And he was definitely the worst the Leafs had ever seen.

At one point during McNamara's tenure, he instigated a civil suit because he had been involved in a car accident. In order to support his case, he insisted in court that he was brain-damaged. Suffice to say, there was no stampede of Leafs fans rushing to the witness stand to argue the point.

He ran the Leafs for six seasons and was well into his seventh when Ballard fired him.

On this occasion, Ballard repeatedly insisted that he would give McNamara the courtesy of a face-to-face meeting. If McNamara couldn't justify his continued presence in the organization at the meeting, said Ballard, he would be gone.

It goes without saying that no such meeting ever occurred. With the Leafs in Hartford on a road trip, Ballard did the deed via a long-distance telephone call.

One of the reasons for the dismissal was that McNamara and the current coach—John Brophy, who had replaced Don Maloney, who had replaced Nykoluk—were at odds. Since McNamara was usually at odds with almost everybody, this was no great surprise.

Part of the reason for this squabble seemed to be that McNamara had taken to unearthing a series of Czechoslovaks to play for the Leafs, whereas Brophy, one of the meanest, toughest players in hockey history, wanted good old Canadian boys. Little wonder, then, that when McNamara was fired in February 1988, one of his favourites, Miroslav Frycer, decided that it was time to pack his bags and move on.

When asked about Brophy at the end of the season, he said, "There's no way I'll ever play for that man again. Ninety per cent of the players hate playing for him, but they're not going to say it. He's the first guy to panic behind the bench when we need a guy to calm us down. He has created a nightmare for this team, this city, for me and my family. I'll never be back."

He wasn't.

McNamara ran the Leafs during the NHL's twenty-one-team era. His teams finished nineteenth, fifteenth, eighteenth, twenty-first, nineteenth and sixteenth. When he was fired, they were twenty-first.

★ ★ ★

In 1984, Gary Lariviere, who later went on to become an assistant coach with the Leafs, was still active as a player and the property of the Edmonton Oilers.

But because Lariviere's home was in St. Catharines, the Oilers offered to lend him to the Leafs' farm team, which at the time was based in St. Catharines, whereas the Oilers' farm team was based in the United States.

· The deal was a good one for both sides, and McNamara accepted the offer. The Leafs got the use of an NHL-veteran defenceman to help out their youngsters on the farm, and the Oilers retained the services of a player who could be called upon readily in an emergency situation.

But as often happens, another NHL team lost an inordinate number of defencemen to injury and called Oilers general manager Glen Sather to inquire about the availability of Lariviere.

Seeing as Edmonton was about to finalize a deal for Lariviere, Sather called McNamara to let him know that the farm team would soon be losing his services. McNamara flew into a rage and told Sather that there was no way Lariviere was leaving St. Catharines. The Oilers were simply out of luck.

"He started screaming and yelling at me over the phone," said Sather. "I said, 'Wait a minute. Are you trying to tell me I can't have somebody that I own?'"

Sather reminded McNamara that the arrangement had been witnessed by a third party. He also pointed out that he had been doing the Leafs a favour, and that McNamara's reaction was somewhat less than honourable.

McNamara finally capitulated, but Sather was not the type to brush it aside. He said that it would be a long time before he ever tried to do another favour for the Leafs.

★　★　★

For two seasons, 1984–85 and 1985–86, the man behind the Leafs' bench was Dan Maloney. Since he had been acquired by the Leafs in what has to go down as one of the most one-sided trades in NHL history—with Toronto coming out on the wrong end, of course—everything possible was done to dredge up some sort of benefit from that deal.

In those days, the Leafs were big on rebuilding, but in their usual backward fashion they rebuilt other teams rather than their own. Such was the case with the Maloney trade. They sent Errol Thompson, a gifted scorer, and two first-round draft picks to the Detroit Red Wings for Maloney. Given the nature of the Leafs' finishes, those draft picks held a lot of potential.

Maloney was one of those people whose playing career ran out before his contract followed suit. Ballard, being the penny-pincher that he was and on the hook for the salary anyway, therefore made Maloney the assistant coach. Then, since Maloney was in the organization when Nykoluk got fired, he became head coach.

Less than three months into his first season, the Leafs were in their usual state of turmoil. A group of veteran players composed of John Anderson, Bill Derlago, Börje Salming and Rick Vaive was the target of Maloney's frequent tirades. Being veterans, they responded in kind. The younger players watched the veterans and coach cursing each other and didn't know how to respond. So they stayed confused. The Czechoslovak players were resented by everybody else, and one player, Jim Korn, was shunned by Czechoslovaks and Canadians alike because he was American and seen to be a pipeline to the general manager.

"At the beginning of the season, it looked like Maloney was going to be the man for the job," said one player, "but now it looks like he has fallen prey to that old Leafs paranoia.

"He thinks everybody is against him and he's just lashing out at everybody. He's got to learn that there's more to coaching than just yelling and criticizing. He's got to encourage some of the guys too."

An NHL scout said, "The Leafs are the worst team in the league behind their blue line. Their only breakout tactic is to crank the puck around the boards waist high at full speed. Most of the time, the forwards couldn't pick it off with a net."

Maloney missed the playoffs in his first year. In his second year, the team finished nineteenth, but such was the playoff structure that they qualified for the post-season festivities. Incredibly, they won a round.

Maloney was fired anyway.

★   ★   ★

McNamara had a fatal attraction for Czechoslovak players, and in that era, one of the very best was Peter Štastný. He was one of the first European players to make a major impact in the NHL, and he did so off the ice as well as on it. He was not only a superb player, he was also a true gentleman who spoke a number of languages, devoured all sections of the newspapers—not just the sports—and fully deserved his eventual induction into the Hockey Hall of Fame.

His brother Anton was less skilled, but he was a professional who was fully deserving of his reputation as a decent player.

Then there was the third brother, Marián, who had enough hockey skills to hang on to a spot in the NHL but had all the personality of a boil.

Needless to say, the Štastný brother McNamara acquired was Marián. The Quebec Nordiques, for whom all three brothers played, had sent a clear message to the NHL when they gave Marián his unconditional release—as far as they were concerned, whatever risk there might be in upsetting Peter and Anton was more than overcome by the desire to get rid of Marián.

At this time, in 1985, the Leafs were a fragile team, and someone like Marián Štastný was the last person who should have been brought into the mix. But he lasted for a year with the team, during which time he missed so many games and practices with headaches that one day, his teammates replaced the nameplate over his cubicle with a handmade sign that said, "Headache."

On one occasion, the Leafs had a four-day break on the road, which was to be spent in Chicago. After the game against the Blackhawks, coach Dan Maloney made a point of urging his players to spend some time together, to go out in groups and get to know each other. He told the team that he wanted every player to go out that night. For emphasis, he added, "And I mean everybody."

When the team bus unloaded at the hotel, the players headed for the elevators. "Want to meet us back here in five minutes, Marián?" asked one player.

There was no answer. Marián wandered off and spent the night in his room.

It was not Maloney's only attempt to get Štastný involved in the team. On another occasion, Maloney suggested that, as a veteran, perhaps Marián could spend a few extra minutes on the ice after practice, passing along a few tips to the younger players.

Štastný quickly pointed out to his coach the error of his ways. In a manner that can only be described as blunt, he told Maloney that when practice ended, so did his obligation to the team.

He did not make public appearances, he said. He did not make speeches on behalf of the team. He did not attend luncheons, and he certainly did not do volunteer work as an unpaid coach. Then he left the ice.

Perhaps he had a headache.

★　★　★

In every draft during the McNamara era, the Leafs were front and centre in the early stages of the proceedings. In 1985, thanks to a season that was even worse than usual—which wasn't easy—they had the first-overall pick.

In second place were the Pittsburgh Penguins who, unlike the Leafs, entered the draft with a well-developed plan of attack. But in order to focus that plan, they wanted to know who the Leafs were going to pick. The Penguins coveted Wendel Clark, but if the Leafs were going to grab him, they would adjust their own intentions accordingly.

With this in mind, Pittsburgh GM Eddie Johnston approached McNamara and asked him who he intended to pick. In return for the information, Johnston offered to give McNamara a player out of the Pittsburgh system.

McNamara refused to go along. Bear in mind, the information wouldn't have impacted the Leafs in the slightest. They had the first pick. It didn't matter who knew their intentions.

As usual, hockey people were left shaking their heads at the way the Leafs did business. "Why would you turn down a free player?" asked one GM.

Apparently, in McNamara's mind, the Leafs were such a power-house that they didn't need any help.

★ ★ ★

Ballard's relationship with his workers, which would have been better suited to a Charles Dickens novel than a high-profile twentieth-century enterprise, wasn't limited to the team itself. He was an equal-opportunity tyrant.

Maple Leaf Gardens had long been known for having good ice, and one of the reasons for this was the chief icemaker, Doug Moore. He worked at Maple Leaf Gardens for decades and was the man who developed the revolutionary Jet Ice system that earned the Gardens its reputation.

Not being in a union, Moore, a first-class stationary engineer, was being paid much less than the unionized men who worked for him, so he asked for a raise.

Ballard's response was quick. He fired him.

He said that Moore had resigned. "I imagine he felt he should put all of his time into Jet Ice," said Ballard, "but I haven't much use for it. We had better ice before we monkeyed around with it."

The truth of the matter was that the Jet Ice process removed all superfluous matter from the water and added certain chemicals to make the ice faster, harder and resistant to chipping. At that point, it had been adopted by thirteen NHL rinks.

"It was money, pure and simple," said Moore. "He doesn't like you asking for more money. But you've got to ask for more money in there. You're never going to get it any other way."

A friend of Moore's said what Moore himself wouldn't. "He was always getting calls in the middle of the night. He was always going in at 2 a.m. But he never complained about it. He was proud of his work.

"He was even in there crawling around, shutting off valves when they had an ammonia leak in there a few years ago. It could have been a disaster if it had happened during a game, but it happened during a night in the summer."

The reason Moore often got calls in the wee hours was that Ballard had cancelled the night shift in the decrepit old building.

"After a hockey game and after those rock shows, there would be all kinds of problems," said Moore. "I didn't really mind it. The long hours didn't bother me.

"I would have stayed on if he'd paid me, but he just doesn't pay. It's a long winter in there. But it may be a blessing. I'm at an age where I didn't really want to be working sixty or seventy hours a week anymore."

Ballard told him to clear out his desk and be out of the building on September 9, 1987. It was thirty years to the day since Moore had started work there.

"I enjoyed working there," he said.

★ ★ ★

Unable to beat anybody on the ice in the 1980s, the Leafs decided to go to war with the media.

It was a battle on many fronts, but the organization that seemed to be perpetually in the vanguard was *The Globe and Mail*. This was the source of much amusement over the next few years as the writers from that paper continued to point out the shortcomings of the Leafs, thereby prompting the Leafs to worry more about defeating the media than defeating their on-ice opponents.

The pettiness probably hit its lowest level at a sparsely attended Sunday-morning practice when Jim O'Leary of the *Toronto Sun* helped himself to a coffee from one of the pots that sat outside the Leafs dressing room. Seeing this outrageous theft of Leafs property and determined to prevent any further heinous acts of this nature, general manager Gerry McNamara came rushing down from the stands and put his jacket over the coffee pots.

McNamara's expertise with technology was apparently on a par with his hockey expertise. The pots were heated by electrical elements, and in a short time, his jacket was on fire. It was not easy for the media to contain their laughter.

There's no need to go into all the Leafs–media altercations here. If you want to read about them, many are documented in William Houston's book *Ballard*. Houston and I were both working at *The Globe and Mail* in those days, so we saw first hand what was going on. Here are just a few examples.

At one of the regular Molson receptions for the Leafs, coach Mike Nykoluk made a speech referring to Fergie Olver and Pat Marsden, the two primary sportscasters for Toronto TV station CFTO, as "hypocritical jerks" and "scum."

Over the years, Ballard had Brian McFarlane, Howie Meeker, Dave Hodge and Bobby Hull removed from Leafs telecasts.

Houston and I were banned from the dressing room for criticizing the team, and I was physically tossed out of the dressing room by Nykoluk. Being a part of the Leafs organization, Nykoluk couldn't even do that properly. He missed the doorway on his first shot and bundled me out on his second.

Assistant coach Dan Maloney told *Globe and Mail* photographer James Lewcun, a man in his sixties, "If I ever see you around here again, I'll bust that thing over your head."

The Leafs refused to give CFRB sports director Bill Stephenson a media pass because he had blamed Ballard for the Leafs' problems. When CKEY radio talk-show host Mark Hebscher tried to organize a demonstration decrying the Leafs' abysmal performances, he was banned, and Leafs players were told not to talk to anyone carrying a CKEY microphone.

When Ballard was finally ordered by NHL president John Ziegler to allow *Globe and Mail* writers in the dressing room, he did so, but banned them from the press box. They bought seats to the games and wrote their post-game stories from a hotel adjacent to Maple Leaf Gardens.

★ ★ ★

In 1988, general manager Gord Stellick, barely thirty years old at the time, decided the Leafs needed some muscle and traded away Russ Courtnall, generally conceded to be the fastest skater with the puck in the NHL, for John Kordic, an enforcer with a host of off-ice problems.

Even though Stellick is still ridiculed for this trade to this day, it must be said that it was an organizational decision. No trade was ever made without Ballard's approval, so he has to be accorded some of the blame. And the coach, John Brophy, was continually pestering Stellick to acquire a tough player.

Furthermore, Brophy wasn't making much use of Courtnall's skills. As a result, Courtnall, who was languishing on the fourth line, had told Stellick he wanted to be traded.

That said, there were better deals to be made. Some research would have revealed the extent of Kordic's psychological problems. The Leafs might have learned, for instance, about the time a discussion in the coach's office ended with Kordic throwing an ashtray at the coach's head.

Kordic did indeed get into a few fights as a Leaf, amassing 446 penalty minutes in his 104 games with the Leafs (and 16 points). But he was hard to handle and was traded to Washington after two years.

Courtnall went on to a career that saw him rack up 744 points, 297 of which were goals.

In August 1992, Kordic got into a struggle with police in a Quebec City hotel and died when he suffered heart failure in the ambulance on the way to the hospital. He had a large amount of cocaine in his system at the time.

★   ★   ★

There are many examples of Harold Ballard's propensity to respond to questions with lies and bluster. But one of the most illuminating came about when the Ralston Purina Corporation decided to file an anti-trust suit against the National Hockey League.

It all had to do with Ralston Purina's decision to end its ownership of the St. Louis Blues in 1983, but that's not really the issue here. There was a subsequent attempt to move the Blues to Saskatoon, a move that Ballard ridiculed, calling Saskatoon the place "where God left his snowshoes."

On August 30, 1984, Ballard, as an NHL governor, was required to give a deposition. What follows is the transcript of his answers, all of which were given under oath.

When Allen Boston, a lawyer representing Ralston Purina, asked Ballard if he had ever been to Saskatoon, he unequivocally said that he had. And the fun began from there. Here's how it went:

A: . . . I have been there.

Q: When was that?

A: Oh, it must have been seven or eight years ago. It could be ten years ago. I think that anybody that has been to Saskatoon in the winter would never want to go back.

Q: Because of snow?

A: Snow and miserable conditions.

Q: Cold weather?

A: It never gets below . . . it never gets any higher than 10 or 15 degrees below zero and it could get down to 40 or 45.

Q: When were you there last?

A: I was at a football game. I guess it must be between eight and ten years ago.

Q: In Saskatoon?

A: In Saskatoon.

Q: Who was playing?

A: The Argonauts, and let me tell you, it was unbearable. And if you weren't a drinker, you were out of luck.

Q: The Argonauts against whom?

A: Saskatoon or Regina it would be, I guess.

Q: So your reference is to Regina, your trip seven or eight years ago?

A: Pardon?

Q: Your trip seven or eight years ago is to Regina?

A: Yes.

Q: On reflection, do you think that your interrogatory
with regard to when you were last in Saskatoon is
not correct or do you think it is still correct?

A: I think it is still correct.

Typical Ballard. He has just lied under oath and has been shown
to have no idea what he's talking about. But he refuses to back
down. He still insists he's correct.

In the same interrogation, he was asked if he knew Mike Griffin.
His answer was short and unequivocal. "No."

Mike Griffin was the NHL's director of information for the
Campbell Conference, the conference in which the Leafs played.
Ballard had met him and talked to him countless times.

Another person Ballard knew well was Bob Sedgewick. In fact,
Sedgewick had been Ballard's backup at NHL board of governors
meetings. At the time of the Saskatoon controversy, he was the Leafs'
alternate governor.

At one point during the taking of the deposition, Boston
showed Ballard a document.

Q: Is that your handwriting?

A: No.

Q: Do you know whose it is?

A: No.

Q: Can you recognize Mr. Sedgewick's handwriting
normally?

A: Yes, I can, normally.

Q: Do you believe this to be Mr. Sedgewick's?

A: I would say yes.

And so it went. Ballard's impact upon the Ralston Purina lawsuit was negligible. The stack of depositions was about four feet

high. But the way in which Ballard lied under oath, then continued to insist he was right, graphically illustrates what type of person was the guiding force behind the Toronto Maple Leafs.

Steve Stavro Donates to His Favourite Charity: Himself

Same circus, different ringmaster. Steve Stavro found a way to take over the Maple Leafs upon Ballard's death in 1991, and until 2003 devoted himself to the task of attaining traditional Leafs ideals—increased profit, high-level incompetence and penny-pinching.

Harold Ballard didn't exhibit a lot of admirable attributes when he was alive. But perhaps he reasoned that he could somehow atone for his multitude of sins once he was dead.

Whatever his reasoning may have been, he drew up a last will and testament that stipulated a considerable windfall for seven charities. In fact, his shares in Maple Leaf Gardens Ltd., the company that owned both the Maple Leafs and the building in which they played, were to be sold and donated to charity upon Ballard's death.

MLG was a public company, and every time Ballard entered hospital, its stock rose sharply. When he regained his health, the stock dropped. That seemed to be a clear indication that, as far as fans and investors were concerned, an end to Ballard's involvement would be a positive development for the company.

This also appeared to be a positive development for the charities. With the value of MLG floating in the $100 million range, Ballard's death would probably drive the value even higher and the charities would be the beneficiaries.

Unfortunately for the charities, however—and unfortunately for Ballard if there were indeed to be some tit-for-tat arrangement once he passed through the Pearly Gates—the ensuing battle for control of the Leafs and the Gardens would see them receive only a fraction of that amount, while Steve Stavro ended up with control of the Leafs and the Gardens.

Thus began the next chapter in the Leafs' litany of poor ownership and, by extension, the next chapter in the long story of the team's ineptitude and its ever-lengthening Stanley Cup drought.

Whereas an owner like Mike Ilitch in Detroit saw it as his duty to provide the fans with a dominant team despite the cost, Stavro cared about little but profit.

In 2001, Ilitch owned a team that had sold out every game the previous year, was a perennial powerhouse and already boasted a lucrative long-range television contract. From a bottom-line point of view, there was certainly no need for Ilitch to increase his operating costs. But he did. He acquired both Brett Hull and Luc Robitaille as free agents, a misnomer if ever there was one. They were far from free—they were extremely expensive. But Ilitch got them anyway because they were available and they would make his already strong team even stronger.

That was in direct contrast to the approach that Stavro was to take with the Leafs.

Had Stavro been as free with his money as someone like Mike Ilitch, and had he given general manager Cliff Fletcher free rein to finish the job he had so promisingly started, there's no telling how far the Leafs might have advanced. But Stavro was not free with his money. Quite the contrary.

Stavro was a grocer by trade, the owner of Knob Hill Farms in Toronto. He owned some racehorses and was a soccer fan, but that was the extent of his involvement with sports. His familiarity with the hockey world of the time was even more minimal than Ballard's.

Yet even though he did not understand hockey, he understood financial manoeuvring, and in April 1994 he made the move that was to negatively impact the fortunes of the Leafs for the next seven years.

In a nifty little financial two-step, Stavro managed take control of 80 per cent of Maple Leaf Gardens Ltd. This was a company worth $105 million, yet Stavro got that 80 per cent control for only $39 million. Said one high-level investor who owned a smaller share of MLG, "Hell, I know fifty guys who would make that deal if they could. I'd do it myself if I could. But I never had a chance. This thing isn't illegal, but it's about as close as you can get."

There was a difference of opinion about that. Some people thought it definitely was illegal.

Whether it was or it wasn't remained to be seen. But it certainly wasn't impetuous. Stavro had been insinuating himself into MLG's affairs since Ballard's death in 1990, and by virtue of that involvement had provided himself with the leverage that he managed to put to full use in 1994.

Here's how it went: after Ballard died, Donald Giffin, Donald Crump and Stavro were named executors of his will. Giffin appeared to have an interest in re-establishing the glory days of the Leafs, but in a classic boardroom power play, Stavro teamed up with Crump to oust Giffin and four other directors of MLG Ltd.

Shortly afterwards, when Giffin died, Stavro and Crump teamed up again to appoint their friend Terry Kelly as his replacement.

As a result of these moves, Stavro was now a major power in MLG, and therefore fully aware of the inner workings of the company. He knew that the Ballard estate was in debt to the tune of $20 million to Molson Companies, and in 1991, Stavro loaned the estate the money to pay off that debt. In return, he received an option to buy all the outstanding MLG stock the estate owned. This proved to be the stepping stone that he needed.

Stavro's detractors said that this was a cozy, secret deal. Brian Bellmore, who was Stavro's friend and attorney—and who later became the power behind the throne in the Leafs organization—disagreed. He said that the estate had tried to raise the money from outside sources but couldn't. Stavro, he said, had been good enough to provide the bailout.

But when Bill Ballard, Harold's older son, then also offered to lend the estate $20 million, presumably to limit Stavro's involvement in the business, he was turned down.

"The executors applied to the Supreme Court of Ontario for direction on the matter," said Bellmore. "It was argued in full public view in February 1991."

Bill Ballard appealed but lost, and the Supreme Court of Canada refused to hear the case.

It was at that point that Stavro exercised the option he had so providently acquired. He had earned the right to buy all the outstanding MLG stock and he did so. He took the 19.9 per cent held by Molson and the 60.4 per cent held by Harold Ballard's estate. Thus he acquired 80.3 per cent of Maple Leaf Gardens Ltd. at a price of $34 a share.

Up to that point, Stavro had been in a clear conflict of interest. As an executor of the estate, he had been entrusted with the responsibility of increasing the price of the stock so that the charities named in Ballard's will would do well. He had a similar responsibility to the other shareholders. But as an individual with an option to purchase that stock, it was in his best interest to keep the share price low.

Furthermore, the $34-per-share offer for a stock that had closed at $28.50 was a clear attempt to encourage private investors to sell their stock to Stavro. If he could increase his holding to 90 per cent, he could make MLG a private company—which he eventually did.

But Stavro had kept his plans secret because release of that information would have driven up stock prices.

There was some screaming from other investors. They decried the $34-per-share price, saying the stock would have been much higher had Stavro made his intentions known. They pointed out that a public company is not supposed to make secret backroom deals.

There was some fallout. Eventually, the public trustee ordered the sale rolled back, then conceded Stavro's right to the shares. The episode dragged on for years, and Harry Ornest, one of the jilted suitors for MLG, was dogged in his determination to prevent Stavro's takeover.

Ornest, who had owned the Toronto Argonauts and St. Louis Blues, also owned a small percentage of the Leafs, and he wanted a much larger portion—or, if that could not be arranged, a much higher settlement than $34 a share. Eventually, the public trustee ordered Stavro to pay $49.50 for each of the outstanding shares.

Ornest was a determined, resolute individual with the mindset of a bulldog. Once he clamped his teeth on Stavro, there was to be no letting go. Ornest would have battled until he won—and he had a very good case.

But Ornest had a history of heart problems, and eventually his ill health forced him to cease his pursuit. From that point on, it was clear sailing for Stavro.

In 1996, Stavro converted the Leafs into a private company, thereby becoming relatively immune to the prying queries of the media and the fans. It was no doubt a great relief to him. The previous year, when MLG was still public and therefore forced by law to hold annual shareholders' meetings, that meeting had turned into something of a circus.

The proceedings were run by George Whyte, ostensibly the chairman of the company, even though he didn't hold a single share. Whyte refused to allow question after question concerning either Stavro's intentions or his earlier actions, saying, "The matter is before the courts."

One shareholder wondered why, if that was the case, the directors whose actions were "before the courts" didn't show just a tiny bit of integrity and step aside until the matter was settled. Whyte wouldn't allow that question either.

Throughout it all, Stavro, the chairman of MLG, sat silently a few feet away. Veteran attendees of shareholders' meetings could never remember another case in which a company's real chairman sat quietly while someone who owned no shares presented himself as chairman and ran the proceedings.

There was no answer to a shareholder's question about why Stavro and his friends had withheld dividends for three consecutive quarters. Even convicted felon Harold Ballard had always kept the quarterly dividends flowing without a break. The suspicion was that, because Stavro knew he was going to make the company private, he wanted to keep as much cash for himself as he could.

Another shareholder wondered why the Mellanby Report, which had projected a tripling of television revenues for the Leafs, had been kept secret by Stavro. Obviously, the prospect of increased revenues would have impacted the proposed $34 share price. In fact, once that information became public knowledge, investment companies valued MLG shares in the $50 to $53 range. Whyte refused to allow the question to be answered.

There were a number of other uncomfortable questions, but not one was rewarded with a satisfactory answer.

That was the last public annual shareholders' meeting ever held by Maple Leaf Gardens Ltd. Before the next one could be scheduled, Stavro had turned MLG into a private company and his questionable dealings could therefore be carried out in private.

In a strange twist of fate, Stavro's actions at that time may have eventually cost him the Leafs. A few years later, his Knob Hill Farms was under tremendous financial pressure. Had MLG been public, its shares would no doubt have been of much greater value than they were when he took the company private. The Leafs had moved into a new building by then—the lucrative Air Canada Centre—and the profits were rolling in.

But by definition, the shares of private companies don't increase in an open market. Furthermore, private shares are not very liquid. You can't just put a few on the market and have someone grab them up, as you can in the case of a publicly traded company. As a result of these factors, Stavro couldn't sell some shares to raise badly needed cash. He was forced to capitulate to takeover offers.

The company that evolved from that takeover is now called Maple Leaf Sports and Entertainment Ltd., but it is still privately held. And it is still extremely profitable—the most profitable in the National Hockey League, in fact. In the 2007–08 season, the hockey-related revenues were $182 million.

Stavro lasted until 2003, when he finally cashed in his share of the Leafs. To the very end, he stood by his twisted version of reality. At the press conference held to announce the changeover, Stavro solemnly intoned that he had "fulfilled the role as guardian of the Leafs as left to me by Harold Ballard's will." That must have been a different will from the one the rest of us remembered and had reported upon. In *that* will, the team was left to charity. Steve Stavro's name appeared nowhere on the list of beneficiaries. But because of that $20 million loan back in 1991, Stavro had acquired the option to buy all the MLG stock owned by the estate. Once he exercised that option, there was next to nothing left for Ballard's designated charities.

And for that matter, Stavro hadn't been a particularly good guardian. If you're a good guardian, you don't have the public trustee filing a statement of claim asking for a review of your actions under the Charitable Gifts Act. There were also breach-of-trust allegations against Stavro.

The new organization, MLSE, was the product of MLG's purchase of the Toronto Raptors of the National Basketball Association from their reluctant owner, broadcasting mogul Allan Slaight. It was to be run by a nine-person board, and as of July 1, 2003, its chairman was to be Larry Tanenbaum, whose lobbying efforts had piqued the NBA's interest in putting a team in Toronto, even though the league awarded the franchise he coveted to a rival group.

And what was Tanenbaum's previous involvement with hockey? Well, he was acquainted with NHL commissioner Gary Bettman, who had once been a big wheel in the NBA. Other than that, there wasn't much.

But he did know money, and he also knew he didn't like the way Stavro had been running things. In fact, the two disliked each other so much that Tanenbaum had refused to even share a boardroom with Stavro, instead sending a delegate to board meetings, first of Maple Leaf Gardens Ltd. and then of MLSE.

Nevertheless, at the press conference to announce the takeover, Tanenbaum offered a warm expression of heartfelt thanks to Stavro. He also said with all the sincerity he could muster, "We have only one objective: to bring home championships." *Of course* that was the case. Who could dispute it? Everyone knew that Tanenbaum had been battling for years to get control of the Leafs just so that he could bring home championships. Profit wouldn't matter in the least.

As the French like to say, the more things change, the more they stay the same.

Ballard, whose primary concern in running the Leafs was his profit margin, had been replaced by Stavro, whose primary concern in running the Leafs was his profit margin.

Now Stavro was gone, and the ownership was much more modern and sophisticated. The owner was not a felon or a grocer; it was now a conglomerate with representatives from a major bank, a pension plan and a large construction firm. But really, it was the same old story. The form changed, but the motive didn't. Profit was the primary concern, and the hockey team was nothing more than a means to that end.

The Light at the End of the Tunnel Gets Extinguished

Had Cliff Fletcher been allowed to do things his way, there would be no need for this book. Fletcher ran the Leafs from 1991 to 1997 and valued winning over greed. When he refused to recognize the error of his ways, the Leafs' window of opportunity was slammed shut.

At one point during their trek through the Stanley Cup wilderness, the Leafs came tantalizingly close to getting it right. The brass ring was right there for them to grab. All they needed was a little fortitude, a little perseverance and a little dedication. But as has so often been the case with this ill-fated franchise, it was not to be. Like Icarus of Greek mythology, once they got close to the sun, they came down with a crash.

Nevertheless, if you consider all the managerial moves that the Leafs have made since they last hoisted the Stanley Cup in 1967, one stands out above all the others as being laden with promise and hope. That was the brilliant decision made by Donald Giffin in July 1991 to hire Cliff Fletcher as president and general manager of the team.

For that brief period between Ballard's death and Steve Stavro's successful fight to gain control of the team, Giffin was in charge, and he made the move that could have put an end to the Stanley Cup drought.

Two months before he was hired by the Leafs, Fletcher was running the Calgary Flames and was representing them at an NHL finance committee meeting in New York. Giffin was there on the Leafs' behalf, and during a break in the proceedings, Fletcher let Giffin know that he was interested in the much-publicized post of "Leafs hockey czar."

There weren't a lot of qualified candidates for that job. After all, the Leafs were in turmoil at every level. The ownership was in the hands of the courts. Over the previous decade, management had batted somewhere around .900 in the bad-trade department. The first- and second-round draft choices for the upcoming season had been frittered away. And the team had just finished twentieth in a twenty-one-team league.

The Leafs had established such a losing tradition that in the years since their last championship in 1967 the Stanley Cup had been won twelve times by teams that weren't even in existence when the Leafs last won. Expansion teams had been born and had matured while the Leafs continued to flounder.

Given those circumstances, Giffin was delighted to learn that a man of Fletcher's calibre was willing to take the job, and matters progressed from there. Had Fletcher subsequently been given free rein to do as he wished, it is not at all unlikely that he would have recreated the strong franchise he had built with the Flames, a team that went to the Stanley Cup final in 1986 and won the Cup in 1989.

But there was to be no repeat performance in Toronto.

Giffin, obviously, was a Fletcher supporter and would have backed him at every level. And Giffin held the balance of power for the moment. But the battle for control of the Ballard estate was still in full swing at the time of the hiring. Not long afterwards, Giffin was nudged aside by Stavro.

Fletcher's hiring had infuriated Stavro, who had envisioned a completely different hierarchy. He himself would be at the top, his friend and accountant Lyman MacInnis would be chief executive officer, and John Muckler would be general manager.

Fletcher might not have been the last person Stavro would have hired, but he certainly would not have received any serious consideration. For one thing, Fletcher was a free-spender. For another, he did everything in a first-class fashion. Those were not attributes highly regarded—or possessed—by Stavro.

Fletcher's salary alone was a sore point. Giffin had signed Fletcher for five years at $850,000 a year. Relative NHL salaries were not made public, but it's almost certain that Fletcher's stipend at the time was the highest of any non-playing team employee in the NHL.

It was also stipulated in his contract that Fletcher had near-total control. Stavro could still get involved in some areas, especially those relating to finances, but for the most part, Fletcher was in charge. This was important because it meant that Stavro's close friend and lawyer, Brian Bellmore, the Leafs' alternate governor, could not exercise any power over Fletcher.

As a result, on the day when Bellmore walked into Fletcher's office and demanded that he trade Félix Potvin for Patrick Roy, Fletcher was under no obligation to pursue the matter. He tried to explain to Bellmore that it takes two to trade, but he was interrupted by Bellmore, who said that he wasn't asking, he was telling. Fortunately for Fletcher, his authority was such that he was able to ignore this patently ridiculous order.

From the day Fletcher took over the Leafs, he was hindered to varying degrees by Stavro and Bellmore. Had he been allowed to follow his own course of action, the Leafs would have evolved into one of the league's powerhouses. No one can ever say with absolute certainty that they would have won the Stanley Cup— there are too many variables along the way to make that concrete assertion. But it *can* be said with absolute certainty that the Leafs would have been legitimate Cup contenders.

Unlike anyone who had run the Leafs for the previous quarter-century, Fletcher knew what he was doing. He had a long-range plan and he started with a vital tenet that had eluded all his pre-decessors: You can't build a hockey team just by building a hockey team.

The team itself—the roster of players—is only one part of a highly complex organization. It needs the right kind of coaches. It needs experienced management as part of a competent front office. It needs a capable support staff of trainers, physicians and so on. It needs a solid scouting staff, and it needs all these groups working together on a cohesive long-term plan.

Let's start with scouting. For years, the Leafs' amateur scouting staff had been composed of two or three of the Ballard faithful who couldn't be shoved into jobs anywhere else. Had the players been horses, the Leafs might have won a string of Stanley Cups. A joke making the rounds asked what was the best way to contact the Leafs' scouting staff. The answer was to meet them at their usual seats just before post time.

No wonder that, at the time Fletcher took over, not a single player drafted by the Leafs later than the third round was playing in the league. The Central Scouting combine provided all the expertise that was necessary to make the early picks. After that, you were on your own. And once the Leafs had to make their own decisions, they failed abysmally, especially with regard to European players who were having a marked impact on the NHL. They had only one: marginal prospect Alexander Godynyuk.

Fletcher immediately shunted old scouting standbys Dick Duff and Floyd Smith into the pro scouting area, which meant it was now their responsibility to give the coach some insight into the team he'd be facing in upcoming games, a luxury never accorded in the past.

Fletcher set up a ten-man amateur-scouting staff under the highly respected Pierre Dorion. He hired former star player Anders Hedberg to scout Europe and look for gems.

Meanwhile, Fletcher himself sought out potential free agents. Sometimes, they weren't potential enough, and he became the subject of tampering complaints. But at least that was an indication that he was targeting the kind of players that teams considered to be valuable.

He moved the farm team from Newmarket, a Toronto suburb, to St. John's, Newfoundland. Newmarket had been ideal for Ballard because players could be shipped back and forth at minimal cost. But Fletcher was more concerned about building a team than saving money and saw St. John's as an ideal locale.

"There is pressure on the players to perform," he explained. "Their development there will be good from that standpoint. When they were in Newmarket, let's face it, that's a bedroom community for Toronto. There was no identity at all."

The overriding idea, Fletcher explained, was that even before they graduated to the NHL club, players would learn to recognize the responsibility that went with wearing the maple leaf on their sweaters.

Fletcher added assistant coaches to the organization—one in Toronto and one in St. John's. Bill Watters, who had been a well-respected player agent, was brought in to act as assistant to the general manager. Fletcher even tried to rebuild the links to the past that had been so callously destroyed by Ballard. There was to be a Leafs alumni lounge, and former players were to be given tickets to games.

Darryl Sittler was appointed to the post of special consultant. Even Ted Kennedy, the revered former captain of the Leafs, who had refused to have anything to do with the team while it was being run by Ballard, came back and took part in a pre-game ceremony at the Gardens.

Despite all these moves, the rebuilding of the Leafs could not take place overnight. When a team is as bad as the Leafs were, and the organization is as dysfunctional as that one was, the regeneration process is not a simple one.

Not everyone accepted that point. When the team started slowly in Fletcher's first season, the usual critics in the media started offering their advice, demanding trades, firings and call-ups. Fletcher ignored them.

"I'm at the stage of my career where I want to get the job done," he explained. "I know it will be done. I'm going to try to do the job based on my twenty years of experience as a manager in the league and I'm not going to be influenced by outside forces because once I start to be influenced by outside forces, then I know we're off the track."

For all intents and purposes, Fletcher was starting with an expansion team. Talent was thin, and future draft choices had been thrown away.

Under the previous regime, the Leafs had been in total chaos. Now, Fletcher faced the task of having to improve the club without creating a similar atmosphere of turmoil and relentless change. This would require a delicate touch, but it was very important.

Throughout the Ballard era, players were always nervous because they never knew what to expect next. Fletcher was trying his best to provide stability.

"I get the feeling that players now are feeling comfortable," said Watters a couple of months into that first season, "and that what is being done upstairs is now being done in a professional sense. There aren't going to be any disasters coming from that area. It's almost like a security blanket.

"The players know who the boss is going to be, and they know that he has done it before, so they're prepared to jump on for the ride."

When Fletcher took over the Leafs, they had missed the playoffs in two of the three previous seasons. They missed the playoffs in his first season as well, but along the way, Fletcher made all the moves listed above and added some trades that set the table for a much-improved Toronto team that was finally able to earn some respect around the NHL.

The first important acquisition came in training camp. Like any capable hockey executive, Fletcher was aware that no team can be successful without a good goalie. In the first of many favourable deals he was to make, Fletcher sent Vincent Damphousse, Peter Ing, Luke Richardson and Scott Thornton to the Edmonton Oilers for Glenn Anderson, Craig Berube and Grant Fuhr.

Fuhr was the perfect goalie for a rebuilding team like Toronto. He had been a Stanley Cup winner and was virtually unflappable. Although some goalies get angry when they don't get enough protection, Fuhr was always philosophical about being peppered with dozens of shots. "Well, it's great for breaking in equipment," he chirped after one such evening.

Then, in midseason, having stabilized the Leafs' goaltending situation by acquiring Fuhr, Fletcher made the biggest trade in the history of the NHL, a ten-player deal with his former team. This one allowed Fletcher to bring in Doug Gilmour, Jamie Macoun, Kent Manderville, Ric Nattress and Rick Wamsley from Calgary in return for Berube, Godynyuk, Gary Leeman, Michel Petit and Jeff Reese.

It may not be the most one-sided trade in hockey history, but it's definitely on the list. Flames GM Doug Risebrough was new at his craft, having held the position only since Fletcher departed for the Leafs. Fletcher, the cagey veteran of the GM wars, knew enough to start it out as a possible Gilmour-for-Leeman deal—which in itself would have been a big win for Fletcher. Then he proposed various additions to the trade, and the two kept talking and adding players until the final deal was consummated.

It was a crucial deal for the Leafs, not only because they got by far the better of it from a talent point of view, but because they added four players who had Stanley Cup rings. The value of such experience in the NHL should never be underestimated, especially on teams that have wallowed in the depths for years.

By the time the season ended, Fletcher had also picked up a few other serviceable and reliable players, including Mark Osborne, Ken Baumgartner and Brad Marsh.

Thanks to Fletcher's moves, the Leafs made huge strides in that one season. But Fletcher was far from finished. The following summer, he added Sylvain Lefebvre, one of the best young defensive defencemen in the game.

In order to maintain stability, Fletcher initially kept the coach he inherited, Tom Watt. But after one year, Watt was fired and replaced by Pat Burns, who had been in Montreal and had won more games than any other coach in the NHL between 1988 and 1992.

As a result, when the Leafs opened the 1992–93 season, they were a genuine team for the first time in years, and they proved the point by rolling into the playoffs with a whopping thirty-two-point improvement over Fletcher's first year.

Fletcher was named Executive of the Year by *The Hockey News,* and Burns won the Jack Adams Award as the NHL's coach of the year. Much more importantly to the fans, the team came within a hair of advancing to the Stanley Cup final.

To this day, those 1993 playoffs tug at the heartstrings of any Leafs fan old enough to remember that season. Ask any one of them for his or her greatest memory in the past forty years, and it will almost certainly go back to one of the three consecutive seven-game series.

It could be Nik Borschevsky's goal in double overtime in the Joe Louis Arena that eliminated the heavily favoured Detroit Red Wings in the opening series. (As it happens, subsequent technological developments have made it clear that the Leafs' Mark Osborne actually scored what would have been the game-winner late in regulation time, but the putative goal was not allowed and, therefore, the glory of the Borschevsky moment remains unsullied.)

It could be Doug Gilmour's wraparound goal to win the opener of the series against the St. Louis Blues. That goal, too, was in double overtime, and it came on the Leafs' sixty-fourth shot of the evening.

It could be the fight between Wendel Clark and Marty McSorley in the Western Conference final against the Los Angeles Kings.

It could be the non-call in game six when Wayne Gretzky's errant stick cut Gilmour, followed by Gretzky's game-winner at 1:41 of overtime. (Kings fans point out that as far as they're concerned, Gilmour had no business being in the game. He should have been suspended for the head-butt he delivered earlier in the series. But that's for fans to battle about. The fact remains that Leafs Nation has not forgotten the Gretzky incident.)

It could be the Gretzky hat trick in game seven that brought the Kings back from a 3–2 deficit to win the series on the road.

Or it could be just the euphoria that built up within Leafs fans from coast to coast as they revelled in the insults fired back and forth by coaches Pat Burns and Barry Melrose, the possibility of an all-Canadian, "Original Six" final between the Leafs and the Canadiens, the excitement of back-to-back-to-back seventh games, and more than anything else, the possibility of the Leafs at long last winning the Stanley Cup.

As it turned out, that was to be the greatest moment of the Cliff Fletcher era. The team he had built stayed strong and advanced to the conference finals again the following season. But the magic was not there in 1994, and the Leafs simply wore down. They defeated the Chicago Blackhawks and San Jose Sharks but were visibly tired in the next round and lost to the Vancouver Canucks in five games.

It is said that coaches have a shelf life. That's why Burns lasted only four years in Montreal despite having a fine winning percentage. In Toronto, his defence-first approach, which seemed to be more focused on getting the puck behind the net than in it, started to wear on the players as well.

All around the league in that era, players were rebelling against defensively oriented coaches. The 1992–93 New York Rangers, for example, had refused to follow Roger Neilson's instructions with the result that Neilson was fired. The next year, under Mike Keenan, what was essentially the same group of players won the Stanley Cup.

Bob Gainey, another defence-first coach who was also GM in Dallas, had seen the way the universe was unfolding in 1995 and resigned from his coaching job. Meanwhile, in New Jersey in 1995–96, the players were ignoring Jacques Lemaire so much that the defending Stanley Cup champions ended up missing the playoffs.

So on March 5, 1996, with the Leafs struggling and in danger of missing the playoffs, Fletcher fired Burns. "Now the onus is on the players," he said. "We feel our team is much more competitive than we've shown in the last two months, and it's going to be up to everyone to get their act together and move forward to confirm a playoff position and to cause havoc in the playoffs."

To get away from the stultifying style of Burns, Fletcher handed the coaching reins to Nick Beverley, a quiet, mellow man who let the players decide the style they wanted to play. As it turned out, the players did crank it up offensively and, as a result, got into the playoffs. But they bowed out in the first round, and with that, Fletcher's days were numbered.

Stavro, who had never supported Fletcher's free-spending ways and whose grocery business was running into difficult times, was not happy about the loss of playoff revenue. NHL players don't get paid during the playoffs, so the revenue the teams receive is just gravy for the owners. But a first-round loss with only three home gates was far less than Stavro wanted, and he started demanding that the more expensive players on the roster be unloaded.

In the summer of 1996, Fletcher had the opportunity to put the jewel in the crown. Gretzky, who had always harboured a love for the Maple Leafs, wanted to play in Toronto. His contract with the St. Louis Blues had expired, and he was a free agent.

Gretzky and his agent, Mike Barnett, talked with a series of teams, but one was the primary target.

"There were four deals I could have had," said Gretzky in a 2009 interview. "Bob Gainey called from the Dallas Stars, but I felt I'd already played in the southern United States and I didn't want to do that again. At that time, Dallas wasn't as established as it became later. Bob gave me a firm offer, and it was a good deal, but I'd been through the thing of building a team in the south and I just wanted to go to a team that was more established.

"The second offer was from Vancouver. I spent fourteen hours negotiating with them, but that fell through. I was really kind of relieved because I really wanted to go to Toronto.

"We called Cliff and asked if he was interested. He said he was, but if I was looking for big money, it was not going to happen. The owner was trying to save money to put it towards a new arena.

"So I said, 'Just put together a reasonable offer and we'll see what we can do.'

"He came back with a deal for $3 million a year with some money deferred. We said, 'Okay, we like that.'

"Toronto was my first choice. It was really where I wanted to go. But Cliff came back and said he had taken it to the owner, and the owner nixed it. The New York Rangers' offer came the next day, so I went to New York."

The elated Fletcher, with the Gretzky contract sealed and delivered but not signed, had taken the proposition to Stavro for what he thought would be a rubber-stamp approval. Wayne Gretzky, a living legend, was to end his career as a Maple Leaf.

Stavro's response was telling. "How many seats will that sell?" he asked.

The answer, of course, was that it wouldn't sell any. Even in the woeful days of the Ballard era, Maple Leaf Gardens had always sold out. The Gretzky deal was vetoed and the greatest player of his day—some would say the greatest player ever—went to the New York Rangers for an annual salary of $6.25 million.

Fletcher persevered and, at the 1997 trading deadline, made what was an excellent deal for the Leafs. He sent Doug Gilmour to the New Jersey Devils for Alyn McCauley, Jason Smith and Steve Sullivan. At least, it would have been an excellent deal had his successors kept the three players instead of frittering them away. But a few weeks later, the Leafs missed the playoffs, and Stavro had the excuse to do what he would have liked to have done six years earlier. He got rid of Fletcher.

The firing was made public on May 24, 1997, but in reality, the Fletcher era ended about fourteen months earlier, when Stavro turned Maple Leaf Gardens Ltd. into a private company. From that point on, the focus changed. The primary concern was no longer the development of a good hockey team. The primary concern—some might say obsession—was profit.

Fletcher was not fired because he did a bad job. Hockey teams go in cycles, and the Leafs were on their way back up. Fletcher was fired because Stavro needed a scapegoat.

Fletcher had a track record of building teams by spending. In Toronto, he made deals to acquire expensive players—Gilmour and Mats Sundin, for instance—and an expensive coach, Pat Burns. When he was forced by Stavro to move out expensive players, and the team was dismantled, it went totally against the methodology Fletcher had followed throughout his entire career. It was Stavro, not Fletcher, who wanted—and got—the jettisoning of such players as Mike Gartner, Dave Gagner and Todd Gill, a series of moves which then made it plausible to ship out Gilmour and Dave Ellett. It was Stavro who vetoed the signing of Gretzky.

"We were told to drop $6 million in salary," said Watters in 2009. "If Cliff and I had to do it again, I think we would have told them what would happen if we dropped $6 million in salary. It was a tremendous blow to the hockey team. When you think about it, they dismantled those teams that we had."

Nevertheless, with fans being what they are, Fletcher was under the gun for the team's failings. As the man responsible, Stavro should have fired himself. Instead, he fired Fletcher.

Even that move, which should have been simple and clean-cut if that's what Stavro wanted, couldn't be done properly. If Fletcher was going to be fired, it should have happened as soon as the regular season ended. Instead, it didn't take place until May 24, more than six weeks later.

It cost Stavro a $2.5 million buyout, but that could easily have been negotiated earlier. The simple fact is that, as usual, there was indecision at the top and an inability to act in a professional, businesslike fashion.

Since the Leafs had missed the playoffs, it seemed fairly obvious that they needed help. And since some of that help could come from the June draft, wouldn't it have made sense to have the new GM in his position for as long as possible leading up to that draft? And shouldn't that new GM have been given the maximum amount of time to acquaint himself with the team's strengths and shortcomings?

With Fletcher gone and a caretaker in place, only two players the Leafs selected in the 1997 draft ever made it to the NHL. They played a total of thirty-two games for the Leafs. One draft year, thirty-two man-games. No wonder the Leafs struggled.

Along the way, Stavro was convinced by other board members that the jobs of president and general manager should be split so that a new president could rein in some of Fletcher's spending. It could be passed off as a corporate restructuring, rather than the money-grab it really was. Stavro explained to the public that since he had decided the team needed a new president, Fletcher, as president, had to be fired. But he could have stayed on as general manager.

This was news to Fletcher. "The real issue is that they wanted a new general manager," Fletcher said. "It was all part of a new corporate structure. If they offered me just the GM's job, I may very well have stayed."

Until August, the Leafs were without *either* a president or a general manager. Then they brought in someone who had never been a president *or* a general manager. Or a coach. Not even a scout. But he could be counted on to keep the costs down. What else could possibly matter?

8

The Reign of the Philosopher King

The Ken Dryden era (1997–2004) was marked by lots of talk. And more talk. And more talk. Little wonder that Dryden finally left hockey for politics. He promised to win the Cup, but didn't. Was anyone surprised? Had he been able to keep promises, he would never have got into politics, would he?

If the guy at the top doesn't know what he's doing, how can he possibly be expected to make the right choice when deciding who he'll hire to work for him?

For instance, if you've never sailed, how can you possibly evaluate the merits of someone who professes to be an excellent sailor? He can tell you whatever he wants about his prowess, but how will you know whether any of it makes sense or whether it's just so much bafflegab?

Ken Dryden was universally praised as the saviour of the Leafs when he arrived on the scene to assume the Leafs' presidency on May 31, 1997.

But how would Leafs chairman Steve Stavro, who hired Dryden, know what makes a good hockey executive? Stavro was a grocer. Had Dryden been a turnip—which might have been an improvement—Stavro would certainly be qualified to make an evaluation of his merits. But Stavro was demonstrably devoid of any hockey knowledge of his own, and was now handing over the operation to a man who had been out of hockey for the better part of two decades.

The appointment came about because Dryden lived in Toronto and moved in the same social circles as a couple of members of the Maple Leafs' board of directors, Brian Bellmore and Larry Tanenbaum. During their conversations, the subject of hockey often arose, and occasionally either Bellmore or Tanenbaum would put out feelers regarding Dryden's interest in returning to the game in a managerial capacity. For years, Dryden rebuffed the overtures, but when Fletcher was fired and the offer was put forward once more, Dryden accepted.

Again, it was an example of the same flaw that has bedevilled the Leafs for so long and continues to do so to this day. If the guy at the top isn't competent, how can it reasonably be expected that those below him will be competent? And if you've got an organization full of incompetents, should it come as a great surprise that the team doesn't rise to the top of the NHL?

Dryden got the job because he happened to be a friend of a couple of guys on the board. And the top guy—Stavro—didn't know enough about hockey to realize that it takes colossal arrogance to believe that someone who has been away from the game for eighteen years can be as good at a job as those who have been working at it day in, day out for all of those eighteen years.

Granted, Dryden is a Hall of Fame player. There are still those in Montreal who say that he would not have been accorded such an elevated status had he played with an ordinary team, but that's debatable. Furthermore, it's not the point. He did not play with an ordinary team. He played for the Canadiens and he played the most difficult position. He won the Stanley Cup six times in an eight-year career, posting a playoff goals-against average of 1.56, and when he took the 1973–74 season off to pursue a law degree, while pressing his demands for a more lucrative contract, the Canadiens did not win the Cup.

And there's no doubt that Dryden is intelligent. In addition to a law degree, Dryden also had earned a degree in history from an Ivy League university—Cornell, to be precise. There was no doubt that he had the intellect to manage an operation like the Leafs. But did he have the expertise? He had retired as a professional player in 1979 and since that time had all but ignored the National Hockey League. By 1997, however, it could fairly be said that he knew no more about the inner workings of the league than any casual fan who watched the games on Saturday nights. He might have known the names of some high-profile players, but he had no idea who the quality players were, what was going on behind the scenes, or what were the vagaries of other league executives. Those crucial nuggets of information that could be of value to anyone interested in improving his team were never going to come Dryden's way. He had a better chance of being hit by a meteor.

Glen Sather, the GM of the Edmonton Oilers at the time, knew Dryden well. They had been teammates on the Canadiens for a year and had even been roommates. But Sather also loved to prick Dryden's bubble, and when he was asked about the hiring, he said, "I have a lot of respect for Ken, but it's a different racket he's in now. The primary goal is screwing the guy next to you while not letting it hurt the game. Sometimes you have to be a street fighter to do that, and Ken has to learn some of that. I don't know if Ken has that mentality.

"Ken has a way of circumventing what he wants to say. He gets his point across, but not right away. Maybe he'll change."

During his hiatus from the NHL, Dryden had moved to England and written *Home Game,* a splendid book about the nature of hockey and its more ethereal aspects. Other than that, little of Dryden's time away from the game had been devoted to staying conversant with the NHL. He had written a novel, *The Moved and the Shaken,* a book so dry it left its readers neither moved nor shaken. He had been on a few governmental committees and written the odd report. He had helped produce a television series based on *Home Game.* In short, he had been such a dilettante and had spent so much time at the government trough that it's a wonder he didn't get offered the post of governor general.

Instead, he became president of the Maple Leafs, another post based largely on pomp and ceremony but demanding little of substance. Because the recently fired Fletcher had been both president and GM of the team, Dryden was easily able to identify his most urgent duty.

"The toughest job will be to hire the right general manager," he said at the press conference to announce his coronation. "He's the key guy to put our organization together. He'll choose the head coach and the assistant coaches. There are lots of available candidates. My job is to sign the one who'll bring the Stanley Cup back to Toronto.

"We want someone who'll be around for a while," he insisted. "We need a stretch of successes, not only two years as we had in 1993 and 1994. That's soon forgotten. We need stretches of five or six years, so people forget the bad years."

Sounds good. Dryden always did sound good. But what did he actually do? Well, let's look at that, with an eye towards those statements.

"Hire the right general manager." He didn't hire a general manager of any sort.

Have the GM "choose the head coach." In fact, Dryden chose the head coach.

Have the GM "choose . . . the assistant coaches." No, the head coach hired the assistants.

"Sign the one who'll bring the Stanley Cup back to Toronto." We all know how that worked out.

Dryden dithered so long about the hiring of a general manager that, two years later, he still didn't have one. He first appointed the incumbent assistant GM, Bill Watters, as acting general manager. Then on August 20, he brought in Mike Smith to act as associate general manager.

Smith carried out most of the normal functions of a general manager for two years, made a total botch-up of the situation and then left after he tried a power grab that didn't work. The bizarre relationship between Dryden and Smith will be elaborated upon in the following chapter, and it typifies the management problems that almost always seem to be at the source of the Leafs' problems.

But throughout the turmoil, Dryden was continuing to hold the post of president, and with Smith on his way out the door, Pat Quinn usurped Smith's position.

Quinn was the coach and didn't really want to be GM. But nor did he want to report to Dryden as general manager. The last thing he wanted was Ken Dryden telling him what to do. Not that he would have paid attention anyway, but he didn't want to give Dryden an excuse to climb down from his ivory tower and get involved in the day-to-day operation of the Leafs.

It is telling that, to seek his promotion, a move he admitted was prompted by a sense of "self-preservation," Quinn went directly to Stavro rather than make his case to Dryden.

The fact is, Quinn didn't get along with Dryden any better

than Smith did. The two rarely communicated directly, and once sat only a few feet apart in an airport lounge for two straight hours without talking to each other. A gaggle of journalists, of which I was one, noted this development with amusement and made sure that at least one of us kept watch to ensure there was no historic breakthrough. There wasn't.

Here's an example of their relationship. Shortly after Quinn's arrival in Toronto as coach, he banished the media from the team bus. It didn't matter much to me, because I rarely made road trips with the Leafs at the time, but it mattered a lot to the beat writers who had travelled on the Leafs' team bus as long as there had been one. When you land in San Francisco late at night and the team hotel is in San Jose, for example, it saves a lot of hassle if you can travel with the team. It's even a great convenience just to make the daily bus trips back and forth between the hotel and the rink in some of Canada's inclement weather.

All the other NHL teams let the writers on the bus. Some teams even encourage the media to travel on their charter flights. The Leafs allowed their tame media—the broadcasters who are in their employ—to travel with them, but the independent newspaper people were banned.

It was suggested that, since I had covered Dryden during his playing days in Montreal and knew him well, I should approach him on behalf of the beat writers.

As was usual for Dryden, he didn't really answer one way or another when asked about Quinn's decision to ban the beat writers. And upon hearing the direct questions that were put to him— "Pat Quinn does work for you, doesn't he? You are his boss, aren't you?"—he simply turned away.

It was a minor incident, but it typified the way things worked— or didn't work—in the Toronto organization. There was a theoretical chain of command, but the reality was that Dryden didn't have the hockey expertise to quarrel with Quinn, who had been involved with a number of organizations in a number of capacities—player, coach, general manager and president.

Quinn had only disdain for Dryden, whom he considered, with good reason, to be a hockey lightweight who was merely indulging his latest whim. Quinn was a hockey lifer, whereas Dryden was described by his friends as someone who spent his working life implementing a series of five-year plans.

It was typical of the Toronto organization that these two men, whose philosophies were radically different and whose personalities were even farther apart, would think they could work together productively.

Dryden had inherited Mike Murphy as coach, but after Murphy had missed the playoffs in Dryden's first year and after Dryden had dodged the issue of Murphy's return for most of the summer, Murphy was finally fired and replaced by Quinn.

But Stavro never thought of saying, "Ken, why did you let Murphy twist in the wind all summer? Weren't you aware by the end of the season that you didn't think he was good enough? If you were going to fire him, why didn't you have the decency to do it earlier so that he had a better chance to get another job?"

Nor, apparently, did Stavro ever say, "Ken, do you realize what you're letting yourself in for by hiring Quinn? This guy is not a yes-man, and he does things his own way. Since you two are not at all alike, won't there be a problem?"

But, of course, Stavro never asked any such questions. How would he know anything about the etiquette of hockey or the personality of the people in the game? He was just an investor. His sidekick, lawyer and alternate governor, Brian Bellmore, saw himself as the hockey expert who would keep Stavro informed, but as every true hockey person in the organization knew, Bellmore's rather curious ideas on the subject were valuable only for the unintentional humour they produced.

When Leafs front-office staffers learned that Bellmore was in the area, they tried their best to make themselves scarce. If Bellmore was not spotted until he was too close to dodge, the emergency expedient of picking up the telephone and pretending to be deep in conversation was often a useful ruse.

So the Leafs at the time were being run by a grocer, a kibitzer and a philosopher king. No wonder they went nowhere.

As one of his first acts, Dryden tried to bring in Bob Gainey to act as general manager and was even willing to give up all-star defenceman Mathieu Schneider as compensation. Elite defencemen are always the most difficult commodity to acquire in the NHL, but Dryden was willing to throw one away to bring in an old playing acquaintance as GM. At that time, Gainey was far from being the respected GM he eventually became, and he didn't even come close to providing what the Leafs needed most—someone who had experience at running an NHL team and had a resumé to prove it.

When it came to the abstract areas of hockey—or abstract areas of anything else for that matter—Dryden was fine. It was because of his efforts, for instance, that the Leafs got out of the league's Western Conference and moved back to the east, where most of their traditional rivals resided. To get his way, Dryden had to make some concessions to the three NHL teams from western Canada, but he didn't mind doing so. He saw the promotion of Canadian hockey as his calling in life, and if his Leafs had to play two games in each of the three western Canadian cities while those teams played only once in Toronto, so be it.

This type of schedule was an inconvenience for the Leafs, perhaps even an unnecessary hardship. But Dryden felt they should endure it for the good of the Canadian game.

There were some Leafs fans, however, who felt that as president of the Leafs, Dryden had misplaced his priorities.

In that era, the small-market Canadian teams were protected from American predators. If a free agent on a Canadian team received an offer from an American team, the Canadian team could retain his rights by matching only 70 per cent of the offer. As part of the Canadian Assistance Program, an NHL fund would kick in the remaining 30 per cent of the player's contract. But if the free agent and the bidding team were both Canadian, the 100 per cent figure was back in play.

So even though Dryden was in a financial position to go after quality free agents like Edmonton's Ryan Smyth, he wouldn't do it because he felt that he would be causing undue hardship to the cash-strapped Oilers.

Dryden did make one excellent acquisition during his tenure as general manager, but it had more to do with the weather patterns of southern Ontario than with his acumen.

It was one of those steamy summer evenings that tend to descend on Toronto in July, and Dryden decided to go for a late-night stroll. While wandering down Dupont Street with his son, he stopped at a twenty-four-hour food market to get an ice cream. Also out wandering around the neighbourhood that night was player agent Don Meehan, who lived on Madison Avenue, which intersects Dupont. He, too, opted to get an ice cream at the store.

The two exchanged pleasantries and started chatting about hockey. One of Meehan's premier clients was goaltender Curtis Joseph, who at the time was a free agent in search of a team. "You should make Curtis an offer," Meehan said.

Dryden's response was that he had no interest in a goaltender. With Félix Potvin holding down that position, he felt that the team was solid for years to come. But Meehan persisted.

Joseph, he said, was a better goaltender than Potvin. Even though

Potvin showed promise, Joseph was a proven commodity. Meehan pointed out that this represented an opportunity for Dryden to significantly upgrade his team without having to give away any players in the process. All Dryden had to do was sign Joseph, then the goaltending position would be rock solid—"and you know how important goaltending is, Kenny," said Meehan.

As for Potvin, because he showed such promise, he could be traded away to a team desperate for goaltending at a decent price. If Dryden signed Joseph, Meehan said, he could solidify two positions for nothing more than a bit of cash. It took Meehan close to an hour to convince Dryden of the merits of his case, but eventually, as his ice cream dripped onto the floor, Dryden agreed.

The deal turned out to be all that Meehan had said it would be. Joseph proved to be arguably the best free agent the Leafs ever signed, and he played four seasons for them—all winners. Furthermore, he was an excellent teammate and loved by the Toronto fans.

And Potvin did indeed prove to be a valuable commodity on the trading market. Three months into the season, he was dealt for Bryan Berard, who was so highly regarded that he had been the first-overall choice in the 1995 entry draft.

But once Quinn took over as general manager, there was little for Dryden to do on the hockey front. He had already been heavily involved in the game-production side of the business, and with Quinn on the scene, he had little choice but to withdraw from the day-to-day operations.

If you go to a Leafs game in the Air Canada Centre today, you'll still see evidence of Dryden's involvement. The mid-game spotlighting of a former Leaf in the stands. The bombastic pre-game announcements, with their overblown, overbearing and overwrought prose. The stylized TML on the sweaters, which many liken to a swastika. The trek through throngs of spectators that the Leafs must make to get to the ice from their dressing room. The artistic tickets with a different theme for every game. The mascot, Carlton the Bear. Relentless ear-splitting intrusions during stoppages, generally with music so loud that it made even Dryden's late father, Murray, sit with his fingers in his ears.

There are many others, but you get the picture. And it must be said that, when evidence came to light that there had been sexual predators in the Leafs' employ during the Ballard regime, Dryden did an excellent job of defusing the situation and dealing with it in a sensitive manner without ever trying to shrug off the team's responsibility.

But when Dryden got involved in the hockey side of the business, he had little to contribute. There is some irony in the fact that when Joseph was trying to negotiate a new contract after four years of excellent service with the Leafs, it was primarily Dryden's intrusion that created the final split.

Meehan and Quinn were working on a new deal, but when Quinn went home to Vancouver for the summer, Dryden opted to get involved in the process. He decided to take a hard line, essentially threw gasoline on the fire and, if you'll pardon the mixing of metaphors, put the final straw on the camel's back.

Dryden had already done a lot to turn Joseph against the Leafs, as will be seen in an upcoming chapter, and his involvement in negotiations that were not part of his job was another contributing factor to Joseph's departure.

Joseph represented the only significant on-ice contribution that Dryden made during his time with the Leafs, and it began by accident and ended in acrimony.

Finally, on May 19, 2004, almost exactly seven years after his arrival, Dryden found a new cause. With a federal election in the wind and a safe Liberal riding on offer, he went off to run for Parliament. Saving the Leafs was no longer a priority. Now it was time to save Canada. And possibly the world.

9

The Russians Are Coming!
The Russians Are Coming!

Mike Smith is the general manager who never was. From the summer
of 1997 to the summer of 1999, he did the work, made the trades, negoti-
ated the contracts. But he never had the title. Because of that, no one can
say he screwed up as GM. But they can say he screwed up.

Mike Smith's stint as general manager of the Maple Leafs was
curious in one major aspect: it never happened.

In their usual bumbling fashion, the Leafs couldn't even get the
titles right. Ken Dryden was president and general manager. But
shortly after his arrival on the scene, he brought Smith into the
organization and gave him the curious title of associate general
manager. Dryden had inherited a capable assistant general manager
in Bill Watters, and he didn't want to relinquish his own status as
GM. He therefore dreamed up a new title for Smith.

So for two years, from the summer of 1997 to the summer of 1999, Smith acted as general manager and is widely believed by Leafs fans to have been the GM. But instead, he operated in some sort of nether region, pulling the strings but not really holding the power.

Early in his career as general manager, Dryden expressed surprise to me that a trade put together by Watters had been initiated and consummated so quickly. I explained to him that there was a reason for this. The team he had dealt with had been forced to act quickly to avoid an unpleasant and potentially explosive situation. That team had on its roster a player who once had an affair with the wife of an NHL goalie. Both players knew about it, and now the team had just traded for the goalie. As a result, they had to get the other guy out of town in a hurry, and the Leafs were the beneficiary. Dryden had no inkling of the background to his deal.

Because of that, and similar incidents showing Dryden to be out of touch with the day-to-day realities of the NHL, it seems quite likely that another story—one which neither party will confirm—is true. The story is that it was because of a practical joke by Glen Sather, then of the Edmonton Oilers, that the Leafs got stuck with Mike Smith.

Given the history and personalities of Sather and Dryden, it certainly seems likely. During their time as teammates with the Montreal Canadiens, Sather had repeatedly taken great delight in pulling practical jokes on Dryden.

On this occasion, it appears that when Dryden was looking for someone to help him with the managerial responsibilities, he sought Sather's advice about Smith, the former GM of the Winnipeg Jets. Sather responded with a glowing recommendation. But the truth of the matter was that Smith had been an astonishingly poor general manager, never having won a single playoff round in his entire NHL career.

He was infamous throughout hockey as someone who was obsessed with a desire to prove that Russian players were superior, and it was clear that he would keep on ruining hockey teams in his relentless quest to justify that stance.

The problem was that, while the Russians could occasionally make some nifty plays in the regular season, they tended to disappear in the playoffs. The situation has changed considerably since then, but at that time, the Stanley Cup was just another trophy to the Russians. They had grown up under the Soviet system in which the IIHF World Championship was considered to be the most important annual tournament. The Stanley Cup? That was just a post-season competition for which players don't get paid. NHL salaries stop being paid on the last day of the season. As far as the Russian players were concerned, a forecheck or a backcheck was nowhere near as important as a paycheque. They could hardly wait to get the post-season out of the way and head home.

Under the playoff system that was in effect in those days, Smith's Jets often had to face the Edmonton Oilers or Calgary Flames, never an enticing prospect. But in 1993, they were up against the Vancouver Canucks, a much less demanding opponent. After four games, the Jets didn't have so much as a second assist from four key players—Evgeny Davydov, Alexei Zhamnov, Sergei Bautin and Igor Ulanov. Spot a connection?

But Smith's relationships with his North American players weren't exactly stellar, either. His evaluation of Kris Draper was that he could not play in the NHL. Had his name been Draperov, he would probably have been a first-liner. But it wasn't, so Smith sold him to the Detroit Red Wings for a dollar. That was in 1993. On February 2, 2009, Draper played in his 1,000th NHL game—all but twenty of them with Detroit. In his tenure with the Wings, Draper has earned no fewer than four Stanley Cup rings.

Winnipeg defenceman Phil Housley held Smith in such regard

that at the Jets' annual post-season party—often held the night before the playoffs began—he grabbed Smith and bounced him off a wall and was about to do considerably greater damage until a few teammates pulled him off the GM.

Eventually, Smith lost the services of Housley, whose name often comes up for Hall of Fame consideration. Smith said that he couldn't afford Housley's contractual demands and had to let him go. But he quickly gave a pair of nondescript Russians, who couldn't even crack the mediocre Jets lineup, one-way contracts totalling $1 million. At this time, the average NHL salary was in the $400,000 range. So Housley was gone, but two Russians were having a great time in the minors on bloated NHL salaries.

There were lots of other Smith transgressions, but Dryden, thanks to his hiatus from the game, didn't know about them. Any recommendation from his old pal Sather would have seemed to be quite reasonable.

There is further corroboration for the suggestion that Sather pulled a fast one on Dryden. By the 1998–99 season, Smith had been employed by the Leafs for a year, and Dryden had come to despise him to the point that the two were barely coexisting. It would stand to reason that by that time, if Sather had indeed burdened Dryden with Smith, Dryden would be in no mood for any further practical jokes from Sather.

In November 1998, I was covering a game between Sather's Oilers and the Leafs at Maple Leaf Gardens and wandered down press row to talk to Sather. Without any serious prompting, he volunteered the information that a proposed all-Canadian tournament for the 1999 pre-season had collapsed because Dryden wouldn't cooperate.

Said Sather, trying to hold back a smirk, "He has forgotten about when he was kissing everybody's butt last year so he could switch conferences. We supported him, and now he has forgotten that he's still a Canadian."

Sather, being no stranger to the propensity of sportswriters to stir up trouble, knew that this allegation would immediately be passed along to Dryden, who was only a few steps away.

"That's outrageous," spluttered Dryden, barely able to contain himself. Then, after a pause, he tersely added, "We have spent more time thinking about this tournament, working on this tournament than Mr. Sather—including a conference call yesterday which I was a part of, Calgary was a part of, Ottawa was a part of, Montreal was a part of. And noticeable by their absence was Edmonton. And it was a long discussion about this tournament."

"Why would Edmonton be absent?" he was asked.

"Now isn't that interesting?" Dryden asked, his voice dripping sarcasm. "That might be a good question for you and your friend who always has an axe to grind."

So it was back to Sather. Why hadn't he been in the discussion?

"I couldn't stand listening to him for an hour," said Sather with a chuckle.

By now, Sather was having great fun. "Kenny is backing out," he persevered. "He has forgotten his roots. The only reason we got a [pre-season] game against [the Leafs] last year was that Steve Stavro is a good Canadian."

Back to Dryden, who by now appeared ready to explode.

"It's completely unfair and inappropriate," he seethed. "I'm mad at axes to grind and idiot questions like this. What fool would ever say such a thing? It's outrageous and it's wrong."

But Kenny, you know who said it. It was Glen Cameron (Slats) Sather.

"Yes," Dryden said. "Slats is wonderful at dropping little balloons. Then who's the first to disappear? Slats. Everybody else is working on it, talking about it, and Sather, who is the hero of every story he tells, including this one, was here watching the practice yesterday when the rest of us were here working on it on a conference call.

"Glen Sather is in a world that is about this big," said Dryden, using his hands to follow the contours of his body, "and it does not go beyond the boundaries of the skin of Glen Sather. Everything is his version of the world. It happens to be, in most instances, very wrong."

That does not sound particularly like a guy who is pleased by the actions of his old friend. It sounds a lot more like someone who is tired of being the brunt of practical jokes.

All this happened just a few weeks after Smith had foisted Alexander Karpovtsev on the Leafs, yet another self-indulgent trade to satisfy his longing to build an organization that contained more Russians than the Gulag Archipelago.

Coming into that season, Mathieu Schneider was a top-notch defenceman. In fact, by the Leafs' own rating system, he was the best that they had.

He was no longer under contract, but the Leafs held his rights, and only three days into training camp, it appeared that an accord had been reached. Schneider would lower his original demand for $3.25 million (U.S.) annually and accept a deal of $2.7 million plus bonuses. It made sense. If he played well, he got more than $3.25 million, but he'd demonstrably be worth it. If he didn't play as well, the Leafs wouldn't have to pay him as much.

Everyone seemed pleased, and the Schneider camp was ready to sign. But suddenly, Smith started making extra demands. He wanted to insert extra clauses that had not been agreed upon. Essentially, he wanted to change the nature of the deal.

Schneider got miffed and returned to his original demand of $3.25 million. Both sides started digging in their heels, and thanks to Smith, what had been a nice, peaceful negotiation had turned into open warfare with Schneider refusing to come to training camp.

Schneider missed the entire exhibition season, and then Smith traded him—to the New York Rangers for journeyman Alexander Karpovtsev and a fourth-round draft pick.

Said one player, "The Leafs gave up an offensive defenceman who can be soft, for an offensive defenceman who's less offensive and softer."

An NHL scout said, "That trade makes no sense to me. Schneider has a lot of talent, and if you think he's soft, ask Paul Kariya or Jon Klemm." Those two had been recent recipients of solid Schneider hits. In fact, the Kariya hit had been so solid it had earned Schneider a three-game suspension.

Said an NHL general manager: "Schneider has some baggage, but so does Karpovtsev. That's a great deal for the Rangers. Potsy hasn't done anything for three years."

And so it went.

As has been pointed out, Smith was not the general manager at this time; Dryden was. Smith's title was associate general manager, but as near as anyone could tell, Dryden had given him the day-to-day managerial responsibilities. Or Smith had taken them, while Dryden adopted a more philosophical role, emerging from his office on occasion to make pronouncements on the state of the game or to pontificate to the masses.

Either way, it was Smith, not Dryden, who virtually gave away Jason Smith.

According to the players, the deal was initiated at the urging of assistant coach Rick Ley, who didn't like the fact that Smith skated hunched over. It was Ley's belief that you had to skate upright to be a decent player. The Edmonton Oilers had no such prejudice. After all, they once had a player who skated hunched over and didn't fare too badly, despite making himself something of a target by wearing the unusual number 99.

The Oilers couldn't believe that the Leafs would settle for so little for Jason Smith—a fourth-round pick and a second-round pick—and jumped at the chance to grab him.

Mike Smith appeared to have some sort of fatal attraction for fourth-round picks. At the trading deadline the previous year, he virtually threw away Jamie Macoun, sending him to the Detroit Red Wings for a fourth-round pick. Macoun subsequently became a key factor in the Wings winning their second successive Stanley Cup.

Jason Smith went on to become one of the most reliable defencemen in the league and the captain of the Oilers. In return, the Leafs got two draft picks, which they used to select a pair of immortals: Jonathan Zion and Kris Vernarsky.

The trades of Jason Smith and Schneider provide a perfect illustration of the wheel-spinning that went on during the Mike Smith regime. On the one hand, Smith didn't argue when Dryden followed Don Meehan's proposal and acquired Curtis Joseph as a free agent to solidify the goaltending situation. That move made backup goaltender Félix Potvin superfluous and everyone knew it. But Smith still managed to deal Potvin for Bryan Berard. Joseph and Berard were solid acquisitions.

But on the other hand, Smith also dealt away fine defencemen like Schneider and Jason Smith. What he got with one hand, he gave away with the other. And perhaps the most damaging aspect of Mike Smith's trade with Edmonton was that it came at one of those rare times when the Leafs were not far from being a genuine Stanley Cup challenger.

Jason Smith was a hard-nosed defensive defenceman, one of those guys who traditionally rise to the fore during the playoff grind. But he was essentially given away at the 1999 trading deadline, a day when quality players like Chris Chelios, Wendel Clark, Vincent Damphousse, Joé Juneau and Ulf Samuelsson switched teams. Instead of acquiring any of those players, all Smith did was turn the Leafs into a Jason-free zone. He sent Smith to Edmonton and traded Jason Podollan for Yanic Perreault, a soft, single-faceted player who could win face-offs but whose skating wasn't up to NHL standards.

For two years, the Leafs stumbled along in this dysfunctional fashion. Smith made the occasional deal, but not one that was likely to lead the Leafs out of the wilderness, perhaps because he was the least accessible GM in the league.

Toronto hockey writers who called other GMs and asked, "Are you talking to Mike Smith about anything?" would invariably get responses along the lines of "I tried to, but he didn't return my call," or "I wanted to, but he was out at a show and hasn't called back."

Dryden was the president and GM, occasionally sticking his nose into the hockey operation but increasingly becoming isolated from the real action. Watters continued as assistant general manager while Smith gradually assumed more and more power, making the trades, dealing with the media and acting as if his title did not contain the qualifying word "associate."

But power tends to corrupt, and finally, Smith decided to go after the GM's title. That might not have been unreasonable, but his mistake was in trying to displace Dryden at the same time. Even Dryden, naive as he was in the ways of the real world, saw through this one.

It was a calculated gamble by Smith. Had he got away with it, he would have been the new chief. But when he lost his gamble, he got the chop, thereby pushing his record in such endeavours to 1–1.

He had staged a palace coup in Winnipeg and pulled it off. On that occasion, the target was John Ferguson Sr., who had given Smith his first NHL job, as an assistant coach with the New York Rangers in the 1970s. When Ferguson moved to Winnipeg to become GM of the Jets, he brought Smith with him. Even so, during the 1988–89 season Smith went over Ferguson's head—or behind his back, depending on your choice of terminology—to get him ousted. Smith then assumed absolute power, reporting only to Jets owner Barry Shenkarow.

In Toronto, Smith pushed to be named general manager, a title he said would reflect his duties. Finally, Dryden offered him the post, expecting, not unreasonably, that as president he would be the man to whom Smith, as general manager, would report. But Smith turned down the offer and returned a counter-proposal suggesting that he would report to Dryden only if he felt like it. He wanted, he explained during the media conference call that was held shortly after his departure, "to report equally to Richard Peddie and Ken Dryden."

Not even Dryden was going to fall for that. Peddie was Dryden's superior, and if Smith were reporting to him, the "equal" status wouldn't last long. It's basic human nature. If you have two bosses and one is clearly more elevated than the other, why bother wasting time with the one who is lower on the totem pole?

Given Smith's reputation, there was little doubt that before long, he would be in Peddie's office sniping about Dryden on a regular basis, just as he did during his conference call. There were none of the usual pleasantries, just a barrage of shots at his former employer.

Here are a few examples. When asked about the phone call he received from Dryden telling him that he was fired, Smith said, "It was quite abrupt for Ken. So actually, it was fairly pleasant."

Reflecting on the previous season's dealings with Dryden, he said, "I ended up quite often trying to keep the door shut so our hockey team could perform and have some peace."

Dryden had made an earlier observation that his relationship with Smith was occasionally difficult. Smith fired back, "I'm not sure what Ken would be comparing that to, because this was his first ride in the management area of professional hockey. There's no question that the first year was a lot different than I expected. This year was, at times, very difficult, keeping this going forward and keeping everybody focused, and Ken found that difficult. I remember seeing him dancing around in the playoffs. It didn't look difficult at that time."

Smith's implications were easily understood. All that was good about the Maple Leafs could be ascribed to the hard work and diligence of Michael Smith. And the aforementioned Michael Smith deserves even more credit because he had to overcome the interference imposed on him by the error-prone Ken Dryden.

After that conference call, there remained no doubt that Smith was out for Smith and no one else. If he would make remarks of that nature with the ravenous Toronto media listening intently, what would he have said in private to Peddie about Dryden if given the opportunity? Isn't it also reasonable to assume that he would not have had the slightest reticence to unburden his soul to Peddie during those times of "equal reporting"?

When Dryden received Smith's counter-proposal, he finally realized what so many people in hockey—and some in the media—had told him. Smith was a dedicated loner. He always went his own way. If you wanted a dictator, he might have been your man—assuming you thought he was an astute judge of hockey talent, which is a separate discussion. If you wanted a team player, it was best to look elsewhere.

Even Dryden admitted after Smith's firing that the two of them did not get along. "Yes, there was a difficult relationship there," he said.

Still, he had offered Smith a contract to be the general manager. But when Smith sent back a revised version that was coming from a completely different planet, Dryden finally had to admit the error of his ways. He said he got "a kind of a feeling that it just wasn't going to work out."

As far as he was concerned, the Leafs were improving, but there were still obstacles to overcome before they evolved into genuine Stanley Cup contenders. "I wasn't confident," said Dryden, "that the feel here was right to meet that challenge."

No kidding. Smith was always at odds with Dryden. He didn't even talk to Anders Hedberg, who was in charge of player development. And he thought assistant general manager Bill Watters was a buffoon.

In fact, the only people he did try to get along with were those who might help him in his quest to get Dryden's job.

To the victors go the spoils. To the losers go the consultancies. And Mike Smith headed off into the sunset—or more accurately, in the opposite direction, to his home in Martha's Vineyard and a job as a consultant.

10

Here's Your Reward for a Magnificent Contribution: Bend Over

Curtis Joseph was a star. He willingly gave the organization a lustre that it didn't deserve. If for no other reason than that, he deserved to be well treated. But the Leafs have a history of embarrassing those who serve them best. Then they wonder why so many stars prefer to play elsewhere.

For some reason, the Maple Leafs seem to be unable to terminate relationships with their stars in an amicable fashion. When Curtis Joseph's contract was winding down, it should have been a simple matter to tell him either that they were interested in retaining his services or they weren't. After all, Joseph's abilities and accomplishments were well established. He'd been their goalie for four years.

But nothing is simple when it comes to the Leafs' financial dealings.

Joseph had done some great work for the Leafs—and for the city of Toronto. He arrived in 1998 as a free agent and used a substantial segment of his salary—more than $500,000 annually—to buy a box at Maple Leaf Gardens and subsequently at the Air Canada Centre, which he donated to the Sick Children's Hospital.

At each game, for the duration of Joseph's stay in Toronto, a number of children, many of them terminally ill, would be treated royally in that box. If their doctors allowed it, they would get the usual kids' treats of hot dogs and soft drinks. Otherwise, they would get as much fun food as their prescribed diets would allow. They all got a picture of Curtis, each one personally autographed to the youngster.

Joseph also visited the hospital frequently, and on more than one occasion when expensive medical equipment was required, he bought it. All of this was done without fanfare.

On the ice, he was everything the Toronto fans had been looking for in a goaltender. He won more than thirty games for three consecutive seasons and was the runner-up for the Vézina Trophy in both 1999 and 2000.

He was the goaltender who led the Leafs to their best season during Pat Quinn's tenure—their trip to the Eastern Conference finals in 2002.

But a few weeks later, in the summer of 2002, none of this mattered.

Of course, the situation should have been resolved long before that. And perhaps it was, but the Leafs, in typical fashion, simply didn't bother to tell Joseph. But there's plenty of evidence that the Toronto front office did not deal with Joseph in good faith.

As the season wound down, they refused to meet Joseph's agent, Don Meehan, to get the negotiations under way. As Joseph said shortly after settling in with his new team, the Detroit Red Wings, "Donnie negotiated in good faith. I don't think they negotiated in good faith—ever. Not at all."

The Leafs, however, had managed to put their usual misleading spin on the matter. Quinn appeared as a guest on a TSN show hosted by Michael Landsberg and said that Joseph had been asking for $11.5 million annually. He added, "We were convinced at a certain level, but not at the eleven-and-a-half-million-dollar level."

Joseph had been in the U.S. when the show aired and hadn't heard about it. When told of the allegation, he responded, "That's insane. That's utterly insane.

"Not at all," he said, continuing to shake his head in disbelief. "Not a chance."

The charitable might call it confusion. Others might call it duplicity. But whatever it was, it happened on all levels, and it plagued the negotiations between the Leafs and Meehan.

Joseph can't escape the feeling that for some reason, the Leafs never intended to keep him. Certainly, that appears to be the case.

According to Joseph, the negotiations, such as they were, never came close to the figures Quinn mentioned repeatedly. Furthermore, the people who had the responsibility for making the decisions, Quinn and Dryden, were involved only sporadically. Most of the talks were between Meehan and Bill Watters, then assistant to the president.

"Somebody came up with 7.2, right at the beginning after Mats had signed," Joseph said. "That was the first and only offer. I think Bill and Donnie were negotiating, then Donnie phoned back and . . ." Joseph made a whistling sound to indicate the offer had been whisked away.

"It ended up being up somewhere around 8.5 as an offer," said Joseph. "But that was at the last minute after [Dominik] Hašek retired. I think until then, [the only serious talks occurred when]

Donnie was negotiating a contract for four years and they pulled it off the table."

It seems odd to start to negotiate a contract within certain parameters, then withdraw it. Why would they do so?

"I have no idea," said Joseph. "There's no communication there. I have no idea. No phone call. No nothing."

That shouldn't come as a shock to anyone. These are the Leafs we're talking about. At that stage, as at so many other stages during the lengthy Stanley Cup drought, the Leafs' front office was in a state of constant confusion.

A full year earlier, Dryden, who communicated with Quinn as little as possible, got involved in the negotiations while Quinn was in Vancouver on vacation.

Quinn was the general manager at that point. Dryden was the president. Contracts are normally the responsibility of the GM, not the president, but in Quinn's absence, Dryden couldn't resist the temptation to try to upstage him.

The people in Joseph's camp believe that it was Dryden who withdrew the offer.

But it's also a matter of public record that Quinn said he had no intention of giving Joseph a four-year deal because at his age, it would turn out to be two years of playing and two years of semi-retirement.

Sounds reasonable. Why sign a goalie as old as Joseph? What goalie has ever played well in his later years? Just Johnny Bower, Jacques Plante, Glenn Hall, Hašek and a few dozen others.

But Quinn's intention to opt for a youth movement seemed like a plausible explanation. However, when Joseph left, he signed Ed Belfour, who was two years *older* than Joseph.

Stranger still, while the Leafs were still publicly announcing that they were offering to "negotiate" with Joseph, Belfour's website was already announcing that he had signed with the Leafs.

It was also Dryden's tinkering—some might call it meddling—that set the stage for the infamous post-Olympic scene when Joseph appeared to refuse Quinn's offer of a handshake.

Dryden loved nothing better than pre-game theatrics. He wrote many of the scripts himself, and they frequently contained melodramatic verbiage that had the press box chuckling and the fans looking around in puzzlement.

After Team Canada won the Olympic gold medal in Salt Lake City in 2002, Dryden was determined to stage a big extravaganza prior to the Leafs' next game.

But Joseph had been inconsequential in the gold medal triumph. He had started the opener, which Canada lost, and never played again.

The whole matter began to evolve as Joseph was driving into Toronto for the first home game after the Olympic break.

"I had got wind that Ken was setting up a big deal bringing in Catriona Le May Doan," he explained afterwards. "I just wanted to get back and play a game—get a win for the Toronto Maple Leafs and be between the pipes. The PR staff was saying that they were bringing in people and going to have a big Olympic thing. So I phoned Ken when I was on the way to the rink and I asked him what it was all about. 'What's it going to be? I don't really have an Olympic highlight film and I don't want to be embarrassed.'"

Joseph says he told Dryden, "I don't want to be honoured. Quinn [as the coach of the Olympic hockey team] did his job and Catriona did her job. Which highlights are they going to show of me?"

He had a simple request. "I wanted to know what was going to be up there, and how was I going to feel. I talked to Ken about it and told him I was really uncomfortable with it. He talked to me for the whole ride in."

But Dryden refused to put the feelings of his goaltender ahead of his baby, the pre-game production that he loved so much. It had to be done his way, he said.

"Of course, I'm put on the spot," said Joseph, "and Pat comes over. I can't take my blocker off. I've got my stick, and everybody makes a big deal of that. It was just putting me on the spot and I didn't like it. I just wanted to get in there and do my job."

So he didn't intentionally spurn Quinn?

"No, I didn't," he said.

But he kept his glove on. "I do that all the time," he said. "I would have to throw my glove off. I just felt very uncomfortable in that situation.

"If they would have asked me or said something about it, it wouldn't have been so bad. I had to ask [director of media relations] Pat Park to find out about it. No communication."

Quinn's rather cryptic take on the circumstance was as follows: "He didn't want to be honoured as an Olympian because he didn't feel part of it, yet someone put him on the ice to honour him." The "someone" was Dryden, and everyone knew it. Quinn wanted to make sure that the blame landed where it belonged.

It was a summer of failure for the Leafs in their attempts to sign free agents. But when they missed out on Bobby Holík, Joseph decided that the team was not serious about building a Stanley Cup winner.

"I thought what a tremendous chance it would be with one-two centres like Mats Sundin and Holík," said Joseph. "But the fact that they never did really negotiate in good faith was a huge factor."

And another star got the Leafs' typical shoddy treatment on his way out.

11

It's Good to Have
All the Tools, but not
if They're Obsolete

Pat Quinn has been around the game all his life and was with the Leafs from 1997 until 2006. He's loyal to his friends, and at one time, he was one of the best coaches in the game. But even for Pat Quinn, the hands on the clock keep on moving. The game changes with or without him.

In many ways, Pat Quinn comes across as one of hockey's living legends. He has been an NHL coach, a general manager and a president. More than once. He was the head coach of Team Canada when they won the Olympic medal in 2002, the country's first in fifty years. He was the coach of the Philadelphia Flyers when they ran up a streak of thirty-five consecutive games without a loss in the 1979–80 season, a feat that still stands as an NHL record. He coached the Team Canada juniors to a gold medal in 2009.

He knows everyone in the game who's worth knowing, and a few who aren't.

When you think of Pat Quinn, you think of the observation that was often made about one of baseball's great personalities, Casey Stengel. "He has forgotten more baseball than most people know," his fans said.

Stengel's detractors had an answer to that. "That's right. And that's the problem. He's forgotten it."

In some ways, Quinn is like Stengel. But when Quinn came to the Leafs, his problem wasn't so much that he had forgotten what he knew about hockey; it was that he no longer had the resolve to implement it.

He knew that NHL coaches of that era relied on hard-working, talented support staffs to give themselves an edge. But he was loyal to a fault and insisted on retaining his old friend Rick Ley as his primary assistant coach. As was mentioned earlier, Quinn and Ley had played together on the Maple Leafs when they first broke into the NHL. Quinn's wife and Ley's wife were the closest of friends. So whenever Quinn got a coaching job, Ley got an assistant-coaching job.

Other teams had assistant coaches who worked hard at their craft. They attended seminars. They studied films. They got involved in networking to keep up on the latest trends. They spent time developing the skills of individual players after practice. They worked on tactics that could maximize the impact of the players' skills. Ley did none of those things.

Ley was a laughingstock to the players, and they enjoyed mimicking his peculiar speech pattern, which involved an occasional involuntary whistle. They pretended to be play-by-play announcers and narrated the action at the end of every practice. Quinn would leave the ice, Ley would look at his watch, skate one circuit of the rink and follow Quinn to the dressing room.

They chuckled at Ley's drinking habits on the team's charter flights. If one of the high-level management people made the trip, Ley would drink white wine out of a large plastic cup, trying to give the impression that he was having beer, not wine.

During Quinn's tenure in Toronto, it was often said that if Ley ever lost his job with the Leafs, he'd be out of hockey. Not only would he not get another post in the professional leagues, he wouldn't even get hired in junior hockey. Those speculations appear to be correct. Has anyone heard of Rick Ley since Quinn left the Leafs?

One player who had been a penalty killer with the Leafs was traded and was astounded at the change when he got to his new team. "When I was in Toronto," he said, "a couple of us guys who were going to kill penalties that night would go to the rink in the afternoon and get some tapes of the team we were going to play. We'd try to figure out what we could expect.

"The first day I arrived here after the trade, I went to the rink for the morning skate and there was a printed package at my stall with a scouting report on the team we were going to play. It gave me their power-play alignments, what they liked to do, who to watch out for, what my responsibilities would be, everything I needed to know.

"There was never anything like that in Toronto. Pat never talked directly to anybody. You were on your own, and Ricky said even less. At least Pat drew up a few things on the board during practice. Ricky just stood there like a cigar-store Indian.

"It was the same during games. Pat was always shouting at the referee. Ricky never said a word."

Toronto players would go for months on end and never have a direct conversation with Quinn. He rarely bothered to talk to the team between periods. The local media would always get a chuckle during post-game scrums when a visiting writer would ask Quinn what he had told his team between periods.

Quinn had a standard response along the lines of, "They know what they have to do."

Translation: "I didn't talk to them."

Quinn didn't take this approach out of any sense of malice. It's just that he was an old-line coach, the second-oldest coach in the league at that time (and he became the oldest when Scott Bowman retired in 2002).

Hockey had evolved considerably since Quinn made his playing debut. In those days, there wasn't even a players' union. And although he had made some adjustments to cope with the changes, he hadn't made enough of them.

In his day, players rarely spoke to coaches. They just listened to them. If a player had a problem, he took a deep breath and knocked on the coach's door, but it would have to be a very serious problem for the player to get to that stage.

It was Quinn's view that the coach taught by drawing diagrams on the board during practice. Everyone would pay close attention, memorize the instructions, follow the plan when the game rolled around, and that would be that.

But times had changed. The game had become much more complex, and a lot of the players spoke English as a second or third language. The message that was purportedly being delivered didn't always get across.

Furthermore, players were much more involved in the team's strategies than they used to be. In Quinn's day, players played and coaches coached. It was that simple. Coaches had not the slightest interest in creating what would today be called a benevolent workplace. In those days, players either accepted the situation or got out.

Today's NHL players take a hand in the coaching. They meet with the coaches, frankly discuss their own strengths and weaknesses and make proposals to maximize those skills.

While Quinn had evolved to the point of always having an open door for those who sought him out, he was perceived as being set in his ways and having a generally aloof demeanour. Most players didn't approach him, and the ones who did were probably the last people on the team who Quinn should have been paying attention to.

Coaches around the league always had a good word for Quinn when they were asked to evaluate him on the record. Off the record, they all admitted that no coach in the league was easier to coach against. He didn't match players; he didn't match lines. He just rolled out his lines in succession—first, second, third, fourth, start again.

When asked about this tendency, Quinn would say that he expected all his players to be able to do a good job under any circumstance. Football quarterbacks must have it all wrong when they try to exploit a rookie cornerback. All players should be able to do a good job under any circumstance.

One result of rolling four lines is that star players don't get double-shifted. That was often a source of friction between Quinn and Mats Sundin. Quinn would use Sundin for sixteen minutes a game. Sundin wanted at least twenty minutes of ice time, and perhaps more. But for Sundin to get his way, Quinn would have to double-shift him and thereby juggle lines. This was something he didn't like to do.

Sundin complained to his teammates but never stood up to Quinn, and he continued to struggle along with less ice time than any player of his talent in the league.

You could count on one hand the number of times that Quinn used the one time-out that each coach is allocated per game. In fact, when he did so against the Ottawa Senators in the last minute of a 2002 playoff game in which the Leafs were down 2–1, it was such a shock that one of the players subsequently was asked what happened.

It seems that, with his goalie pulled and a face-off in the Ottawa end, Quinn wanted to send out Robert Reichel as the sixth attacker.

"No," said Reichel.

"Go on out there," said Quinn.

"Not now," said Reichel. "I'm tired."

So in order to give Reichel a breather, Quinn had to use his time-out.

Throughout all these transgressions, Quinn knew better. But he was like an aging craftsman. When you're young, the finished work must be perfect. If you're a young carpenter, a nail that doesn't go in straight is pulled out and replaced, and any damage is touched up with filler. Later in life, you leave the nail in crooked. The piece isn't going to fall apart because of one crooked nail.

Similarly, when you're young, you like to drive a sporty five-speed car and run through the gears. When you're older, you want a sedan, and you're quite content to set it on cruise control. For most of his tenure with the Leafs, Quinn was in cruise control.

If there had ever been a strong hockey man at the top of the Toronto organization, he would have called Quinn into his office and demanded a more conscientious performance. He would have told Quinn to coach to the full capacity of his abilities. He would have told Quinn to find a better assistant coach, and if Quinn found that to be unpalatable, then one would be found for him.

When Sam Pollock was running the Montreal Canadiens in the 1970s, and the team was arguably the best the game has ever seen, coach Scott Bowman was regularly upbraided by Pollock. Even though he was behind the bench of a dynasty, Bowman always knew that every move was being scrutinized, and if he made a mistake, he would hear about it.

At that time, Bowman and Quinn were probably the two best coaches in the game. Decades later in Detroit, Bowman was still the best at his job, but he had evolved. He no longer bothered to spend much practice time on the ice. Sometimes he wouldn't go out at all, preferring to watch from the stands. On other occasions, he'd go on the ice for the first part of the practice.

But he had two excellent assistant coaches in Dave Lewis and Barry Smith. Bowman didn't spend a lot of time talking to players, but he did spend a lot of time talking to captain Steve Yzerman, and messages were passed back and forth. Lewis and Smith talked to the other players. Frequently.

Quinn, on the other hand, had Rick Ley as an assistant coach, with some help from Keith Acton. Although Acton was capable enough, he had little authority, and the players knew he was well down the pecking order from the Quinn-Ley coupled entry.

Quinn had Sundin as a captain, but he never used him in the capacity that Bowman used Yzerman. For starters, he would have needed an overriding strategy to impart, and there wasn't one. For Quinn, it was just a matter of facing—reacting to—challenges as they arose.

There was no doubt that Quinn knew his hockey. He hated the media with a passion, but to his credit, he never let his disdain get in the way of his responsibilities. Whenever he was asked a hockey question, he always provided an intelligent, well-reasoned answer. Some of those answers were fascinating and laden with insight. But the players insisted that he never passed such insights on to them.

Because of this, it's reasonable to assume that if Quinn had ever been prodded from above, he might have pushed the Leafs even farther than they went under his tutelage. He got them to the conference final in both 1999 and 2002. In 1999, they never really looked as if they would beat the Buffalo Sabres, and they didn't, going down in five games. But in 2002, they lost in six to the Carolina

Hurricanes. In three of those games, Carolina won 2–1 in overtime. Under coach Paul Maurice, Carolina was an extremely well-prepared team. Every player knew exactly what his job was, just as he knew exactly what to expect from each of the Leafs.

Is it unreasonable to assume that if the Leafs had been afforded the benefits of the same degree of preparation, they could have won one or two of those three games? And if that were the case, could the Leafs have won that series and faced the Detroit Red Wings in the Stanley Cup final? And once in the final, could the hockey gods have smiled on them with a few good breaks and . . .

No one knows. But we do know, beyond the slightest shadow of a doubt, that top to bottom, the Hurricanes' coaches did more to help their team than the Leafs' coaches did to help theirs.

But who was going to put Quinn's feet to the fire? Stavro didn't know anything about hockey. Dryden wasn't going to do it, having long since been cowed by Quinn. Dryden tried to do everything he could to take the team to the fans. Quinn did everything he could to hide it from public scrutiny. Dryden installed TV cameras in the dressing room. Quinn had them removed. Dryden approved a new set of media-access regulations. Quinn refused to abide by them. Dryden knew where he stood, as did anybody close to the situation. Quinn had as much disdain for Dryden as he had for the media. Perhaps even more.

That's why, when Mike Smith was fired as associate general manager in June 1999, Quinn, coming off a strong playoff performance, quickly went to work to stabilize his situation and make sure that he did not find himself in a position of having to report to Dryden.

Smith had been the de facto GM, even though Dryden held the title, and despite some difficult moments, Quinn and Smith coexisted fairly well.

As a primary shot across Dryden's bows, Quinn started to wonder out loud about his legal status. His contract stated that he answered to the man who was in charge of hockey operations, but when Dryden and Smith started to feud, Dryden turned some of Smith's responsibilities over to Anders Hedberg. Because Quinn reported to Smith, he wondered, therefore, whether his contract could be fulfilled and if not, whether perhaps it had been breached.

It was something of a stretch, and there was nothing to it, of course, but it set the tone. At the June entry draft in Boston's FleetCenter, Quinn ignored the proceedings going on behind him and talked about his future. When he joined the Leafs, he said, he had thought that he was going to be the coach and have no other duties. With Smith gone, he admitted, he might have to reconsider his status.

What he didn't say directly, but certainly hinted at, was that he didn't think Dryden was capable of making the right hockey decisions.

When asked outright if he could work for Dryden as GM, he said, "That's an unfair question." In other words, he couldn't.

Even though Smith had a number of failings, including a fatal attraction for players from Moscow Dynamo, he knew what was going on in the NHL and, unlike Dryden, what had gone on for the previous two decades. Quinn did not want to be lumbered with Dryden making personnel decisions, hence his remark about "self-preservation" when explaining why he might be interested in the GM's job.

Two weeks later, he was named general manager.

The problem was that, even though Quinn had been a GM before—with the Vancouver Canucks—his record in that regard had not been particularly good. The team's success rate at the entry draft was extremely poor, and the only young player of any note to be acquired by the Canucks during Quinn's decade of service arrived under a cloud.

It happened in 1989, when a number of teams asked the league about a young Russian prospect, Pavel Bure, and were told that he was not eligible for the draft. But with the 113th pick, the Canucks selected him anyway. Despite vehement protests from other clubs, a curious ruling from NHL president John Ziegler allowed the choice to stand. Coincidentally enough, Ziegler's decision was followed by an equally momentous decision on the part of the Canucks: they dropped a long-standing lawsuit against the league.

In Toronto, Quinn was to face a further difficulty in that he was to be both coach and general manager. Even though coaches and general managers throughout the league were unanimous in their complaints that they didn't have time to do one job properly, Quinn proposed to do both.

He did have a good front office, and could expect help from both Hedberg and Watters. But other GMs had front-office help as well and they didn't have to coach.

Before long, even Quinn had to admit that he had placed himself in an untenable position. The season was only two weeks old when he confessed that, even though he felt comfortable with the existing situation, he was already aware of its shortcomings.

"It wasn't something I wanted," he admitted. "Right now, it's working. I don't know how it is going to work long-term. I don't think the best situation is a manager-coach for a lot of reasons. But it is a fact right now and we will deal with it. Someday, that is going to change.

"We were kind of in a stop-gap situation," he continued. "Suddenly, Mike was gone, and he wasn't intended to be gone. Nobody expected that. At least, we didn't. So you shore up and you try to make the best of it and I think someday, along the way, some steps will be made, probably to bring in a manager. I want to coach."

Quinn was only too well acquainted with the nature of the

difficulties. He had encountered them during his stay in Vancouver, where he had also been coach and general manager for a little more than two years. To get out of that situation, he had named Rick Ley as coach, but Ley lasted only one full season before Quinn fired him and took over both jobs again.

In fact, until the Canucks were sold by the Griffiths family to Orca Bay Ltd., Quinn also served a term as president, so there wasn't a direct parallel between the situations in Vancouver and Toronto. But there were similarities.

"Until Orca Bay came in, I had responsibility over everything as the president, so it was a different circumstance," Quinn said. "I saw that when I was coaching there, I wasn't doing the job I wanted to do as a coach because I felt that I was running all around, so neither job was getting done properly.

"That's why I stepped away, but I stepped away to the job I was hired to do in the first place. But I was hired to coach here and that's what I want to do. I want to coach."

That may have been what he wanted to do—and it should have been. But it was to be four full years before Quinn was able to get out of the dual role, a role that by his own admission was not the one he wanted and definitely was not ideal.

The Leafs of that era were not ideal, either. They were respect- able in 1999–2000, Quinn's first year as coach–GM, finishing sev- enth in the overall standings and topping the Northeast Division. Fortunately for them, they drew the Ottawa Senators in the first round, a team they regularly dominated in the playoffs. But in the second round, they lost to the New Jersey Devils.

Midway through the next season, they were struggling and playing like a team that had lost its direction. Quinn was regularly asked about the cause of his team's problems, and over the course of a few such interviews, five reasons were given:

(1) The power play. It wasn't working because the players wouldn't do what they were supposed to do.

(2) The officiating. It was never good.

(3) Trade rumours. The media had created a climate that caused the players to be distracted and therefore unable to do their jobs.

(4) The schedule. It was either the back-to-back games or the rigours of travel. Either way, it was causing difficulties for the Leafs.

(5) Poor practice habits. The players weren't working as hard as they should in practice and were therefore incapable of performing well in games.

That was it. Those five reasons were resurrected in various incarnations time after time.

Strangely enough, there was never any hint that the coaching might be a bit flawed. After all, practices are run by the coach. If the practices are not going well, is it only the players who deserve the blame?

The same logic applies to the power play. Quinn was its architect. Was it ineffective only because players weren't doing what they were supposed to do?

In both instances, the coach is presumably making certain demands on the players. If those demands are being ignored, could it not be a sign of a larger problem? The coach has twenty or so players at his disposal. Can he not find five who'll follow his orders on a power play?

As for media distractions, that was nothing more than Quinn attributing his own characteristics to others. He is one of the most media-intolerant people in hockey history, but his players weren't that way.

Officiating and the schedule? Every team in the league had

similar complaints, so while Quinn's observations in that regard were often entertaining, they certainly weren't the reason for the Leafs' woes.

The situation was getting so precarious that in early 2001 Quinn undertook a radical departure from his established coaching methods. In a move that shocked everyone on the team, he actually solicited players' opinions.

He handed out a questionnaire asking the players how they felt about such matters as practices and team strategy. The responses were not, to put it charitably, overwhelmingly favourable. So for a month or so, Quinn pretended they didn't exist.

Eventually, development coach Paul Dennis put together a summary of the responses and discussed them with Quinn. To the shock of no one, Quinn decided that he disagreed with the players and went back to ignoring them.

But two months after the questionnaire had been distributed, with the team in a slide and in danger of missing the playoffs, Quinn could close his eyes to the problem no longer. As if the questionnaire hadn't been a radical enough departure from the norm, Quinn now went off the deep end. He actually held one-to-one interviews with the players.

There was no precedent for this. Quinn did not usually talk to players. In fact, the Leafs were the only team in the league that sent their players home at the end of the year without exit interviews. But these were drastic circumstances, and they called for drastic measures.

The Leafs bucked up a bit after that, perhaps out of shock, and even though they slipped to the middle of the pack that year—tied for fourteenth in a thirty-team league—they did indeed get into the playoffs.

As usual, they pasted Ottawa in the opening playoff round, but once again followed that "success" with a loss to the Devils.

And what was the prime complaint voiced by the players in those discredited questionnaires? That there was no accountability on the Leafs, a fact that they saw as a direct result of Quinn's double role.

When you're a general manager, you don't coach the same way as someone who doesn't have the dual responsibility. A coach just wants to win, and he uses his team the way he sees fit to attain that end. But a coach–GM wants to make his managerial decisions look good. As a result, the top line consists of the highest-priced forwards whether they deserve to be there or not. The GM has to justify the contracts he awarded.

Similarly, a player who was acquired in a trade has to be given every opportunity to look good because, in the process, he'll make the GM look good.

The primary case in point with the Leafs at that time was Dmitri Khristich, a player who was universally despised by his teammates. He was given all the ice time he wanted in the hope that he might someday prove that management was right in acquiring him. He never did. In fact, Khristich generally got more ice time than Mats Sundin. He played on all the power plays, sometimes even for the full two minutes. Even when the Toronto fans took to booing Khristich every time he touched the puck, Quinn refused to reduce his ice time, saying that he wanted to help the winger regain his confidence. Quinn's tolerance of Khristich was probably the most notable example of his attempts to justify one of his deals, but to a lesser degree, there were a number of others.

Robert Reichel was one of them. He was given an inflated contract by Quinn and, to justify that decision, Reichel was accorded a spot on the second line, a reward that his play did not warrant. It was because Quinn tried to make Reichel look good that he sent him out in situations where the goalie had been pulled—even if, as mentioned earlier, he had to use his time-out to do so.

Contrast that with Quinn's treatment of a low-priced player he had inherited. Steve Sullivan was a nifty little forward who had been acquired in Cliff Fletcher's 1997 deadline-day deal. Even though he had been playing well, when the Leafs went to Ottawa for a game in 1999, Quinn scratched him. Sullivan had dozens of relatives coming to that game, so after the morning skate, he went to Quinn's office and asked to be put back into the lineup.

Quinn, furious that a player should question his omnipotence, snapped at Sullivan, and the two had words. Quinn's next salvo in this war that didn't need to happen was to put Sullivan on waivers.

What a productive move that was. Sullivan was a valuable prospect and, as such, was quickly snapped off the waiver wire by the Chicago Blackhawks. Over his next six seasons, he racked up 461 points in 520 games. The Leafs, of course, got nothing back. There's no return for a player claimed on waivers.

Yet despite all the Leafs' problems and despite the widespread awareness that Quinn was overextended in a double role—and in fact was the only coach–GM in the league—a new contract was worked out over the summer.

By October 2001, the negotiations were, for all intents and purposes, complete. But as was always the case in matters that involved Dryden, the process dragged on much longer than necessary, and it was not until mid-January 2002 that the new deal was announced.

It was a three-year contract, and although most of the specifics were not made public, some aspects were widely reported and never contradicted. Quinn would be paid about $7 million over three years, and he was to be given veto rights over his successor in the GM post.

It didn't seem likely, however, that this veto would need to be exercised. Quinn admitted that it was "possible, at least for the length of the current extension," that he would continue in both jobs.

Quinn's rationale for maintaining the status quo was that he had a strong support team in Mike Penny, the director of player personnel, and in Watters, the assistant to the president. (Watters was soon to have his title changed to assistant to the GM, which made sense, since a person who does nothing has no great need for an assistant.)

But Penny was another friend of Quinn's and the guy who had been in charge of Quinn's scouting in Vancouver, where the record had been nothing short of dismal. Watters was capable enough, but every team had an assistant GM. They also had a GM who did the managerial work—which the Leafs didn't.

While the Leafs insisted that the future was in good hands, a number of more skeptical observers pointed out that the fairly deep organization that existed at the time was due to the drafting skills of Anders Hedberg and Nick Beverley. Since both of them had since moved on, the organization could be expected to erode under Penny. They were right.

But nothing is static in hockey. Gradually, the blame for the Leafs' woes was shifting away from Quinn and towards Dryden.

Dryden had been the president for five years, and in that time, what had been accomplished? Toronto had won six playoff rounds, three of them against the Ottawa Senators, who seemed to be incapable of playing well against the Leafs in the post-season.

Thanks to a bizarre contract approved by Dryden, the Leafs had the only coach in the league whose approval was needed to name the next GM.

Dryden spoke well—and at great length. He could pontificate on the virtues of hockey and its place in the fabric of Canadian society. He could represent the team in difficult times. But the on-ice product was not significantly improving, partly because in an era of unlimited league-wide spending, the Leafs were notably tight-fisted.

Dryden vehemently denied those charges. "It has really been irresponsible—in terms of the commentary over the unwillingness to spend and the rest of it," he said. "You just look at the clear facts of it all."

Well, the clear facts were that the Leafs ranked first in ticket prices but fifth in payroll. Another clear fact was that the team had publicly justified its latest price increase by saying that the revenue thus generated would be used to acquire elite-level free agents. It wasn't. The Leafs were still in dire need of a top-notch defenceman.

Even so, when Stavro was punted aside by the new board early in 2003, it was Quinn who was under the gun. Dryden's old buddy Larry Tanenbaum, who had talked him into taking over the presidency in the first place, was now a prime mover in the organization.

Sure enough, when the Leafs went out in the first round that spring, Quinn was removed as general manager and replaced by John Ferguson Jr., whose contributions—or lack thereof—will be discussed in the next chapter.

There was no real love lost between the two men, and Ferguson didn't do much to help Quinn's cause. Or vice versa. Quinn stayed behind the bench for a decent regular season in 2003–04, but the subsequent playoffs produced the usual result: a win over Ottawa followed by a loss in the next round—to the Philadelphia Flyers for the second year in succession.

Commissioner Gary Bettman shut down the league the next year, and in 2005–06, Quinn came back but the Leafs didn't make the playoffs. He was then fired.

"I only missed the playoffs once," said Quinn. "Most places, you don't get let go for missing the playoffs once. I was just in the wrong place at the wrong time. Mr. Stavro was gone and Mr. Tanenbaum was in. He wanted his own people."

As his Toronto career progressed, Quinn eventually showed that he was capable of modifying his style and making changes for the better, but his prompting came from the media rather than from within the organization.

There had never been the slightest doubt that his hockey knowledge was magnificent. But because he never received any prodding from above, because no one above him in the hierarchy had either the courage to stand up to him or the knowledge to battle him on hockey matters and make the most of his ability, he stuck to his old ways—methods that had been successful two decades earlier but were out of touch with the modern game.

When Quinn went to the Olympics, a number of Maple Leafs who were there playing for nations other than Canada reported being approached by Team Canada players who always had a variation of the same question: "How do you guys ever win with this guy behind the bench?"

Nevertheless, two facts are incontestable. Canada won the gold. And Quinn had top-flight assistants to support him.

Two facts were also incontestable after the world junior championship of 2009: Canada won the gold. And Quinn had top-flight assistants to support him.

Shortly before this book went to press, Quinn was hired as head coach of the Edmonton Oilers and given a top-flight assistant in Tom Renney. It is therefore not at all unlikely that the Oilers will finally live up to the potential that fans have seen in them for years.

Had anyone in the Leafs organization ever bothered to insist that Quinn avail himself of a solid support staff—which the team could certainly afford—the results of Quinn's tenure might have been much more positive.

In Toronto, Quinn's old-line mentality led him to believe that he didn't need to bother with the accoutrements of modern hockey, such as an expanded coaching staff.

Another factor believed to have assured Quinn's demise as general manager was an offhand remark made just before he headed home to Vancouver in July 2003.

The Leafs, said Quinn following his team's first-round playoff exit, were now engaged in a full-scale youth movement.

A full-scale youth movement?

Imagine, if you will, that you're one of the directors of Maple Leaf Sports and Entertainment Ltd. Four months earlier, your general manager stocked up on veteran free agents—Doug Gilmour, Phil Housley, Owen Nolan and Glen Wesley.

In the June draft, your team had not a single first-round pick, the result of your GM's decision to mortgage the future to provide for the present—more specifically, in making the Nolan acquisition. In fact, for those four players mentioned above, your GM gave up his first-, sixth- and ninth-round picks in 2003; his second- and fourth-round picks in 2004; and two excellent young players, Brad Boyes and Alyn McCauley, whose respective ages were twenty-five and twenty. The average age of the four free agents he acquired was thirty-five.

And now your GM is saying that he's in a youth movement? He's going to develop the young talent that's in the organization? *What* talent? He gave away two of its brightest prospects and a bunch of other draft picks of indeterminate value. If there was that much talent in the organization to begin with, the team wouldn't have headed for the golf course after the first round of the playoffs. At that point in Leafs history, even the most optimistic fan wouldn't have been able to name three decent prospects in the entire organization.

The summer of 2003 was notable for its overabundance of free agents. When free agents were hard to get, Quinn had wanted every one of them. Now that they had become easily available, he suddenly decided he was going to develop from within and create a youth movement?

A few days before Quinn's announcement of this stunning development, both Paul Kariya and Teemu Selanne signed with the Colorado Avalanche for a combined bargain-basement salary of $7 million. Quinn apparently wasn't interested. At twenty-eight and thirty-two respectively, they must have been too old for his youth movement.

No wonder that by the time Quinn returned to Toronto for the following season he was no longer general manager.

Unfortunately for Leafs fans, however, the chronic problem had not been solved. There was still that dearth of competence at the top. The MLSE board members knew that they no longer wanted Quinn as general manager, but they had not the slightest clue when it came to finding a suitable replacement.

Nevertheless, they had no choice. Quinn was gone. A replacement was needed.

12

If You Can't Do It Yourself, Hire Someone Else Who Can't

The coach hired his own GM. Two guys who had failed miserably at a job evaluated candidates for that very job. A food company executive hired a hockey company executive. This could only have been the Toronto Maple Leafs continuing their quest for ever-elusive high-level leadership.

In the summer of 2003, the board of directors of Maple Leaf Sports and Entertainment approved a three-man search committee that would have been laughable if it hadn't been so pathetic. Come to think of it, it was laughable anyway.

There was Richard Peddie, whose business experience came from his days as an executive with various food companies. If you wanted to learn how to put the cream filling in a Hostess Twinkie, Peddie was your man. Finding someone to run a hockey team? Unless the Pillsbury Doughboy and the Jolly Green Giant were the prime candidates, you had the wrong selector.

The other two were Dryden and Quinn, whose primary qualification to pick the Leafs' general manager was that they had both failed horribly at the job. Moreover, Quinn was the coach. Only the Leafs would put a coach on a search committee to select his general manager.

It did not seem to bother anyone that it would take a cattle prod to get any two of these three into the same room at the same time.

Dryden, who liked to let people think that he still had some clout within the team, assured the media that the Leafs' new GM would be "a star." Those who remembered Dryden's assurances about his first GM—when he ended up with no GM at all and only associate GM Mike Smith to show for his efforts—took it all with a grain of salt.

Peddie, having the fanciest title—president and chief executive officer of Maple Leaf Sports and Entertainment Ltd.—did his best to take charge and decided to seek some advice. He asked Bill Daly, who was then the chief counsel for the National Hockey League, for his views. It must be said that Daly is very good at his job. In fact, he has since been promoted and is now the league's deputy commissioner. But in his role at the time, he had nothing whatsoever to do with hockey operations. Any hockey fan could have told him that the NHL's New York office was probably the last place in the world to undertake such a quest, but this is Richard Peddie we're talking about. At least Daly had the good grace to stay out of the matter.

There were many potential candidates, but because the Maple Leafs operation was so badly run, a number of them immediately rebuffed any overtures. Of course, the Leafs denied this fact. To do otherwise would be an admission that their operation was widely seen as a laughingstock, and surely that could not be the case.

When all was said and done, the Leafs, amazingly, hired John Ferguson Jr., who had spent five years as assistant general manager of the St. Louis Blues before becoming the team's director of hockey operations eighteen months before he joined the Leafs.

So much for Dryden's assurance that the new GM would be "a star." He was anything but. He was a glorified talent scout for the Blues—not an organization desperate to make room in the arena rafters for its next Stanley Cup banner.

At the televised press conference held in late August to announce Ferguson's appointment, I asked Peddie if the Leafs had approached anyone other than the four candidates who had been widely mentioned—Ferguson, Bob Nicholson, Neil Smith and Steve Tambellini. Peddie said they had not.

Immediately, my cell phone rang. I pretended that it wasn't mine because I should have turned it off before the proceedings began. When I checked later, I found a brief message from one of those candidates that the Leafs said did not exist. "He's lying," the message said.

Neil Smith had been the GM of the New York Rangers when they won the Stanley Cup in 1994. Steve Tambellini had been an NHL player and was an up-and-coming executive with Quinn's former team, the Vancouver Canucks. He subsequently became general manager of the Edmonton Oilers, and hired Quinn as coach after the Oilers missed the playoffs in 2009. Bob Nicholson was in charge of Hockey Canada and an old friend of Quinn's.

Because Quinn had close ties to Tambellini and Nicholson, they were not held in high regard by Dryden and Peddie. Neither wanted to see the evolution of a strong coach–GM alliance.

And because Smith had considerable expertise as a GM, Quinn

didn't want *him* around. As had been shown, Quinn liked to run his own show, and Smith, who had once employed the forceful Mike Keenan as his coach, wasn't likely to allow that to happen.

Consequently, Ferguson, the candidate with the least impressive portfolio—and therefore the least reason to be opposed by the three wise men—got the job. Ferguson got the job not because of what he was but because of what he wasn't.

Peddie subsequently explained that baseball's New York Yankees had a young general manager in Brian Cashman and a veteran field manager in Joe Torre. Peddie reasoned that since the Yankees were perennial winners, this sort of January–December tandem could work well for the Leafs. (Which must explain why Peddie contacted Daly. After all, he lived in New York; wouldn't that make him an expert on the Yankees' situation?)

Apparently, the fact that the Yankees' annual payroll invariably tended to be larger than the gross national product of most African nations did not strike Peddie as being a factor in their success.

Peddie also tried to suggest that he was delighted to hire Ferguson because he had always wanted a talented youngster in the Cashman mould. But if that was the case, why had they interviewed the experienced Neil Smith?

Similarly, why did they approach a number of high-profile hockey people to see if they'd be interested in the job? It was clear they had done so, even though they denied it.

As for the selection process, it provided a perfect example of how not to carry out such an endeavour.

The potential candidate would arrive at the Air Canada Centre and start with Peddie, who laid out his vision for the team. Strong financial returns played a prominent role in this scenario, as did the expertise of one Richard Peddie, the shining star in the MLSE boardroom. Then the candidate was sent down a floor to see Dryden (that's *sent,* not *taken*), who had his turn. He, too, expounded his vision for the team. And for hockey. And for world peace. And for an end to poverty.

Finally, and perhaps symbolically, the putative candidate was sent down to the basement to talk to Quinn, who professed not to be terribly interested in the whole procedure but was willing to have a chat since he had nothing else to do, and the candidate was in the building anyway.

Here was a storied franchise, one of the true iconic franchises in hockey, if not all sports, and it hired the youngest GM in the league, a man with no experience in the job, and a man about as far from being a star as the Leafs were from being a dynasty.

But because he wasn't a threat to any of the king-making triumvirate and because he wouldn't do anything to alter the course of the vision that each one had for the organization, he was seen as the ideal general manager. Those circumstances, of course, doomed him to failure, but no one worried about that. Once again, there was a leadership void at the top of the Maple Leafs organization. Without true direction at the top, there was never going to be any true direction at the lower levels.

The coaching situation provided a perfect example of Ferguson's dilemma. By that time, Quinn had become a very poor coach. That was the view of his peers who freely admitted in private conversations that no one in the league was easier to coach against. It was also the view of all his players, and since players aren't likely to exert themselves for someone they don't respect, the only sensible course of action for the new GM was to make Quinn's firing a priority.

But Peddie had made it clear that any candidate who suggested during the interview process that he favoured firing Quinn would be left off the short list. And Quinn certainly wasn't going to vote for someone with designs on dismissing him. So the new GM was already saddled with a coach who was long past his best-before date.

Furthermore, this was the era before the salary cap. To compete, a general manager generally needed a good-sized budget. Would Ferguson get that?

In his initial press conference, Ferguson started by answering all the questions in a confident, forthright manner. Then came a question about the budget.

He dodged that one, muttering something about the team's success being a function of the players' performances—as if no one else in the building had adequate hockey expertise to work that out.

A little later, he was asked if the Leafs had sufficient cash to compete. For the only time in the entire news conference, he looked towards Peddie as if seeking guidance. Then he dodged the question again.

In the scrum that invariably follows formal hockey press conferences, the matter of the team's budget was again broached. Did he have the authority to sign Joe Nieuwendyk, who was a free agent at the time? Ferguson didn't want to talk about specific players.

There was no reason not to do so. It was pointed out that he couldn't be accused of tampering for talking about a free agent. He didn't want to do it anyway.

So the question was expanded to include any high-priced free agent. Did Ferguson have the authority to sign one or didn't he?

"I don't want to tip our hand to any agents or any of our competitors," he said. "We'll reserve the right to make decisions. In fact, I have an obligation to make recommendations that will improve our club. I'll make those decisions and recommendations as I see fit."

In other words, "No."

Thus began the John Ferguson Jr. era.

It was to last for four years and just under five months, but fortunately for Leafs fans, the league was shut down for one of those years, thereby preventing Ferguson from make any further personnel mistakes.

He started off well enough, grabbing the much-coveted Nieuwendyk. His other off-season free-agent signing, defenceman Ken Klee, wasn't bad either. But his subsequent acquisitions in the 2003–04 season left something to be desired.

Petr Tenkrát and Clarke Wilm were signed as free agents. Craig Johnson was claimed off waivers. Drake Berehowsky came in a trade. No need to place a call to the Hall of Fame's selection committee yet.

But then Ferguson, apparently not having been copied in on Quinn's memo regarding the youth movement, shipped away his first-round pick in the 2004 draft and his second-round pick in the 2005 draft as part of a deal to acquire the thirty-six-year-old Brian Leetch. That was followed by the sacrifice of a fourth-round pick to get the forty-one-year-old Ron Francis. The moves amounted to a desperate attempt on Ferguson's part to make some sort of playoff impact with the Leafs. If you consider the winning of one round to be a success, then it worked. The Leafs, as they did so often, eliminated the Ottawa Senators. But the euphoria was short-lived.

That proved to be the one and only playoff round the Leafs would win during Ferguson's tenure.

It should not come as any surprise that there never seemed to be a clear-cut modus operandi during the Ferguson era. Granted, there were the usual Pollyanna-ish assurances that the arrival of the Stanley Cup would create the fairy-tale happy ending, but Ferguson did nothing to convince the fans either that he knew what he was doing or that they should have confidence in his ability to take the team in the right direction.

Eventually, in the summer of 2006, Ferguson was able to make a coaching change. Citing the team's inability to make the playoffs as a reason, he fired Quinn and promoted Paul Maurice, the coach of the Leafs' AHL farm team the Toronto Marlies. Maurice, who had taken the Carolina Hurricanes to the Stanley Cup finals in 2002, lasted just two years and missed the playoffs on both occasions.

Many observers felt that much of the blame for Quinn's short-comings as coach should go to Ferguson himself. He had misallo-cated his budget in the first year of the salary-cap era and had lost two key forwards, Nieuwendyk and Gary Roberts. The two close friends went to the Florida Panthers after Ferguson decided to play hardball with Roberts.

As Roberts explained, "He played the card they always play in Toronto—that people will stay there for less money because every-body wants to be a Toronto Maple Leaf. Unfortunately, he played that hand a little too long and he lost."

Every summer throughout his tenure, Ferguson would be in the bidding for the best free agents, but they would always land somewhere else. In 2005, after the league had been shut down for a year and literally hundreds of free agents were available, Ferguson could do no better than land six nondescript players who were in no great demand elsewhere.

The biggest names were Eric Lindros and Jason Allison. But Lin-dros was far past his prime, to put it tactfully, and Allison may well have been the slowest skater in the league at the time. Those were their good points. On the down side, Lindros was rarely healthy (he played only thirty-three games for the Leafs) and Allison had been out of hockey for two years.

Most general managers liked to use their free agents as building blocks—long-term acquisitions who become instrumental in the team's development. Neither Lindros nor Allison put in even one full season with the Leafs.

The other four free-agent acquisitions that summer were Alex-ander Khavanov, Mike Hoffman, Jean-Sébastien Aubin and Brad Brown, all marginal players.

Despite his perennial quest for free agents, Ferguson would occasionally insist that the team intended to build through the draft and develop its own players. This is never an easy task when you keep giving away draft picks, but Ferguson implied that he and the Leafs' scouts were smarter than everyone else's and, as a result, would easily compensate for the poor draft seeding.

Therefore, when the Leafs drafted a pair of goaltenders—Justin Pogge with their first pick (ninetieth overall) in 2004 and Tuukka Rask with their first pick in 2005 (twenty-first overall)—there was much bravado issuing forth from the front office concerning the vaunted status of this pair. The Leafs clearly considered them to be the two best young goaltending prospects in the world.

At that point, you could have made a good case to support that claim. Granted, Rask was better, having stopped no fewer than fifty-eight shots to earn a shutout for Finland in the World Junior Championship, but no one could dispute that these two could reasonably be expected to have solid NHL careers ahead of them.

So, did Ferguson nurture the pair and develop them? Not on your life. He threw one of them away. He sent Rask to the Boston Bruins for another goaltender, Andrew Raycroft. Although Raycroft had won the Calder Trophy as the NHL's top rookie in 2004, his play had fallen off badly the year before. In fact, he had all the hallmarks of a flash in the pan. His goals-against average had ballooned from 2.05 to 3.71. His record had gone from 29–18–9 to 8–19–2.

Certainly, Ferguson needed to do something about his goaltending. Back in the summer of 2004, when everybody knew that a lengthy lockout was coming, he re-signed the thirty-nine-year-old Ed Belfour to a three-year deal. Belfour had perennial back problems and underwent surgery just before the lockout began. Since this was a "hockey injury," the Leafs had to pay him while he recuperated during the dark year.

But even if Ferguson were given the benefit of the doubt about his belief that Raycroft was the man to succeed Belfour, there was absolutely no reason to trade a player, especially one of Rask's calibre, to get him.

Because of Raycroft's dismal season, the Bruins had not the slightest intention of re-signing him. Tim Thomas had emerged, had clearly outplayed Raycroft and was the number one goalie in Boston. Young Hannu Toivonen appeared to be ready to stay at the NHL level.

Raycroft had worn out his welcome, and the hockey world knew that the Bruins were simply going to turn him loose. All Ferguson had to do was wait until July 1 and he could have grabbed Raycroft as a free agent and retained his two young prospects as well.

But when Ferguson came sniffing around, the Bruins got Raycroft to sign a qualifying offer of $1.38 million that tied him up for a year. (They reasoned, correctly, that not even Ferguson would trade for a player who could attain free-agent status a week later.)

Then, on June 24, with the groundwork in place, Ferguson shipped Rask to the astonished, but delighted, Bruins for Raycroft.

Ferguson then tore up the one-year deal and gave Raycroft—who turned out to be somewhere between mediocre and awful—a three-year, $6-million (U.S.) contract. To justify his decision, Ferguson said the Leafs couldn't simultaneously develop two young goalies in the minors and one would have had to have been discarded anyway.

Really? Then why did the Leafs draft goalies in back-to-back years? Did they have no faith in their drafting ability? Why did they give away the better one? Why couldn't they let one develop in Canada and one in Europe? After all, one was Canadian and one European.

There were, of course, no answers to those questions. And once again, the Leafs had jettisoned a player who might well have become an important part of their evolution.

Eventually, even Ferguson had to admit his mistake, and in the summer of 2007, he traded away more draft picks—another first-rounder and a fourth-rounder—this time to San Jose for forward Mark Bell and goalie Vesa Toskala.

Was Ferguson trying to build through the draft, or was he frantically running around applying Band-Aids wherever he could? Who knew?

Another strange move was the acquisition of Pavel Kubina in 2006. Kubina came as a free agent from the Tampa Bay Lightning and was a quality defenceman. As a result, bidding was lively and Ferguson had to give him a five-year, $21.25-million contract.

But the problem was that Kubina was coveted because he was an excellent point man on the power play. In fact, he was just as good as Bryan McCabe and Tomáš Kaberle, both of whom were already on the Leafs' roster.

Unless Ferguson had some yet-to-be-unveiled plan for an innovative power play that used three defencemen on the blue line, the acquisition didn't make a lot of sense. The Leafs had many problems, but a shortage of offensive defencemen wasn't one of them.

As might be expected, Kubina rarely got sufficient ice time to display his best qualities, and the Toronto fans complained that the large salary was unjustified. That wasn't Kubina's fault, but it was Kubina, not Ferguson, who got booed.

The following summer, Ferguson finally noticed that his team needed an offensive forward. But in keeping with his penchant for picking up one-year wonders, he signed free agent Jason Blake. It was another high-priced deal—$20 million for five years.

Blake had a curious background. He was an American who was still playing college hockey when he was twenty-five. He didn't score more than eight goals in an NHL season until he was twenty-nine. That was in 2004.

Playing with Alexei Yashin for the New York Islanders in 2006–07, he had a forty-goal season, a development that almost every hockey observer saw as one of two things. It was either a result of Yashin's ability to set him up, or it was a fluke.

Ferguson saw it another way. He saw Blake as the genuine article, albeit a guy who had suddenly blossomed at the age of thirty-three. The score on that evaluation was Rest of the World 1, Ferguson 0.

Blake got off to a poor start with the Leafs. It was quickly followed by a poor midseason and a poor finish. He was, to put it mildly, not a favourite in the dressing room and he ended the year with only fifteen goals. But by that time, Ferguson wasn't around to try to justify his decision.

By November, the buzzards were circling in plain view. The previous summer, the MLSE board had let it be known that they were considering hiring a mentor to help Ferguson. That's not the kind of action that can be taken as a vote of confidence. The idea was that a managerial veteran like Scott Bowman or John Muckler would come in to help Ferguson learn his craft. To show their faith in Ferguson, the board would extend his contract.

But the plan never came to fruition, and neither did Ferguson's extension.

Then, in November, Peddie admitted to Mike Zeisberger of the *Toronto Sun* that Ferguson's hiring had probably been "a mistake." It was now clear that a change was inevitable. All that remained to be done was the usual MLSE bumbling, prevarication and time-wasting.

On January 22, 2008, after a disastrous west-coast road trip, the axe finally fell. Ferguson was fired and Cliff Fletcher came back for his second tour of duty.

Harold Ballard, Leafs captain George Armstrong and Stafford Smythe show off the Stanley Cup in the 1967 Stanley Cup parade.

One of the most-loved guys in the organization's history was King Clancy. He's on the left with one of the most-hated guys in the organization's history, Punch Imlach, in this 1969 photo.

Darryl Sittler (27) and Lanny McDonald leave the ice at Maple Leaf Gardens after a game during the tumultuous 1978–79 season. Not long after this game, Imlach shipped McDonald to the Colorado Rockies.

Darryl Sittler races against the clock in "Showdown," an intermission feature of the *Hockey Night in Canada* 1979 telecasts. A squabble with Punch Imlach and Harold Ballard over his right to participate led to him shunning the captain's C.

The older he got, the less Harold Ballard liked the media, and when they showed up, he often told them—in the clearest of terms—to get away from him. That's what he was doing here.

The Leafs' best chance to end the Stanley Cup drought came when Cliff Fletcher, right, was brought into the fold by an interim management team headed by Donald Giffen. In May 1992, Fletcher hired Pat Burns to coach the team.

Pat Burns, always animated behind the bench, tries to get his point across to the players during a 1993 playoff game. Assistant coach Mike Murphy shows the tension of the situation.

Wayne Gretzky celebrates one of his three goals during game seven of the Campbell Conference final in 1993. Leafs fans were hoping for a Stanley Cup matchup against the Montreal Canadiens, but Gretzky's Kings went to the dance instead.

By August 1994, two of the most popular people in Toronto were Doug Gilmour and Pat Burns. The two were all smiles at the press conference to announce that Gilmour was to become the Leafs' captain.

Steve Stavro, left, a grocer, won the battle for control of the Leafs after Harold Ballard's death and, by 1997, was able to get rid of Fletcher, who spent far too much money for Stavro's liking. Ken Dryden, seen at right, came in to run the team, even though he'd had only minimal contact with the NHL since 1989.

Ken Dryden, president of the Leafs, and Richard Peddie, president of Maple Leaf Sports and Entertainment Ltd., leave Maple Leaf Gardens in September 1999 after telling the media of their plans to sell the once-hallowed hockey shrine. As of 2009, it remains vacant.

Another one of the Leafs' infamous moments came on November 29, 2000, when they managed to blow a five-goal lead against the St. Louis Blues. Assistant coach Keith Acton and coach Pat Quinn look on. The players are, from left to right, Igor Korolev, Darcy Tucker, Shayne Corson and Gary Roberts.

Goalie Curtis Joseph and coach Pat Quinn chat at a morning skate during the 2000 playoffs against the Ottawa Senators. The Leafs beat the Senators, of course, but their hopes for the cup ended when they lost to the New Jersey Devils in the subsequent round. The Quinn–Joseph relationship soon went south as well.

Ken Dryden's face tells it all. Well, most of it. Dryden was announcing that Curtis Joseph had turned down overtures from the Leafs and signed with the Detroit Red Wings. What Dryden didn't mention was that his meddling played a major role in Joseph's departure.

John Ferguson Jr. was hired as a compromise to be the team's general manager. By April 2006 he had decided that he could lay the blame for his unsuccessful tenure with the Leafs on the coach. He is seen here arriving for the press conference to announce that Pat Quinn had been fired.

In November 2008, Brian Burke (right) arrived to save the Leafs. Here, he talks about himself to NHL commissioner Gary Bettman at a February 2009 function. Actually, Burke may not have been talking about himself, but the odds are good that he was.

"I apologize to the fans," said MLSE chairman Larry Tanenbaum. "In my lifetime, we're going to bring that Stanley Cup back to Toronto."

There was not the slightest doubt about the truth of that statement. The Hockey Hall of Fame is in Toronto, and that's where the Stanley Cup resides. As for the Leafs winning it, that's another story. If that's Tanenbaum's plan, he must be counting on remarkable longevity.

"It has been very clear all along," said Peddie of the Ferguson experience. "We've been missing the playoffs and it has been a struggle this year. I told him, 'Win and you'll get a contract extension,' but that didn't happen."

Fortunately for Peddie, no one insisted that such a condition be applied to his own continued employment.

"It has become clear that change and a new direction is needed," said Peddie. "And it's in the best interests of the Leafs and of John to begin the transition immediately."

He was talking about a change of direction at the managerial level. He should have considered applying the same principle a little farther up the food chain.

13

Eleven Years Too Late, Cliff Fletcher Gets Free Rein

In February 2008, the Leafs went back to the best general manager they'd had since they won their last Stanley Cup. The 2008 entry draft proves to be very fruitful, and a lot of deadwood became someone else's problem. But in the long run, was too much of the future given away?

Cliff Fletcher was supposed to be nothing more than a caretaker, a guy who would keep the team on an even keel until a full-time general manager could be acquired.

In other words, the Leafs' upper echelon knew that Ferguson couldn't do the job, but hadn't got as far as deciding what they were going to do next.

It was clear that the Leafs weren't going to make the playoffs, and minority owner Larry Tanenbaum offered his hockey wisdom on that development as it related to the firing of Ferguson: "To be able to bring a Stanley Cup here, it's hard to do that when you don't have playoffs."

Fans everywhere stood in open-mouthed amazement. Could this be true? Here was a concept that no one had ever considered. No wonder Tanenbaum held such a position of power with a National Hockey League team.

It was, of course, widely assumed that Fletcher would eventually be succeeded by Brian Burke. But the Leafs denied it. After all, Burke was under contract to Anaheim for another year, and he had insisted that he had no interest in the job.

Based on those facts, and the usual standard of integrity in the NHL, Leafs fans therefore knew beyond a doubt that the job had to go to Burke. But in the meantime, the charade had to be acted out. Burke had to insist that he already had a job. The league had to insist that there would be no tampering. The Leafs had to form a search committee that would consider all candidates.

Eventually, by a marvellous stroke of good fortune for the Leafs, the Anaheim Ducks decided that Burke could seek opportunities elsewhere, the league decided that there had been no tampering and the Leafs decided that Burke was the best available candidate. To see the universe unfold in such a fortuitous fashion almost brings a tear to one's eye.

In the interim, Fletcher was in charge, and he wasn't about to sit around idly. After all, an excellent case could be made that Fletcher's record as a general manager was far superior to Burke's, so there was no reason for Fletcher to think that any actions he took would not be good for the team.

With that in mind, he made a lot of moves. They weren't all good, but that's the nature of being a general manager. Even the best GMs make some questionable decisions. The trick is to make more good moves than bad, and Fletcher did that.

In fact, a single move in Fletcher's "plus" column overshadowed all of the minuses of his second term: the acquisition of defenceman Luke Schenn.

The Leafs were to draft seventh in the 2008 draft, but Fletcher gave the New York Islanders his third-round 2008 pick as well as his second-round pick in 2009 in exchange for a flip of first-rounders. That meant he moved up to fifth and was able to grab Schenn, who would not have been available had Fletcher simply elected to pick seventh.

It was a brilliant move that even Fletcher's own support staff didn't recognize. In the Leafs' 2008–09 media guide, every active player has a page devoted to him. There is no page for Schenn. In the guide's next section, every serious prospect has a page devoted to him. There is no page for Schenn.

As it turned out, Schenn was not only too good to be sent back to junior hockey, he was the Leafs' best defenceman over the course of the 2008–09 season. In fact, there were those who made the case that he was the best player to emerge from the 2008 draft. Supporters of Steven Stamkos and Drew Doughty would argue, but there's no denying that Schenn was a superb choice and should be the anchor of the Leafs defence for years to come.

In his nine months on the job, Fletcher transformed the team and set the stage for Burke. He fired coach Paul Maurice, who simply had not been able to get the team to play up to its perceived potential, and brought in Ron Wilson, who had been released by the San Jose Sharks for the same reason. Of course, it must be said that the perceived potential was a lot higher in San Jose than it was in Toronto.

Whether it's deserved or not, Wilson has the reputation of being a coach who can improve a team substantially but can't get it over that final hump. With the Leafs, he was going to have plenty of time before he had to worry about hump day.

And since he was a long-time friend of Burke—not that anyone knew Burke was coming, of course; it was just coincidence—he would be a good man to have in the organization.

Fletcher got rid of players who weren't likely to help the Leafs in the long run—goalie Andrew Raycroft and forwards Darcy Tucker and Kyle Wellwood, for example. He trimmed the payroll, shipping out defenceman Bryan McCabe and a fourth-round pick for Mike Van Ryn, a similar player who was younger and less expensive. He also allowed team captain Mats Sundin to leave as a free agent when his contract expired.

He unloaded players who hadn't lived up to potential, sending injury-prone defenceman Carlo Colaiacovo and inconsistent winger Alexander Steen to St. Louis for winger Lee Stempniak. He picked up draft picks in exchange for spare parts Hal Gill, Chad Kilger and Wade Belak.

He signed free agents Jeff Finger, Curtis Joseph and Niklas Hagman. He gave up draft picks to acquire Jamal Mayers, Mikhail Grabovski and Ryan Hollweg.

If there are grounds to criticize Fletcher, they are to be found in that last statement. Grabovski turned out well, but Mayers and Hollweg were not close to being worth the prices paid.

Even though the drafting of players is certainly not the only important aspect in the building of a team, it must still be taken very seriously. In his second go-around as GM of the Leafs, Fletcher brought in a second-round pick, a third-round pick and two fifth-round picks. But he traded away two third-round picks in 2008, a fifth-round pick in 2008, a second-round pick in 2009, a fifth-round pick in 2009, a second-round pick in 2010 and a fourth-round pick in 2010. In addition, the NHL forced the Leafs to forfeit their 2009 fourth-round pick as punishment for giving defenceman Jonas Frögren a bonus that was not allowed under the collective bargaining agreement.

There are only seven rounds to the draft these days, so if you're going to give away that many picks, you'd better feel confident that your scouting staff is capable of spotting free agents that the other twenty-nine teams have missed.

Perhaps the Leafs do feel that way. The last fifty years have shown that there's not the slightest reason to do so, but it could happen.

The sun could come up in the west, too.

14

Plenty of Pomp,
So Little Circumstance

Brian Burke was to be the latest saviour of the Toronto Maple Leafs.
His qualifications were phenomenal—he told us so himself. As long as
no one bothered to check his record—and no one in the Toronto mass
media did—everyone could agree that it was only a matter of time
before the next Stanley Cup parade.

Amidst much fanfare in Toronto, the Brian Burke era began on
Saturday, November 29, 2008. A few days earlier Burke had issued
a typically pompous decree announcing that he would be indulging in no business matters during the week. He was in Boston visiting his family for U.S. Thanksgiving, he said, and therefore, all other
considerations would be secondary until after the weekend.

But on Thursday afternoon, November 27, right in the middle
of the National Football League's Thanksgiving Day games, the local

sports media were tripping over each other to claim to be the first to break the news of Burke's signing with the Leafs. Curiously enough, not a single person in the Toronto media commented on this discrepancy.

For that matter, nobody mentioned some even more glaring inconsistencies. Earlier in the year—on January 17, to be exact—Burke had been a guest on the TSN show *Off the Record*. He was asked by host Michael Landsberg, "Do you want the job in Toronto as general manager?"

Burke's answer was succinct and unequivocal.

"No."

On January 25, Burke visited Toronto. At the time, he was still the general manager of the Anaheim Ducks. Since there had already been considerable speculation that he might end up running the Leafs, the media asked him about the possibility. His answer was characteristically disdainful and condescending: "I have no intention of going anywhere else," he said. "I've said so repeatedly to anyone who will listen. I'm not sure which part of it I'm not saying in English. We really love it in Anaheim. We work for special people there and we want to stay."

Just in case he hadn't made his point, he added: "I have a job that I love . . ."

And this: "I'm not going anywhere."

As for his views on the Leafs' search committee of Gordon Kirke and Richard Peddie: "They'll be able to take their pick of guys who aren't under contract. I don't intend to be on their list."

Ten months later, the hockey world was ready for Burke's inauguration in Toronto. Out of respect for the gravity of the moment, Burke showed up for the 2 p.m. press conference in his finest regalia. His tie was fastened at the throat. Usually, he wanders around with his tie loosened—as he did for his subsequent media scrum and his nationally televised interview on *Hockey Night in Canada*.

For the press conference, his jacket was buttoned up and his shirt was tucked in—both of which are also unusual for Burke. In fact, he usually discards the jacket at the earliest opportunity. He didn't even bring along his paper cup—the one into which he spits constantly as a regular user of smokeless tobacco. In short, he was on his best behaviour for the coronation.

And naturally, he seized the moment to pontificate. It's not mere coincidence that some of Burke's colleagues in the National Hockey League's managerial ranks refer to him as Pope Brian. He has all the answers and he issues them as if they were papal bulls.

On this particular Saturday, he assumed his best Burkian frown (he rarely smiles, especially in the presence of media) and delivered his decrees.

On being named GM and president of the Leafs: "You're talking about the Vatican if you're Catholic. You're talking the centre of the hockey universe. You're talking about one of the most important jobs in hockey."

On what a Stanley Cup would mean to the city: "The guy that turns this team around and wins a championship here, they're going to name schools after him."

On the kind of team that a hockey genius expects: "We require as a team proper levels of pugnacity, testosterone, truculence and belligerence."

On the future of those lucky enough to be a part of the impending Leafs juggernaut under Burke: "Everyone will get a chance to show they want to stay and do it my way and be part of the future here."

The Toronto media drooled with anticipation. In the newspapers and on the websites, they spewed out vast amounts of adulation and adoration. The only columnist who took a stance that was not slavishly pro-Burke was Bill Lankhof in the *Toronto Sun*. Lankhof pointed out that this was not Burke's first managerial job, and in the previous three, a fair number of errors had been committed.

As for Burke's status as a messiah who would lead the Leafs to glory, Lankhof wrote, "That first Moses, it might be recalled, ended up wandering in a wilderness and never did make it to the Promised Land himself."

It was not an anti–Burke piece, but it was balanced, and on that November weekend in Toronto, that was a genuine rarity.

It is indeed possible that Burke will supervise a series of developments that will someday culminate in a Leafs captain hoisting the Stanley Cup. He is not a fool, and he did come to the Leafs with ten years of experience as a general manager.

He has a law degree from Harvard, although it is widely assumed that he skipped class the day the first amendment to the United States Constitution was being studied. That's the one that guarantees freedom of speech. As far as Burke is concerned, you get to speak freely only if you agree with him.

Anyone in the media who points out his shortcomings can expect that Burke will go to his superiors in an attempt to get him fired. He has made numerous attempts of that nature, and in some cases has been successful. He justifies such actions by claiming that those with whom he disagrees were lying. These "lies" usually turn out to be nothing more than an interpretation of the facts that differs from Burke's own views. And a radio announcer he got fired in Vancouver didn't even mention Burke at all—he made a remark about Todd Bertuzzi's wife that offended Burke.

No one can make the case that Burke is incompetent. But the case can most certainly be made that he is not the genius that many—including himself—believe him to be.

Let's look at his managerial background—something that no one in the Toronto media seemed willing to do.

He started his career with the Hartford Whalers, a team that had made the playoffs for seven consecutive seasons. Once Burke got there, they finished out of the running.

But he was much better in Vancouver. There, he won a playoff round. Granted, it took six seasons to do so, but Burke has an explanation. His payroll, he says, was lower than that of many teams, and he therefore couldn't afford to corral stars in the pre–salary cap era.

In fact, his Canucks missed the playoffs twice during his tenure, and not all the teams that finished above them had higher payrolls. In the lone year when his Canucks actually won a round, they subsequently lost to the Minnesota Wild, a team with a considerably lower payroll.

On the occasion when Burke's Canucks got their single playoff victory, they were following their usual form and were trailing 3–1– even though they had knocked out the St. Louis Blues' star defenceman Al MacInnis with a separated shoulder. Then the entire Blues team contracted the flu in a form so debilitating that they often had to rush to the dressing room between shifts, and the Canucks came back to win.

Despite this glorious achievement, Burke left the Canucks after a contract dispute. Once again, as was the case in Hartford, the parting was acrimonious.

Nevertheless, as Burke's backers point out, he won a Stanley Cup in Anaheim. True enough. And a stopped clock is right twice a day.

In Anaheim, Burke took over an up-and-coming team from Bryan Murray—a team that had advanced to the seventh game of the Stanley Cup final only two seasons earlier.

Because he inherited Rob Niedermayer, he was able to persuade Rob's brother Scott to join the team as a free agent. Even Burke, a notorious self-promoter, couldn't find it in himself to brag about that one. When asked about it during the subsequent season, he said, "People always say we did a great job signing Scott last summer. But anybody who takes credit for signing a Hall of Fame player when he's an unrestricted free agent is an imbecile."

As it happened, Niedermayer's acquisition wasn't enough to get the team back to the Cup final, but the Ducks did win two playoff rounds. The Burkian legend was born. Two playoff rounds won in only one season. Wow! Twice as many as his entire career to that point!

Next, Burke received a huge boost from Chris Pronger's wife, who decided she hated Edmonton. Although Pronger had finished only the first year of a long-term contract with the Oilers, he demanded a trade, and Burke made the deal to get him. For this one, Burke has to be given credit. Pronger was a dominant defenceman and as such was in great demand around the league. Burke put together an offer that outbid all the other suitors.

But even that wouldn't have been enough had it not been for what is considered in the Detroit area to be the worst call in the history of playoff hockey. In the dying moments of game five of the Western Conference semifinal, the Red Wings appeared poised to take a 3–2 series lead. The Ducks were moving up ice and Detroit's Pavel Datsyuk was skating alongside his check, as players do thousands of times a game. Suddenly, referee Don Koharski's arm shot up and Datsyuk, a four-time winner of the Lady Byng Trophy, was penalized for interference. On the subsequent power play, a shot deflected into the goal off the shaft of Nicklas Lidström's stick to tie the game, and the Ducks won in overtime.

So a very good case could be made that the three people most responsible for Burke's Stanley Cup win are: (1) Bryan Murray for providing the team Burke inherited, especially Rob Niedermayer; (2) Chris Pronger's wife; and (3) Don Koharski.

The year after the Stanley Cup victory, Burke's team returned to form and went out in the first round. So if we take out the Stanley Cup year, Burke came to Toronto having won the whopping total of three playoff rounds in nine years. Even if you include the Cup year, he had won only seven rounds in ten years. This is hardly the stuff of which a legend is made.

Nevertheless, the Toronto media fell all over Burke. In the *Toronto Star,* Damien Cox praised him for his drafting acumen, pointing out that he had manipulated the deal that brought Daniel and Henrik Sedin to Vancouver in 1999. Why this was such a momentous achievement is not clear. The Sedins have been good, but no one puts them in the superstar category. And their knuckles aren't dragging on the ground from the weight of Stanley Cup rings.

While praising Burke's drafting ability in 1999, Cox somehow managed to overlook the 2000 and 2002 drafts. The only pick to graduate to the NHL from Burke's entire 2000 draft list was Nathan Smith. He played all of four games for the Canucks before becoming a career minor-leaguer. By July 2009, when he was signed to a one-year deal with the Wild, Smith had played in twenty-one NHL games.

In 2002, Burke had an even worse day at the draft table. Not a single one of his selections ever played a minute in the NHL.

As part of the euphoria surrounding Burke's arrival in Toronto, there were even some suggestions in the media that Burke might upgrade the Leafs' goaltending. What precedent there would be for a move of that nature was not clear. When Burke arrived in Anaheim, he inherited superstar goaltender Jean-Sébastien Giguère. Fortunately for the Ducks, Burke didn't have to go out and get a goalie himself.

During his tenure in Vancouver, such was not the case. At one point, he acquired Kevin Weekes and labelled him "the goalie of the future." Weekes was gone within a year. At another point, he acquired Félix Potvin. In his usual humble fashion, Burke said, "In Félix Potvin we have acquired a goaltender who I think is one of the better goaltenders in the NHL. When I first came to Vancouver, I expressed dissatisfaction with the state of affairs of our goaltenders.

I repeatedly stressed that theme. We have been trying to upgrade at this position for some time, and I feel we have done that."

In that same soliloquy, Burke said he had become tired of seeing his team quickly fall behind by a goal or two. With Potvin, that was no longer the case. They quickly fell behind by three or more.

In his six years in Vancouver, Burke went through no fewer than thirteen goaltenders. In addition to Weekes and Potvin, there were Alex Auld, Martin Brochu, Dan Cloutier, Bob Essensa, Johan Hedberg, Corey Hirsch, Manny Legace, Alfie Michaud, Tyler Moss, Corey Schwab, Peter Skudra and Garth Snow.

Some of them went on to become good goalies elsewhere. But they couldn't perform well for Burke's team. Was that only coincidence?

Burke is never slow to tell anyone who will listen that he's a man of his word. He arrived in Vancouver in 1998 after assuring the Canucks' ownership group that he would get along well with coach Mike Keenan and that the owners would certainly never find themselves having to pay both a working coach and a departed coach. "I'm thrilled to have Mike Keenan as my coach," he said publicly. "It's not something that I am saddled with. It's something I have been blessed with."

Right from the beginning of that season, Burke was unable to come to contractual terms with star forward Pavel Bure. Negotiations dragged on for months—while Bure sat out—until the new year. All that time, as the team struggled, Burke kept telling the media that he would make no evaluation of Keenan's work until the Bure trade had been completed and Keenan was given a respectable amount of time to work with the newly constituted team.

Two days after making the Bure deal, Burke fired Keenan. So much for being a man of his word. And he didn't even have the decency to tell Keenan in person. The task fell to a member of the team's public relations staff, Chris Bromwell.

Similarly, when Burke got the job in Toronto, he said on a number of occasions over the subsequent few weeks that everyone in the Leafs' management should consider his job to be safe. Two months later, the news leaked out that Burke had fired director of player personnel Al Coates.

When asked about it by the local media, Burke said, "I have no comment on that." Nobody bothered to press him for an answer.

At the end of the season, Burke fired three members of the training staff and two pro scouts. Assistant GM Joe Nieuwendyk, another executive Burke had inherited, had already seen the writing on the wall and departed for the Dallas Stars.

Burke makes no secret of the fact that he sees himself as superior to the other general managers in the league. When he was outbid for some free agents in July 2001, he said, "I'm going head to head with people who are crazy, as far as I'm concerned." He also said he was "embarrassed" by the actions of his colleagues.

On another occasion, he expressed a similar view, saying, "Other than my annoyance with the way this business is being run, if we're going to have asinine, insane, inflationary signings, it suits me fine that most of them have been in the East so far."

He was still smarter than everyone else in the summer of 2007. When everyone else said that Bertuzzi wasn't worthy of anything more than a one-year deal, only Burke had the foresight to give him a two-year deal. Then he bought out the second year of that contract. The resultant payout to a player who had left the scene was a factor in the Ducks being so cash-strapped early in the 2008–09 season that they had to send Bobby Ryan, the second-overall draft pick behind Sidney Crosby in 2005, to the minors because his salary couldn't be accommodated under the salary cap.

In the same summer that Burke was signing Bertuzzi, Kevin Lowe, the general manager of the Edmonton Oilers, signed Dustin Penner away from Burke's Ducks. There was absolutely nothing wrong with this. Under league rules, Lowe had every right to tender an offer sheet to Penner. He did so, and Penner accepted.

But Burke, who for some reason held the opinion that Lowe should have informed him of his intentions in advance, was furious. It was his contention that by signing Penner to a five-year, $21.25-million deal, Lowe had somehow upset the pay structure of the NHL. Again, it was a matter of Burke knowing better than all of his colleagues.

"Thanks to the Edmonton Oilers," he told the *Los Angeles Times,* "the second contract has disappeared. You go right now from the entry level to what used to be the third contract thanks to two offer sheets from Kevin Lowe."

After hearing Burke fire a number of public insults his way, Lowe finally fired back.

"Where do I begin?" he asked during an interview with Team 1260, an Edmonton radio station. "He's a moron, first of all. Secondly, he really believes that any news for the NHL is good news. Thirdly, he loves the limelight, and I don't think anyone in hockey will dispute that. Lastly, he's in a pathetic hockey market where they can't get on any page of the newspaper, let alone the front page of the sports, so any of this stuff carries on."

Lowe also disputed Burke's contention that the NHL salary structure had been unduly inflated by the Penner signing.

"The reality," he said, "is Rick Nash's contract a number of years ago, [Patrice] Bergeron's and [Ilya] Kovalchuk's—that's what set the standard. That has been going on for decades."

There were lots of others: the six-year, $27-million contract for Nashville's David Legwand; $24 million over six years to Nathan Horton in Florida; $16 million over four years to Patrick Sharp and so on.

As for Burke's constant pronouncements on the state of the

game and his know-it-all attitude, Lowe said, "I'm sick and tired of it. I know everybody in hockey is. I know our peers are like, 'Well, that's Burkie.' This guy is an absolute media junkie and I guess that he's achieving what he wants because he gets his name in the headlines. But the reality is, I hate the fact that my name is linked to his. He's an underachieving wannabe in terms of success in the NHL.

"He won a Stanley Cup? Great. I've won six Stanley Cups. You want to count rings? Who cares? It's just a little pathetic that he carries on."

There were plenty of bad trades during the course of Burke's career as well, but it must be said that every general manager makes bad trades at some point—not as bad as Andy McDonald for Doug Weight perhaps, but bad nonetheless. What cannot be ignored, however, is the way in which Burke tends to ravage a team, leaving very little behind when he departs. He left the Canucks in 2004, and the next season (following a dark year thanks to the lockout), the team missed the playoffs. Had it not been for a sharp move by Burke's successor Dave Nonis, the Canucks might have languished at the bottom of the NHL for years. But Nonis managed to pry all-world goaltender Roberto Luongo out of Florida and the Canucks were able to return to respectability.

The legacy from Burke's six years of drafting in Vancouver was almost nonexistent. The Sedin twins were there, as were defenceman Kevin Bieksa and forward Ryan Kesler. But little else.

R.J. Umberger, Burke's first-round draft pick in 2001 and a highly rated player, had made the mistake of asking for a contract that was certainly well within market parameters.

Of course, Burke never was known for his ability to judge the market. When forward Trent Klatt suggested that the Los Angeles Kings would give him more money than the Canucks were offering,

Burke said, "If Trent Klatt gets more money from L.A., God bless him. I'll drive him to the airport."

Klatt did get more—about 50 per cent more, as a matter of fact—but he had to drive himself to the airport.

When Burke similarly played hardball with Umberger, the youngster refused to give in to Burke's bullying. He sat out a year and was then traded away without ever playing a game for the Canucks. In return for this first-round draft pick, Burke got Martin Ručinský, who played all of thirteen games for Vancouver and mustered three points.

The only other guy left behind after Burke's departure who was close to an NHLer was Fedor Fedorov. And he was close only because his brother was Sergei Fedorov. Even Burke couldn't defend his own pick on this occasion. Some years later, when there was speculation that the Canucks might go after Sergei Fedorov, Burke said, "Why would we be interested in acquiring Fedorov? We already have one Fedorov too many."

So that was the Burke legacy in Vancouver—a smattering of decent players, a couple of good ones and a depleted farm system.

It was the same story in Anaheim. When Burke departed early in the 2008–09 season, he left behind a ravaged organization. Only seven NHL-level players were under contract for the 2009–10 season, and four of them—Ryan Getzlaf, Giguère, Corey Perry and Teemu Selänne—had been inherited by Burke from the previous regime.

Yet the Toronto media were universal in their assurances that Burke would rebuild the Leafs and make them into a force in the league. The headline in the *National Post* over Bruce Arthur's column on the Burke beatification was "Colourful philosophy paints bright future."

Arthur's article wasn't any worse than any of the others. In fact, it pretty much reflected the common view. It said that Burke's arrival represented a change of course: "What it does mean is that the days of the Toronto Maple Leafs as a national laughingstock—and local joke in the more clear-eyed quarters—are done. At some point, this team will deserve its prime-time slot on *Hockey Night in Canada,* rather than simply command it."

That may or may not be so. It happens to be Arthur's belief, and he's therefore quite free to present it. He followed that up with a statement that wasn't as well grounded in reality but quite typical of the approach taken by the Toronto media. "But finally, the Leafs have someone with the heft and stomach to rebuild the franchise, top to bottom and side to side," he wrote.

Again, that may or may not be so. Perhaps Burke can rebuild a franchise. But he has never done it before. In fact, he has laid more franchises to waste than he has built.

Who knows? Perhaps in Toronto, using the wisdom that he gained from his earlier failures, Burke can indeed build a franchise. And it must be said that his signing of undrafted free agents in the spring of 2009 was definitely a step in the right direction. In Christian Hanson, Tyler Bozak and Robert Slaney—along with Viktor Stålberg, a sixth-round draft choice in 2006 who signed after his junior year at the University of Vermont—Burke got four kids who are cheap but may blossom. The upside on those moves is considerable, the downside negligible. Burke also made a potentially rewarding move when he signed Swedish free-agent goaltender Jonas Gustavsson to a one-year deal in July. The twenty-four year-old Gustavsson was the top goalie in the Swedish Elite League in the 2008–09 season.

Even so, these moves came long after the media implied that Burke has a track record of franchise-building already in place. He doesn't.

Much was expected from Burke when it came time for the 2009 entry draft, and he played a key role in raising those expectations. The Leafs were scheduled to draft seventh overall, but he made no secret of his desire to trade up and select either John Tavares or Victor Hedman. And if he didn't land either player, he was on record as saying, his sights were set on Brayden Schenn, a potential power forward who happened to be the younger brother of the Leafs' Luke. He also revealed that he was in talks with Boston to acquire Phil Kessel, a thirty-six-goal scorer in 2008–09, in exchange for defenceman Tomáš Kaberle.

In the end, the Kessel deal fell through, and Burke failed in his attempts to draft from any slot other than the one in which he began: seventh. Not only that, but the Los Angeles Kings, with the fifth pick, selected the younger Schenn. To cap off a not-so-great day, as Burke took the stage to announce his pick, Nazem Kadri of the London Knights, the crowd at Montreal's Bell Centre—who had been chanting "six-ty sev-en"—greeted him with a chorus of boos.

Whichever way it plays out, the Burke era—scheduled to run for at least six years—started with a bang. All other news was secondary on that day. Whether Burke is or is not the man to lead the Leafs to the holy grail of the Stanley Cup remains to be seen.

For many Leafs fans, no small number of whom hold down media jobs, this was the first step on a path to glory. Certainly the media approach came nowhere close to mirroring a *Toronto Sun* survey earlier in the week in which respondents for and against Burke were roughly 50–50.

Instead, the honeymoon was under way. Now only time would tell whether Burke was indeed the saviour or just another in a long list of false prophets.

15

Doom at the Top

Just in case you wondered who makes the decisions at the upper levels of Maple Leafs Sports and Entertainment, you'll be happy to know that they're all equally qualified. They know how to make money. Please don't ask about hockey.

The jubilation with which Brian Burke was hoisted onto the Maple Leaf Sports and Entertainment bandwagon bore a remarkable similarity to that of an earlier event staged with similar hoopla by the same corporation.

That was the acquisition of Bryan Colangelo to run the Toronto Raptors, MLSE's money-losing franchise in the National Basketball Association. Like Burke, Colangelo was given the dual titles of president and general manager. Like Burke, Colangelo was to be the man who would lead the Raptors to a string of titles. Although it's not a matter of public knowledge, their salaries are believed to be identical.

With the aid of a little nepotism, Colangelo had established himself as a top-notch basketball executive by running his daddy's team, the Phoenix Suns. He arrived in Toronto in February 2006 and his team has yet to win a playoff round. In fact, instead of winning championships, it seems to be getting steadily worse. In 2008–09, it didn't even make the playoffs in a league where it's not uncommon to join the post-season festivities with a sub-.500 record.

Richard Peddie, the president and CEO of MLSE, has repeatedly pointed to his acquisition of Colangelo as one of the corporation's great achievements. Now, Peddie sees the acquisition of Burke in the same light. Unfortunately, however, there has never been any great evidence that Peddie has the tiniest clue about how to operate a sports franchise. In fact, the same thing can be said about the entire nine-man MLSE board.

Three of them represent the Ontario Teachers' Pension Plan which, by virtue of its 58 per cent share of MLSE, is the majority owner. One board member is the son of a former mayor of Toronto—a mayor whose political downfall was certainly no cause for consternation on the part of the city's beleaguered citizens. One is a former television network executive. One represents a bank. One runs a construction company. And so it goes. Nowhere on the board is there anyone who has ever had an iota of direct involvement with a professional hockey team at ice level.

As of December 2008, when he picked up another 7.5 per cent of the firm, Larry Tanenbaum became the second-largest shareholder in MLSE. Through his company Kilmer Sports Inc., he now owns 20.5 per cent. The Toronto-Dominion Bank holds 14 per cent and the remaining 7.5 per cent is owned by CTVglobemedia.

Tanenbaum got into the hockey business because he was trying to bring an NBA team to Toronto. He failed—the franchise he coveted was awarded in 1993 to rival bidders John Bitove Jr. and

Allan Slaight. Tanenbaum then bought a minority stake in Maple Leaf Gardens Ltd. from Steve Stavro, who needed the capital. The company was renamed Maple Leaf Sports and Entertainment.

Bitove and Slaight's basketball team, the Raptors, played their first games in 1995–96 and made the SkyDome their temporary home while construction began on their arena, the Air Canada Centre. In 1996, Peddie was installed as the Raptors' president.

When the stakes got too high for Slaight's liking, he exercised a shotgun clause in his partnership agreement with Bitove, essentially forcing his partner to buy him out or be bought out. The move backfired—Bitove couldn't raise the necessary money, and Slaight ended up owning the whole thing. Construction of the Air Canada Centre proceeded, while the Leafs made noises about building a palatial hockey arena on top of Union Station. Ultimately, that proved impractical, and Stavro and Tanenbaum took the Raptors and their arena—by now 20 per cent complete—off Slaight's hands. The building, designed for basketball, was hastily reconfigured to accommodate the Leafs.

Thus, it has been Peddie and Tanenbaum—a pair of basketball men—more than any other board members, who have been making all the hockey decisions for MLSE.

Someday, perhaps, the corporation will acquire the services of someone who is a genuine top-notch hockey man and give him some authority. Peddie and Tanenbaum would say that they have done that with Burke, but in other quarters, there is considerable doubt that Burke meets the primary qualification.

In the meantime, the Leafs will probably struggle along, tantalizing their fans every few years with a run in the general direction of the Stanley Cup, but never quite grasping the ultimate prize.

16

It Can Be Fixed
—and Here's How

There is a way that the Leafs can develop a winner, and if they're willing to be fairly free with their money—never one of their strong points—it can be done in a reasonable period of time. It won't be easy and it won't be automatic. But the opportunity is there.

"If there's a blueprint available that guarantees success in any professional sport, I haven't seen it yet."
—Cliff Fletcher, November 20, 1991

The board of directors of Maple Leaf Sports and Entertainment is composed of executives whose primary concern is making money. Even though they all talk a good game and insist that they'd love to see the Leafs win a championship, can anyone seriously believe that the Ontario Teachers' Pension Plan bought controlling interest of this team with the overriding aim of finding a fancy piece of silver-ware to fill an empty spot in some trophy case?

They're there for profit. All of them. All the time.

However, having said that, it should be pointed out that they do want to win the Stanley Cup. Even though many Toronto fans say that MLSE doesn't care about improving the team because every seat is sold anyway, that's not quite true.

MLSE desperately wants to win because doing so would provide a huge boost for the corporate coffers. The salaries of NHL players are based on the regular season. Once the playoffs begin, players get no paycheques, just a relatively small bonus from the league for each round they win.

For the team owners, the playoffs are the gravy train. Ticket prices are jacked up for the opening round and escalate steadily after that. In Toronto, where ticket prices are already the highest in the league, that means a whopping windfall in the playoffs.

It's hard to attach a precise number to that windfall because it has been so long since the Leafs have been in the playoffs—five years as of 2009—that it's not clear what playoff prices would be. Even so, it's not at all unreasonable to assume that on any given playoff night, the Leafs' profit—from tickets alone, not counting the obscene cost of food and drink in the Air Canada Centre—would start at $3 million and go to an amount in excess of $5 million.

A Stanley Cup run would therefore bring in something in the range of $35 million–$40 million.

That's why the MLSE board members can say, without a hint of deception, that they're doing everything they can to get the Leafs to win a Stanley Cup.

For more than forty years, the Toronto Maple Leafs have ranged from marginally inept to totally incompetent. They have had some brief moments of respectability, but those moments have been more than offset by lengthy stretches as laughingstocks.

In fact, by the spring of 2009, their incompetence had reached such a level that *Sports Illustrated* adjudged them the worst-managed team in the National Hockey League. "Unfortunately, the dysfunctional relationship between the two principals—Richard Peddie and Larry Tanenbaum—continues to trickle down to the on-ice product," said the magazine, "as MLSE is too busy running too many sports properties and breaking ground on too many real estate projects to pay enough attention to the Leafs."

What should they have done? There are many answers to that question, but most of them come too late. The hockey world in which those answers could have been useful no longer exists.

Beginning with the 2005–06 season, the National Hockey League imposed a salary cap on its teams with the intention of creating what commissioner Gary Bettman called "cost certainty" and "a level playing field."

Prior to that, the teams had been free to spend as much as they wanted—not that the Leafs ever took advantage of that situation. Extravagant spending was rarely the modus operandi of any of the Leafs' various management teams over the decades.

Ballard was notoriously cheap, as has been shown. Stavro's famous response to the opportunity to sign Gretzky—"How many seats will he sell?"—tells you everything you need to know about the priorities during that regime.

After Teachers' bought Stavro out in 2003, any major expenditure required the approval of the MLSE board. Although the company certainly imposed spending limits on its hockey operations, it must also be said that any time the Leafs' general manager went to the board asking for extra money, he invariably got what he wanted.

The payroll gradually slid upwards as Pat Quinn attempted to stay employed, but the problem at that point was not one of financial support; it was one of focus. Quinn was allowed to bring in some high-salaried players, or jack up the salaries of Leafs who were due to have their contracts extended, but his spending was generally misdirected.

By the time Bettman shut down the league and killed the 2004–05 season, the Leafs were near the top of the league in payroll spending, along with franchises like the New York Rangers and Detroit Red Wings. As far as the Leafs' on-ice results were concerned, however, they were much more like the Rangers than the Red Wings. In other words, they spent big money on the wrong people.

But once the salary-cap restrictions were imposed on the league, the Leafs had to conform like everyone else.

Or did they?

After the lockout, the Leafs, now under general manager John Ferguson Jr., mismanaged their allotted amount. They couldn't persuade the best of the unrestricted free agents to come to Toronto, so they compensated by throwing ridiculous amounts of money at second-rate free agents who had yet to be picked up by anyone else. Apparently, it never dawned on anyone in the Leafs' front office that there was a reason that these guys were still available.

But there was another key aspect of the collective bargaining agreement (the document that laid down the rules for the salary-cap restrictions) and it should have been seized upon by the Leafs. Even though the amount that could be spent on players was strictly controlled, there was no limit to the amount a team could spend elsewhere in its hockey operations.

The Leafs were the most profitable team in the league. They had money coming out of their ears. Ticket prices were the highest in the league, and television revenues were staggering. In most ways the Leafs were—and are—Canada's team. As a result, they sold—and continue to sell—phenomenal amounts of Leafs-branded paraphernalia.

At one point in 2006, I wrote a column for the *Toronto Sun* hypothesizing that the Leafs were making close to $100 million

(Canadian) in annual profit. The column was based on the limited financial information that was available about the Leafs, but a lot of it was indisputable.

A little research, for example, would reveal the total gate receipts for each home date. Simply take the number of seats, multiply by the ticket prices in each range, and calculate the result. Ditto for the corporate boxes. Then you added it up and multiplied by 45—the 41 regular-season home games plus four pre-season games sold at full price. Since the Leafs never had an empty seat or box, the resultant figure would yield a total for the season that could be presumed to be accurate.

At NHL commissioner Gary Bettman's press conference during the Stanley Cup final that year, I mentioned my hypothesis regarding the size of the Leafs' profit. Bettman shrugged it off, but his second-in-command, Bill Daly, was livid. He vigorously disputed the figure.

Daly is a fair guy, and you can invariably get a straight answer from him, so I told him that in the interest of accuracy, I would like to know where my suppositions broke down. I said I would send him the column that provided the numbers and he could send back a list of false assumptions that he believed I'd made. I sent the column, but never heard back from Daly. For him, this was very unusual. The only logical conclusion to be drawn was that the figures were accurate.

Even with their failures on the ice, the Leafs continue to pull in big money. Because the NHL now has a form of revenue sharing, each team has to submit its revenue information to the league. According to an informed insider, the Leafs' hockey-related revenues for the 2007–08 season were $182 million.

So with all this money, what was to stop the Leafs from developing a superb scouting staff? What was to stop them from luring the best general manager in the league away from whatever team employed him at the time? What was to stop them from building the league's largest and most effective support staff of pro scouts, bird dogs, specialized trainers, administrative assistants and anyone else from hypnotists to aromatherapists who might come in handy in the attempt to push the team to the top?

The answer to all those questions was the same in every case. Absolutely nothing.

But, as has so often been the case over the decades, the Leafs misread the situation and blew their opportunity to make significant advances.

The post-lockout era, with its salary cap and "level" playing field, handed them a great opportunity. No matter what Bettman said, that new playing field was not at all level. In 2003–04, seven teams had payrolls over $60 million (U.S.) The salary cap in 2005–06 was $39 million. This meant that those seven teams had been handed a gift of more than $20 million, which they could use to improve their team in every way.

But the Leafs just shrugged and continued to shamble down the same old time-worn path. They signed a few free agents, but to put it mildly, not one of them was likely to provide any long-term help for the team.

To reiterate, here is the Leafs' free-agent crop from the summer coming out of the lockout: Jason Allison, Jean-Sébastien Aubin, Brad Brown, Mariusz Czerkawski, Eric Lindros, Mike Hoffman and Alexander Khavanov.

Among the players who were free agents that summer were Sergei Gonchar, Paul Kariya, Adam Foote, Sergei Zubov, Martin Straka, Alex Kovalev, Pavol Demitra, Mikael Samuelsson, Markus Näslund and about three hundred others. But the Leafs could manage only to get Lindros and friends.

Here's how their Toronto careers unfolded:

Allison: Played one season (17 goals, 43 assists, 60 points) and became a free agent.

Aubin: Played two seasons as backup goalie with a 12–5–4 record and became a free agent.

Brown: Played only for the Marlies farm team. Became a free agent.

Czerkawski: Played 19 games (4 goals, 1 assist, 5 points), then was placed on waivers and claimed by Boston.

Lindros: Played 33 games in one season (11 goals, 11 assists, 22 points) and became a free agent.

Hoffman: Played only for the Marlies farm team. Became a free agent.

Khavanov: Played 66 games in one season (6 goals, 6 assists, 12 points) and became a free agent.

With all the opportunities the Leafs had awaiting them as hockey resumed after the lockout, this was the best they could do? Ferguson must have been really pleased with himself.

So the question arises, how should a general manager respond if he wants to build a team in the salary-cap era?

As Fletcher pointed out almost two decades ago, there is no formula that guarantees a winner. But because of the restrictions that are now in place which limit the options available to every NHL team, there is a path that makes more sense than others.

Some of what follows may be a bit complex, but that can't be helped. There is no simple way to build a Stanley Cup–winning team. You can't just say, "Follow these easy steps to certain victory."

Yet for some reason, an astonishing number of people who should know better think that they have that elusive easy answer. You can find these people on radio and television, and usually the ones who are the most vociferous are also the least knowledgeable.

People who think they have an infallible formula for building a

Cup-winning hockey team are like gamblers who show up at the casino with a system. Nothing makes casino owners happier. There is no foolproof system; there are only fools who think they've developed one.

Similarly, there are those who think they have figured out an easy way to build a Stanley Cup winner. "Blow it up," they say.

"That's all?" you ask. "Then what?"

"Oh, you just blow it up and start over."

Of course, if you've blown it up, you'd pretty well have to start over, wouldn't you?

And how would that help? Well, the theory is this. The Leafs should get rid of every player of consequence and stockpile the draft picks that they will get in return. The Leafs should play a goalie who's not ready for the National Hockey League.

The proponents of this theory don't actually say that the Leafs should throw games, but they do want management to put the team into a position that would create the same result. They want the Leafs to finish last—and not just for one year. For year after year.

If you ask them what comes next, their plans become increasingly vague. They haven't really thought that far ahead. But when pressed, they'll mumble something about the Pittsburgh Penguins and insist that everything will fall into place in the fifth year.

Sounds perfect. You're the worst team in the league for four years, and then you're the best team in the league in the fifth. Nothing to it. We should have thought of this before.

Since the people who expound this theory are apparently incapable of subjecting their proposal to an in-depth examination, let's do it for them. Let's call their team the Sharpies.

Let's assume that in year one, the Sharpies do indeed finish last and get the first-overall draft pick. Or do they? Right off the bat, that basic assumption is wrong. The last-place team is no longer guaranteed the first draft pick—there's a lottery. In the ten years from 1997 to 2007 (not counting the 2005 draft, which was a thirty-team lottery because there had been no preceding season upon which to base the order of selection), the last-place finisher got the top pick only three times.

So the Sharpies have thrown away the season in a quest for the top draft pick—the next Sidney Crosby or Alex Ovechkin or Steven Stamkos—but if precedent holds, someone else will likely get him.

But let's assume that the Sharpies get lucky. They win the lottery and get the top pick. And the next year, they finish last again. Apparently, the star they took with the first-overall pick in year one wasn't good enough to get them out of the basement single-handedly.

But Sharpies fans who endorsed the blow-it-up theory are happy because their team finished last again. The Sharpies are back in the lottery. One more time, they need to get lucky. It's extremely unlikely, but they do so and get the first pick again.

In year three, despite the two great young stars that they drafted, they still manage to finish last. And they get lucky again. With luck like this, the Sharpies' general manager is wasting his time in hockey. He should play roulette for a living. But this is what the widely held theory demands, so we'll go along with it.

Still, let's pause here and ask ourselves a few questions: Can anyone seriously think that any team is going to get a string of top young players and keep finishing last? If these kids that the Sharpies are drafting are so good, why isn't the team winning enough games to get out of the basement? Are there no other bad teams in the league? Are there no borderline teams that suffer a series of debilitating injuries and have a much worse season than everyone anticipated? Are there no teams with dysfunctional management and poor coaches that have an awful season? Is there no team with dressing-room turmoil that finishes below the Sharpies with all their young talent? Is there no one else in the league believing the blow-it-up theory is a good one and deciding to take the same course as the Sharpies?

How far out of touch with reality do you have to be to propose a theory calling for a team to finish last for four years? And yet there are those who not only put forth this suggestion but do so with such arrogance that they feel comfortable ridiculing anyone who questions their approach.

So much for the rant. Let's persevere. The Sharpies have some-how managed to finish last for three years in succession. Now they head into year four and suddenly find that they're facing a slight problem. The kid they drafted in the first year has completed his standard three-year entry-level contract.

Now, either this kid will be a great player or he won't. If he isn't, the Sharpies have wasted one year of their five-year plan. They threw away a whole season in the hope of getting lucky in the draft lottery and acquiring a great player. Instead, he turns out to be a flop—or, if not a flop, then certainly not the kind of player they can build a team around.

Anyone who doesn't think that can happen should look at the list of first-overall draft picks over the last couple of decades. Note the names of players like Patrik Štefan, Chris Phillips, Bryan Berard and Alexander Daigle.

Štefan suffered a series of concussions, and Berard lost most of the vision in one eye. But even when they were fully healthy, nei-ther looked likely to guarantee a team's success. Phillips was ade-quate, but certainly no one would see him as a franchise player. And Daigle was a monumental flop.

The point is that even if you get the first-overall pick, it does not come with a guarantee of excellence. In fact, as of this writing in 2009, of the last twenty players drafted first overall, only one has ever won a Stanley Cup. At any time in his career! That was Vincent Lecavalier, who won once with Tampa Bay.

Think of it. Twenty first-overall draft picks and they have one Stanley Cup between them. Yet many Leafs fans spent the 2008–09 season hoping that their favourite team would lose every game so that they could draft first, select John Tavares and live happily ever after.

Which forces us to make still another concession to the proponents of the blow-it-up theory. We've already conceded that they'll get all the luck they need to win lottery after lottery. We've conceded that there will be no other bad teams in the league so they can keep finishing last. Now we'll also have to concede that all their picks will be great ones.

But that presents another problem. Because the Sharpies were so smart and drafted an impact player in year one, and because he became everything they wanted him to be, he'll now, after three years, want the maximum contract—an amount equal to 20 per cent of the payroll allowed under the salary cap.

The Sharpies could offer him less if they want. But if some other team decides he's worth the 20 per cent and makes an offer, the Sharpies will either have to match that offer or lose him. Granted, if they do lose him, they'll get compensatory draft picks in return. But draft picks can't help them until they've been converted into players, and that takes time. If you're the Sharpies' management, you've already asked your fans to be patient while you lost game after game after game for three years. Now you want them to wait even longer until these new draft picks come around?

So here the Sharpies are, only three years into their five-year program. They've had everything go their way for three full years—an incredible prospect at best—and they're still planning to finish last again, but now financial problems are looming on the horizon.

The reason is obvious: if the kid you drafted in year one wants 20 per cent of the amount available under the salary cap after year three of your plan, the kid you drafted in year two is also going to want 20 per cent of the amount available under the salary cap the next year.

Heading into year five, the year when all this privation is supposed to magically pay off, you've got two players who are earning 40 per cent of your entire payroll.

An NHL roster has twenty-three players, so you're going to have to convince the other twenty-one that they can share the remaining 60 per cent of the cap amount.

Does it need to be pointed out that after year five, the Sharpies will have another kid coming along who will want his 20 per cent? And another one the year after that?

So obviously, from a financial point of view, the concept of blowing up the existing team and building a Stanley Cup winner with the subsequent draft picks has some serious flaws.

Help from free agents? That's not likely. Free agents take four aspects into consideration when making their decision: (1) money, (2) the franchise location, (3) a chance to shine and (4) the chance to win.

The Sharpies can't provide the first one because they're already overextended by virtue of the money that is going to the draft picks. The second depends on the individual. The third might work, but it probably won't because the free agent will assume that prime ice time is going to go to the young draftees. The fourth is nonexistent as far as the free agent is concerned. He will see the team as a perennial cellar dweller.

We must therefore assume that the Sharpies' roster will consist only of kids and fringe players. There's nothing else. It was blown up, remember?

As a result, there are also psychological factors to consider. Hockey players like to win. They're competitive people, and losing grates on them. If you have a team that is losing year after year for four years, those players won't be able to just shrug off that experience overnight and become winners in the fifth year.

Long before that opportunity arises, they will have become convinced that they're not capable of winning. They'll start to believe that they're inferior to teams with a winning tradition. They'll see themselves as losers, and in any sport, confidence is a major factor. If you don't believe you can win, you won't. Why would these hockey players, after four years of finishing dead last, have even the slightest reason to display any self-confidence?

Furthermore, what would be the impact of all these losses on these young stars who were first-overall draft picks? When you come to the NHL out of junior hockey, success at the higher level is still a long way away. No matter how outstanding an individual might be, if his team is consistently the worst in the league, he will find it extremely difficult to convince himself that he can ever be a winner in the NHL.

Another aspect that has to be considered is what is generally referred to as team chemistry. When a team is losing, blame is invariably placed. That's not unreasonable. If a team is being outscored game after game, someone isn't doing his job, and in professional sports, there's not much room for sympathy. It's a results-based lifestyle and if the results aren't there, someone is going to get blamed.

Some players will perform better than others and will start to criticize those who are letting down the team. But these matters are not always black and white. If a pass goes awry, was it the fault of the guy who made the pass, or should the guy who was to receive the pass have put himself in a more advantageous position?

If a puck goes in the net, is it always the fault of the goalie? Or should the defenceman have done a better job of covering his man? Or did a forward not come back to pick up a trailer?

It's always the same on losing teams. Before long, the fingers start pointing. Those who are blamed defend themselves and point fingers elsewhere. Soon, guys who should be close friends and should be working together are at odds with each other. They argue and bicker. Sometimes, fights break out. Some guys will go to the coach to complain about a teammate.

The team will splinter into factions as players try to justify their respective stances and place the blame on players in one of the other groups. Next, players in one clique try to make sure that players in the other clique don't have anything to brag about. So an easy pass to an open teammate is ignored because the intended target is someone in the wrong clique. Instead, a difficult pass to a friend is attempted.

The result of all these machinations is that the team becomes even more dysfunctional.

And what about the coach? If the team is doing so badly that it's consistently finishing last, is the same coach going to remain in place for four years? Almost certainly not. But with each coach comes a change of focus. What your young players learned under one coach might have to be ignored for the new coach. So development time has been wasted.

Granted, the original premise of the blow-it-up theorists is in place. The team is consistently losing. But at what cost to the psyche of the players? And is any ground being gained in the process?

When you get right down to it, the whole premise of rebuilding exclusively through the acquisition of first-round draft picks is fatally flawed. If it weren't, the Columbus Blue Jackets would be a dynasty by now. The theory of stocking up on first-rounders as the only way to build a team sounds very seductive. Unfortunately, it's totally wrong.

Let's try to look at it as analytically as possible.

The basic assumption is that the first-overall draft pick is the single most valuable commodity. You can take any eighteen year old in the world, so he should be worth the most. The next most valuable is the second-overall draft pick. And so on.

So let's try to establish a numerical value based on that assumption. If you have a first-overall draft pick, you get 30 points. Second overall is worth 29. Third overall is worth 28—all the way down.

That way, if we add up all the numbers, we should be able to figure out which teams have been the most advantageously placed when making their draft selections.

Let's start with the 2008 entry draft and go back eight drafts. There are two reasons for that. First, it takes us back to the point at which the current thirty-team format came into in existence. Second, an eight-year span should be long enough to make an evaluation. The popular wisdom, as we've seen, is that it takes five years to build a contender from scratch.

So using that 30, 29, 28 formula, here are the standings for the teams with the most advantageous draft picks over the past eight years:

1.	Columbus	204
2.	Florida	195
3.	Chicago	192
4.	Washington	187
5.	Montreal	179
6.	Pittsburgh	178
7.	Minnesota	170
8.	Atlanta	167
9.	Los Angeles	166
10.	Anaheim	158
11.	Phoenix	146
12.	Edmonton	137
13.	N.Y. Islanders	136

14.	Nashville	130
15.	San Jose	127
16.	Carolina	126
17.	Buffalo	125
18.	N.Y. Rangers	120
19.	Boston	110
20.	Calgary	106
21.	Philadelphia	101
22.	Ottawa	98
23.	St. Louis	95
24.	Vancouver	80
25.	Tampa Bay	69
26.	Colorado	63
27.	Toronto	49
28.	New Jersey	46
29.	Dallas	26
30.	Detroit	18

For those not mathematically inclined, this chart clearly shows that over the last eight years, Columbus's typical first-round draft position has been twenty-eight slots higher than Detroit's.

Yet Detroit has been the most powerful team in the league over that span and Columbus made the playoffs for the first time in 2009, then got swept in the first round by the Red Wings.

And look who's right behind Columbus. It's Florida, a team that hasn't made the playoffs since 2000, despite all those great first-round draft opportunities. Next is Chicago, a team that is finally showing signs of having a bright future but before 2009 had made the playoffs only once since 1997.

If these first-round draft picks are so valuable, why haven't these teams, which are consistently drafting higher and more frequently in the first round, shown better results?

The trend is clear. Most of the recent Stanley Cup winners are at the bottom of the list. Most of the perennial losers are at the top. (The operative word being *most*. The Leafs are twenty-seventh in this ranking, yet have missed the playoffs four years running. Chalk it up to their ability to find a way to be inept, no matter what.)

Add together all the first-round draft picks the Red Wings have had over those last eight years—there were actually only three of them—and altogether, they get a score of eighteen on our chart. That's the amount awarded for one thirteenth-overall pick.

And even that observation paints a rosier picture than really existed because one of those Detroit first-round picks was Jiří Fischer, who had to retire from hockey at the age of twenty-five because of a heart condition.

Columbus, meanwhile, has picked someone from the top ten no fewer than eight times. Similarly, the Panthers have had seven picks in the top ten in those eight years.

If you go back farther and add a couple of years to the study—which skews it a bit for obvious reasons—the picture doesn't change much. The New York Islanders take over the top position, followed by Chicago and Florida. Not many Stanley Cups there.

Still at the bottom are the same three teams—Detroit, Dallas and New Jersey—that have been consistently powerful despite a poor performance by the Stars in 2008–09.

What the numbers seem to show is this: it can help to have high draft picks, but that's only a part of the picture.

You also need to draft well in the later rounds. And your scouting staff has to be on top of the situation. Those first-rounders have to be used wisely.

This is the area in which the Leafs could have made up some ground. Their scouting staff is far from being the largest in the league, even though it's fairly obvious that the key to the success for teams like Detroit, Dallas and New Jersey is to draft well in the later rounds. To outdraft the other teams in the league, you have to find the gems that others miss, and the best way to do that is to have more people on the ground than your competition.

There are many anecdotes to support this theory, but one of the best has to do with Joel Otto. For those who don't remember him, he was a dominant player for the Calgary Flames in their glory years. He played a major role in helping the Flames win a Stanley Cup in 1989 after getting to the Stanley Cup final in 1986. His battles with Hall of Famer Mark Messier were legendary, and it is generally conceded that he was the only player in the league who could physically dominate Messier in his prime.

But Otto got to the NHL only because a Calgary scout happened to be at a game involving tiny Bemidji State University in Minnesota. He was there to see someone who was playing for the opposition. He wasn't there to see Otto because in its media releases, the school's athletic department had mistakenly listed him as being only five feet, nine inches. When the scout saw that Otto was in fact a six-foot, four-inch, 220-pound hulk, the wheels started turning, and the rest, as they say, is history.

The Flames got Otto because they had a scout where no one else did, and if you ever sit around a table full of scouts at dinner, you'll hear lots of stories like this.

A team like the Leafs, with its coffers overflowing, should have scouts at more amateur games than any team in the league. And if they were to do so, they'd acquire the Joel Ottos of the world.

They might even get to the point that they could go to a game of Miami University of Ohio, where Danny Boyle played. They might see someone like Boyle, who went on to win a Stanley Cup with the Tampa Bay Lightning—yet was never drafted.

Vancouver's first-line forward Alex Burrows was never drafted, either. Nor was Anaheim Ducks goaltender Jonas Hiller. In 2002, with the last pick in the draft, the Red Wings took defenceman

Jonathan Ericsson, who is so highly regarded that in the 2009 post-season he was given more ice time than Nicklas Lidström in many games.

But drafting well isn't enough. You also have to make astute trades, and again, money can go a long way towards helping in that regard.

Some people in hockey have the ability to notice traits that others don't. They have the ability to spot a player who for one reason or another has been neglected and realize that he can help the team.

Here's a classic story to illustrate that point. In the 1970s, when Scott Bowman was coaching the Montreal Canadiens, he was a close friend of Roger Neilson, later an NHL coach but at that time a coach of the Peterborough Petes in junior hockey. Neilson was also employed as a Montreal bird dog, and one day he called Bowman to say that he had a kid who was the best face-off man in the game.

"The junior game," corrected Bowman.

"Any game," insisted Neilson.

Bowman took this news to Sam Pollock, general manager of the Canadiens. Pollock did a check on the kid and found that he'd been drafted by the Leafs. Pollock's reputation was such that if he simply approached Toronto GM Jim Gregory and asked to trade for the kid, he would set off alarm bells.

Instead, he called Gregory and gave him the old car-dealership line. He was overstocked. He had to cut his inventory and was willing to do so at bargain-basement prices. He had a player, Greg Hubick, who was going to be past his prime if he didn't get a chance to play in the NHL soon, but he wasn't good enough to play for Montreal, so Pollock, ever the philanthropist, was going to give him away.

Pollock insisted that he didn't really care who he got back—but he had to get some sort of warm body for appearances sake.

To prove his point, he suggested that Gregory send him a list of five prospects in his organization—any five prospects—and he'd pick one.

Pollock had nothing to lose. It was true that Hubick couldn't play for Montreal, so he was giving up nothing of value. Yet there was always a chance that Neilson's youngster would be on the five-player list. Gregory submitted the list and sure enough, there he was!

That's how the Montreal Canadiens got Doug Jarvis, who went on to take all the key face-offs for the Canadiens as they rolled to four consecutive Stanley Cups. Jarvis also established an NHL iron-man record, playing no fewer than 964 consecutive games.

Hubick? The Leafs kept him for a while, then shipped him to Vancouver. His entire NHL career did not total a full season.

This all took place in the middle of the Ballard era. The Canadiens had their scouts and bird dogs all over the continent. The Leafs' scouts tended to sit in Maple Leaf Gardens and exchange stories in the coffee shop while waiting for the Ontario junior teams to come into the building to play the Marlboros. Or they would hang around one of the Toronto racetracks in case any bright prospects showed up there.

No wonder the Leafs were so bad for so long.

But there is a lesson here in that there is an area in which today's Toronto franchise can make some inroads. Again, it's largely a matter of using money to build a strong organization, an approach that has simply not existed in Toronto in the post-1967 era.

So let's see what we've got so far. There's a need to draft well. There's a need to use a strong financial position to build a large and capable staff. But without some further management moves, that still won't be enough. As was made clear earlier, if you rely totally on the draft, you'll run out of time and salary-cap space before you can win anything.

You're going to have to bolster your draft picks with smart trades. Again, the expertise provided by an extensive, highly capable staff will facilitate your moves in that area.

There's also a chance that you can occasionally pick up a college free agent of some worth. There have been a few high-profile players to emanate from that source—Adam Oates, Curtis Joseph and Jason Blake being among them.

Brian Burke pursued that avenue and made what could turn out to be a good move in March 2009 when he signed an undrafted twenty-three-year-old, Christian Hanson, from Notre Dame University. Shortly thereafter he added Tyler Bozak from the University of Denver.

But at some point, you're still going to have holes and you're going to have to fill them by signing unrestricted free agents.

If your staff has done everything right by this point, you'll have good young players whom you drafted, good mid-range players whom you picked up in your astute trades, and some good veterans whom you grabbed as free agents.

Now the question becomes one that the Leafs of the past would not have had to worry about: How do you pay them? In other words, how do you fit them all in under the salary cap?

It's never easy. Up to this point, some teams, notably the Pittsburgh Penguins and Detroit Red Wings, have been lucky. They've convinced key players to give them hometown discounts. They've got players who could be commanding more money on the open market but who, for one reason or another, have decided to play for less.

If you can get your best player to take this tack, you're in good shape because then the general manager can be justified in going to other players and saying, "Look, we can't pay you more than Nick Lidström. He's our best player," or, "Look, we can't pay you more than Sidney Crosby. He's our best player."

But for a couple of reasons, we have to take the hometown discount out of the equation. For one thing, it varies with the individual and can't be counted on. For another, within the community of player agents, there is pressure to end these discounts because they have a trickle-down effect that impacts every salary in the league.

So what the good general managers do is identify seven top players. Ideally, this group will be composed of one goalie, two defencemen and four forwards.

These seven can share as much as 60 per cent of the total payroll. In today's game, that would be roughly $5 million per player. The other sixteen players would have to share the remaining 40 per cent, which would average out to something in the $1.5-million range.

These numbers can be massaged a little bit, but this kind of breakdown is the ideal.

The top seven guys are the core of the team. You don't really need more than one elite-level goalie, and there are so many good young goaltending prospects these days that the goalie market is flooded. Therefore, barring a really serious injury, a tandem of one high-priced veteran goalie and one decent journeyman at a much lower price should serve you well throughout the course of the season.

You also need to have two elite defencemen. These are the guys who will be out in the shutdown situations. They're also the guys who will run the power play and do the lion's share of the work on the blue line.

The four high-priced forwards form the basis of your two scoring lines. Because you were so astute in your trades and your drafts, you'll have two pairs of quality forwards. Each pair will be supplemented—and presumably complemented—by a lower-priced player who can do the dirty work for the line. He'll dig pucks out of the corners. He'll stand in front of the net. He'll make sure the other two don't get banged around much.

The third and fourth lines will be primarily checkers. They'll be eager, hard-working, honest players who know that if they perform well, they'll someday get a crack at the coveted spots on the first two lines. Ideally, they'll be balanced, with some offensive ability, but their primary purpose will be defensive.

It takes a skilful general manager not only to identify the players who can fill these roles but also to acquire those players for his team. He must constantly balance the salaries and must always be alert to changes in status. Should those key players start to slip, he must make immediate adjustments. With so much of the cap space devoted to these players, it is absolutely essential that they earn their money.

They say that to win in hockey, your best players have to be your best players. This is especially true in a salary-cap world.

The structure mentioned above is as close to a formula for success as there is in today's game. Nothing is foolproof. Injuries can destroy the best of plans, as can a sudden and unanticipated reversal of form. But if the Leafs truly want to build a quality team that has a serious chance to win the Stanley Cup, this is the model they have to follow.

Forty Years in the Wilderness, Plus Two: The Leafs' Stanley Cup Drought, Year by Year

Since 1999–2000, NHL teams have been awarded a single point for a loss in overtime. And since 2005–06, the same has occurred after games lost in a shootout. The tendency has been to treat overtime losses as something other than a loss—many would suggest that the 2008–09 Leafs, with 34 wins, 35 losses and 13 overtime losses, were just one game under .500.

If that were true, they should be near the middle of the pack.

A more honest accounting would be that they lost 48 of 82 games—a miserable record worthy of a twenty-fourth-place team.

With that in mind, the percentages for the years since 1999–

2000 have not been arrived at by dividing points by games played. Rather, points for overtime and shootout losses have been disregarded. From 1999–2000 to 2003–04, the traditional formula (W + ½T) ÷ GP has been used. Since the lockout, wins have simply been divided by games played. The idea is to promote more accurate comparisons of teams from different eras.

Key to abbreviations:

GP—games played	Pct.—winning percentage
W—wins	GM—general manager
L—losses	G—goals
T—ties	A—assists
OTL—overtime losses	PIM—penalties in minutes
GF—goals for	MIN—minutes (played in goal)
GA—goals against	GAA—goals-against average
Pts—points	ShO—shutouts

1966–67

70 GP • 32 W • 27 L • 11 T • 204 GF • 211 GA • 75 Pts • .536 Pct.
Division: N/A
Finish: 3rd of 6
Playoffs: Won Stanley Cup
Coach: Punch Imlach
GM: Punch Imlach

The Maple Leafs win the Stanley Cup, defeating the Montreal Canadiens in six games. Since then, they have not won the Cup—or even played in the Cup final. In that same stretch, the Canadiens have won the Cup no fewer than ten times. In February, Imlach sits out ten games due to exhaustion. King Clancy fills in behind the bench for a ten-game stretch, during which Toronto wins seven and ties two.

In June, a draft is held to stock the six expansion teams. Each of the six established clubs is allowed to "protect" eleven skaters and a goalie. Among the players claimed by expansion teams are goaltending prospect Gary Smith, twenty years Johnny Bower's junior, who goes on to play 527 games in the NHL; defenceman Bob Baun, who had fallen out of favour with Imlach; Ed Joyal, a centre who scores 108 goals over the next five seasons; left wingers Mike Corrigan (152 goals in 594 games) and Lowell MacDonald (175 goals in 460 games); and right winger Bill Flett, who scores 202 goals over nine and a half NHL seasons.

Red Kelly tells Imlach he has been offered the job of coach of the Los Angeles Kings. Imlach doesn't file Kelly's retirement papers, accuses the Kings of tampering and claims Kelly as fill during the expansion draft. Kings owner Jack Kent Cooke settles the dispute by trading minor-league defenceman Ken Block to the Leafs. Block plays a single NHL game, for Vancouver.

Top Scorers

	GP	G	A	Pts	PIM
Dave Keon	66	19	33	52	2
Frank Mahovlich	63	18	28	46	44
Ron Ellis	67	22	23	45	14
Bob Pulford	67	17	28	45	28
Red Kelly	61	14	24	38	4

Goaltenders*

	GP	MIN	GA	GAA	W–L–T	ShO
Johnny Bower	27	1431	63	2.64	12–9–3	2
Terry Sawchuk	28	1409	66	2.81	15–5–4	2

* **Throughout this chapter, goaltenders who have played a minimum of 25 games per season**

Team Leaders

Games: George Armstrong, Tim Horton, 70
Goals: Ron Ellis, 22
Assists: Dave Keon, 33
Points: Dave Keon, 52
PIM: Jim Pappin, 89

Leafs Among League Leaders

Johnny Bower, 8th in games played in goal (27), 6th in wins (12), tied for 5th in shutouts (2), 5th in GAA (2.64)

Ron Ellis, tied for 2nd in shorthanded goals (2), tied for 1st in game-winning goals (7)

Bruce Gamble, 9th in games played in goal (23), 9th in GAA (3.39)

Jim Pappin, tied for 8th in power-play goals (6), tied for 1st in game-winning goals (7)

Terry Sawchuk, 7th in games played in goal (28), 5th in wins (15), tied for 5th in shutouts (2), 6th in GAA (2.81)

Awards

Dave Keon, Conn Smythe Trophy (playoff MVP)
Tim Horton, Second Team All-Star on defence

Notable Draft Choices

J. Bob Kelly (2nd round, 16th overall), left wing, Port Arthur Marrs
As a Leaf: 0 GP, 0 G, 0 A, 0 Pts, 0 PIM
Career: 425 GP, 87 G, 109 A, 196 Pts, 687 PIM

1967–68
74 GP•33 W•31 L•10 T•209 GF•176 GA•76 Pts•.514 Pct.
Division: East
Finish: 5th of 6 (5th of 12 overall)
Playoffs: Did not qualify
Coach: Punch Imlach
GM: Punch Imlach

As is so often the case, a star is discarded for less than he's worth. The Leafs send Frank Mahovlich, Peter Stemkowski, Garry Unger and the rights to Carl Brewer (then playing for Muskegon of the semi-pro International Hockey League) to Detroit for Paul Henderson, Floyd Smith and Norm Ullman.

Toronto is the only "Original Six" team to post a losing record (10–11–3) in games against the expansion clubs of the West Division.

Out
Eddie Shack, LW—traded to Boston for centre Murray Oliver, May 15, 1967
Bob Baun, D—claimed by Oakland in expansion draft, June 6, 1967
John Brenneman, LW—claimed by Oakland in expansion draft, June 6, 1967
Kent Douglas, D—claimed by Oakland in expansion draft, June 6, 1967
Larry Jeffrey, LW—claimed by Pittsburgh in expansion draft, June 6, 1967
Terry Sawchuk, G—claimed by Los Angeles in expansion draft, June 6, 1967
Red Kelly, C—rights traded to Los Angeles, June 8, 1967
Frank Mahovlich, LW—traded to Detroit, March 3, 1968
Pete Stemkowski, C—traded to Detroit, March 3, 1968

In

Murray Oliver, C—traded from Boston, May 15, 1967

Paul Henderson, LW—traded from Detroit, March 3, 1968

Norm Ullman, C—traded from Detroit, March 3, 1968

Top Scorers

	GP	G	A	Pts	PIM
Mike Walton	73	30	29	59	48
Bob Pulford	74	20	30	50	40
Ron Ellis	74	28	20	48	8
Dave Keon	67	11	37	48	4
Murray Oliver	74	16	21	37	18

Goaltenders

	GP	MIN	GA	GAA	W–L–T	ShO
Johnny Bower	43	2239	84	2.25	14–18–7	4
Bruce Gamble	41	2201	85	2.32	19–13–5	5

Team Leaders

Games: Ron Ellis, Murray Oliver, Bob Pulford, 74

Goals: Mike Walton, 30

Assists: Dave Keon, 37

Points: Mike Walton, 59

PIM: Pete Stemkowski, Tim Horton, 82

Leafs Among League Leaders

Johnny Bower, 9th in games played in goal (43), tied for 7th in
    shutouts (4), 2nd in GAA (2.25)

Bruce Gamble, tied for 10th in games played in goal (41), tied for
    8th in wins (19), tied for 5th in shutouts (5), 4th in GAA (2.32)

Bob Pulford, tied for 2nd in shorthanded goals (3)

Norm Ullman, tied for 4th in goals (35), 7th in points (72), 7th in shooting percentage (15.4—stats include games with Detroit)

Mike Walton, tied for 9th in goals (30), tied for 4th in power-play goals (11), 9th in shots on goal (238)

Awards
Tim Horton, First Team All-Star on defence

Notable Draft Choices
Brad Selwood (1st round, 10th overall), defenceman, Niagara Falls Flyers

As a Leaf: 100 GP, 6 G, 27 A, 33 Pts, 71 PIM

NHL Career: 163 GP, 7 G, 40 A, 47 Pts, 153 PIM

WHA Career: 431 GP, 42 G, 143 A, 185 Pts, 556 PIM; Avco Cup with New England, 1973

1968–69
76 GP•35 W•26 L•15 T•234 GF•217 GA•85 Pts•.559 Pct.
Division: East
Finish: 4th of 6 (5th of 12)
Playoffs: Lose quarter-final, 4–0, to Boston
Coach: Punch Imlach
GM: Punch Imlach

Leafs make the playoffs but are swept in four straight games (including defeats of 10–0 and 7–0) by the Boston Bruins. Immediately after the final game, Punch Imlach, who by now has managed to alienate everybody, is fired. Jim Gregory, former GM of the Toronto

Marlboros juniors, takes over as GM. John McLellan is promoted from the farm team in Tulsa to coach.

On October 16, defenceman Jim Dorey makes his NHL debut against Pittsburgh and is assessed a then-record 48 minutes in penalties. Imlach rewards him with a $100 bill and tells him, "That's the kind of hockey we want." Imlach gets it in spades in game one of the playoffs. Fourth-liner Forbes Kennedy takes on Bruins goalie Gerry Cheevers, defenceman Ted Green and forward Johnny McKenzie and is ejected from the game. Both backup goalies are fined for jumping the boards to take part in the melee. Kennedy never appears in another NHL game.

Out

Jim Pappin, RW—traded to Chicago, May 23, 1968

Brian Conacher, C—claimed by Detroit in intra-league draft, June 12, 1968

Larry Hillman, D—claimed by N.Y. Rangers in intra-league draft, June 12, 1968

Duane Rupp, D—claimed by Minnesota in intra-league draft, June 12, 1968

Allan Stanley, D—claimed by Quebec (AHL) in reverse draft, June 13, 1968

Bill Sutherland, C—traded to Philadelphia, March 2, 1969

In

Pierre Pilote, D—traded from Chicago, May 23, 1968

Larry Mickey, RW—claimed from N.Y. Rangers in intra-league draft, June 12, 1968

Bill Sutherland, C—claimed from Minnesota in intra-league draft, June 12, 1968

Forbes Kennedy, C—traded from Philadelphia, March 2, 1969

Brit Selby, LW—traded from Philadelphia, March 2, 1969

Top Scorers

	GP	G	A	Pts	PIM
Norm Ullman	75	35	42	77	41
Dave Keon	75	27	34	61	12
Paul Henderson	74	27	32	59	16
Murray Oliver	76	14	36	50	16
Ron Ellis	72	25	21	46	12

Goaltenders

	GP	MIN	GA	GAA	W–L–T	ShO
Bruce Gamble	61	3446	161	2.80	28–20–11	3

Team Leaders

Games: Murray Oliver, 76
Goals: Norm Ullman, 35
Assists: Norm Ullman, 42
Points: Norm Ullman, 77
PIM: Jim Dorey, 200

Leafs Among League Leaders

Bruce Gamble, 3rd in games played in goal (61), tied for 2nd in wins (28), tied for 8th in shutouts (3), 8th in GAA (2.80)

Dave Keon, 1st in shorthanded goals (6), tied for 8th in game-winning goals (6)

Murray Oliver, tied for 8th in shorthanded goals (2)

Norm Ullman, tied for 7th in goals (35), tied for 3rd in power-play goals (13)

Awards

Tim Horton, First Team All-Star on defence

Notable Draft Choices

Brian Spencer (5th round, 55th overall), left wing, Swift Current
Broncos
As a Leaf: 95 GP, 10 G, 20 A, 30 Pts, 192 PIM
Career: 553 GP, 80 G, 143 A, 223 Pts, 634 PIM

1969–70

76 GP • 29 W • 34 L • 13 T • 222 GF • 242 GA • 71 Pts • .467 Pct.
Division: East
Finish: 6th of 6 (7th of 12)
Playoffs: Did not qualify
Coach: John McLellan
GM: Jim Gregory

For the first time since 1958, the Leafs finish in the basement. It won't be the last time.

Ace Bailey's number 6 is "unretired" and given to winger Ron Ellis. Seven games into the regular season, Dave Keon is named captain. He succeeds George Armstrong, who is currently on his third retirement (he rejoins the team in mid-November). Johnny Bower, having fallen to third on the depth chart, plays the final game of his NHL career on December 10—a 6–3 loss to Montreal. On March 3, defenceman Tim Horton, who has been in the Leafs organization since 1947, is traded to the New York Rangers.

Out

Larry Mickey, RW—claimed by Montreal in intra-league draft, June 11, 1969
Tim Horton, D—traded to N.Y. Rangers, March 3, 1970
Pierre Pilote, D—retired

In

Marv Edwards, G—claimed from Pittsburgh in intra-league draft, June 11, 1969

Jim Harrison, C—traded from Boston, December 10, 1969

Top Scorers

	GP	G	A	Pts	PIM
Dave Keon	72	32	30	62	6
Norm Ullman	74	18	42	60	37
Mike Walton	58	21	34	55	68
Ron Ellis	76	35	19	54	14
Murray Oliver	76	14	33	47	16

Goaltenders

	GP	MIN	GA	GAA	W–L–T	ShO
Bruce Gamble	52	3057	156	3.06	19–24–9	5
Marv Edwards	25	1420	77	3.25	10–9–4	1

Team Leaders

Games: Ron Ellis, Murray Oliver, 76
Goals: Ron Ellis, 35
Assists: Norm Ullman, 42
Points: Dave Keon, 62
PIM: Rick Ley, 102

Leafs Among League Leaders

Ron Ellis, 7th in goals (35)

Bruce Gamble, 6th in games played in goal (52), tied for 6th in wins (19), tied for 3rd in shutouts (5)

Dave Keon, tied for 8th in shorthanded goals (2), 5th in shots on goal (284)

Norm Ullman, tied for 10th in assists (42)
Mike Walton, tied for 6th in game-winning goals (6)

Awards
None

Notable Draft Choices
Darryl Sittler (1st round, 8th overall), centre, London Knights
As a Leaf: 844 GP, 389 G, 527 A, 916 Pts, 763 PIM
Career: 1096 GP, 484 G, 637 A, 1121 Pts, 948 PIM

Errol Thompson (2nd round, 22nd overall), left wing, Charlottetown
  Royals.
As a Leaf: 365 GP, 126 G, 119 A, 245 Pts, 70 PIM
Career: 599 GP, 208 G, 185 A, 393 Pts, 184 PIM

1970–71
78 GP • 37 W • 33 L • 8 T • 248 GF • 211 GA • 82 Pts • .526 Pct.
Division: East
Finish: 4th of 7 (6th of 14)
Playoffs: Lost quarter-final, 4–2, to N.Y. Rangers
Coach: John McLellan
GM: Jim Gregory

Pearls before swine, anyone? Late in the season, the Leafs make an excellent trade, getting Bernie Parent from the Philadelphia Flyers. Two seasons later, he becomes one of several Leafs to jump to the rival World Hockey Association. He returns to the NHL after a one-year absence but refuses to rejoin the Leafs, who are forced to trade him to Philadelphia, where he becomes the best goaltender in the world and wins back-to-back Stanley Cups.

The Leafs also acquire, in separate deals with St. Louis, veteran netminder Jacques Plante and defenceman Bob Baun. As a result, goals against drop from 242 to 211.

In game two of the quarter-finals, played at Madison Square Garden, Vic Hadfield steals Parent's face mask and throws it into the crowd. Plante finishes the game.

In a symbolic break from the Stanley Cup–winning era, the Leafs introduce a new logo, with a stylized eleven-point leaf, and redesigned uniforms.

Out

Murray Oliver, C—traded to Minnesota, May 22, 1970

Pat Quinn, D—claimed by Vancouver in expansion draft, June 10, 1970

Floyd Smith, RW—traded to Buffalo, August 31, 1970

Bob Pulford, LW—traded to Los Angeles, September 3, 1970

Brit Selby, LW—traded to St. Louis, November 13, 1970

Terry Clancy, RW—traded to Montreal, December 23, 1970

Bruce Gamble, G—traded to Philadelphia, February 1, 1971

Mike Walton, C—traded to Philadelphia, February 1, 1971

In

Jacques Plante, G—traded from St. Louis, May 18, 1970

Guy Trottier, RW—claimed from N.Y. Rangers in intra-league draft, June 9, 1970

Garry Monahan, C—traded from Los Angeles, September 3, 1970

Bob Baun, D—traded from St. Louis, November 13, 1970

Bernie Parent, G—traded from Philadelphia, February 1, 1971

Top Scorers

	GP	G	A	Pts	PIM
Norm Ullman	73	34	51	85	24
Dave Keon	76	38	38	76	4
Paul Henderson	72	30	30	60	34
Ron Ellis	78	24	29	53	10
Bill MacMillan	76	22	19	41	42

Goaltenders

	GP	MIN	GA	GAA	W–L–T	ShO
Jacques Plante	40	2329	73	1.88	24–11–4	4

Team Leaders

Games: Ron Ellis, Jim Harrison, Garry Monahan, 78
Goals: Dave Keon, 38
Assists: Norm Ullman, 51
Points: Norm Ullman, 85
PIM: Jim Dorey, 198

Leafs Among League Leaders

Dave Keon, tied for 6th in goals (38), tied for 9th in points (76), 1st in shorthanded goals (8), 3rd in game-winning goals (9), 7th in shots on goal (277)

Bernie Parent, tied for 9th in shutouts (2), 10th in GAA (2.72—stats include games with Philadelphia)

Jacques Plante, 5th in wins (24), tied for 4th in shutouts (4), 1st in GAA (1.88)

Norm Ullman, tied for 10th in assists (51), 6th in points (85), tied for 7th in power-play goals (11)

Awards
Dave Keon, Second Team All-Star at centre
Jacques Plante, Second Team All-Star in goal

Notable Draft Choices
Rick Kehoe (2nd round, 22nd overall), right wing, Hamilton Red
  Wings
As a Leaf: 184 GP, 59 G, 72 A, 131 Pts, 32 PIM
Career: 906 GP, 371 G, 396 A, 767 Pts, 120 PIM; Lady Byng
  Trophy, 1981

1971–72
78 GP • 33 W • 31 L • 14 T • 209 GF • 208 GA • 80 Pts • .513 Pct.
Division: East
Finish: 4th of 7 (6th of 14)
Playoffs: Lost quarter-final, 4–1, to Boston
Coach: John McLellan
GM: Jim Gregory

Harold Ballard buys the late Stafford Smythe's shares of Maple
Leaf Gardens, giving him 71 per cent of the stock. But he can't be
a hands-on owner right away: he's sentenced to three three-year
prison terms—to be served concurrently—after being found guilty
of multiple counts of fraud and theft.

Coach John McLellan is hospitalized during the season because
of ulcers, and misses fifteen games. King Clancy again fills in, posting a record of 9–3–3.

In the summer of 1972, Ballard fires Tom Smythe, son of Stafford
and grandson of Conn. Tom had been a part of the Leafs organization

since the age of six, when he was appointed stick boy, and had risen to the post of GM of the junior Toronto Marlboros. He learned of his firing by reading about it in the *Toronto Star.*

Out

George Armstrong, C—retired

Jim Dorey, D—traded to N.Y. Rangers, February 20, 1972

In

Don Marshall, LW—claimed from Buffalo in intra-league draft, June 8, 1971

Pierre Jarry, LW—traded from N.Y. Rangers, February 20, 1972

Top Scorers

	GP	G	A	Pts	PIM
Norm Ullman	77	23	50	73	26
Paul Henderson	73	38	19	57	32
Dave Keon	72	18	30	48	4
Ron Ellis	78	23	24	47	17
Jim Harrison	66	19	17	36	104

Goaltenders

	GP	MIN	GA	GAA	W–L–T	ShO
Bernie Parent	47	2715	116	2.56	17–18–9	3
Jacques Plante	34	1965	86	2.63	16–13–5	2

Team Leaders

Games: Ron Ellis, Garry Monahan, 78

Goals: Paul Henderson, 38

Assists: Norm Ullman, 50

Points: Norm Ullman, 73

PIM: Rick Ley, 124

Leafs Among League Leaders

Ron Ellis, tied for 4th in game-winning goals (7)

Paul Henderson, 10th in goals (38), 8th in power-play goals (12), 4th in shooting percentage (19.9)

Bernie Parent, 7th in games played in goal (47), tied for 10th in wins (17), tied for 7th in shutouts (3), 8th in GAA (2.56)

Jacques Plante, tied for 10th in shutouts (2), 9th in GAA (2.63)

Awards

None

Notable Draft Choices

George Ferguson (1st round, 11th overall), centre, Toronto Marlboros

As a Leaf: 359 GP, 57 G, 110 A, 167 Pts, 236 PIM

Career: 797 GP, 160 G, 238 A, 398 Pts, 431 PIM

Pat Boutette (9th round, 139th overall), centre, U. of Minnesota–Duluth

As a Leaf: 349 GP, 59 G, 82 A, 141 Pts, 520 PIM

Career: 756 GP, 171 G, 282 A, 453 Pts, 1354 PIM

1972–73

78 GP • 27 W • 41 L • 10 T • 247 GF • 279 GA • 64 Pts • .410 Pct.

Division: East

Finish: 6th of 8 (13th of 16)

Playoffs: Did not qualify

Coach: John McLellan

GM: Jim Gregory

The Leafs finish behind the Buffalo Sabres, who are in only their third year of existence. They also finish with fewer points than the Atlanta Flames, who are in their first season, and five of the six 1967 expansion teams. Ballard is released from prison after serving approximately one-quarter of his term.

The World Hockey Association begins play, and finds many Leafs who are willing to jump leagues. Jim Harrison, Guy Trottier, Brad Selwood, Rick Ley and Bernie Parent all sign contracts with the new league, while Brian Spencer and Bill MacMillan are claimed in the expansion draft and Bob Baun suffers a career-ending injury in a game against Detroit. Paul Henderson, after scoring the game-winning goals in games six, seven and eight of the Summit Series, is injured for much of the year and manages only 18 goals in 40 games. In March, Jacques Plante is traded to Boston for a first-round pick, used to draft defenceman Ian Turnbull.

At the end of the year, John McLellan, citing health problems, resigns as coach. He is replaced by former Leaf Red Kelly.

Out

Brad Selwood, D—claimed by Montreal in intra-league draft, June 5, 1972 (signed as a free agent with New England of WHA)

Bill MacMillan, RW—claimed by Atlanta in expansion draft, June 6, 1972

Brian Spencer, LW—claimed by N.Y. Islanders in expansion draft, June 6, 1972

Jim Harrison, C—signed as a free agent with Alberta of WHA

Rick Ley, D—signed as a free agent with New England of WHA

Bernie Parent, G—signed as a free agent with Miami (moved to Philadelphia) of WHA

Guy Trottier, RW—signed as a free agent with Ottawa of WHA

Don Marshall, C—retired

Bob Baun, D—suffered career-ending injury in game, October 21, 1972

Jacques Plante, G—traded to Boston, March 3, 1973

In

No regular players acquired via trades or intra-league draft

Top Scorers

	GP	G	A	Pts	PIM
Darryl Sittler	78	29	48	77	69
Rick Kehoe	77	33	42	75	20
Dave Keon	76	37	36	73	2
Norm Ullman	65	20	35	55	10
Jim McKenny	77	11	41	52	55

Goaltenders

	GP	MIN	GA	GAA	W–L–T	ShO
Jacques Plante	32	1717	87	3.04	8–14–6	1
Ron Low	42	2343	152	3.89	12–24–4	1

Team Leaders

Games: Ron Ellis, Garry Monahan, Darryl Sittler, 78

Goals: Dave Keon, 37

Assists: Darryl Sittler, 48

Points: Darryl Sittler, 77

PIM: Mike Pelyk, 118

Leafs Among League Leaders

Dave Keon, tied for 7th in shorthanded goals (2), tied for 9th in game-winning goals (6)

Jacques Plante, 7th in GAA (2.81—includes games with Boston), tied for 8th in shutouts (3—includes 2 with Boston)

Darryl Sittler, 4th in shots on goal (331)

Awards

None

Notable Draft Choices

Lanny McDonald (1st round, 4th overall), right wing, Medicine Hat Tigers

As a Leaf: 477 GP, 219 G, 240 A, 459 Pts, 372 PIM

Career: 1111 GP, 500 G, 506 A, 1006 Pts, 899 PIM; Stanley Cup with Calgary in 1989

Ian Turnbull (1st round, 15th overall), defence, Ottawa 67's

As a Leaf: 580 GP, 112 G, 302 A, 414 Pts, 651 PIM

Career: 628 GP, 123 G, 317 A, 440 Pts, 736 PIM

1973–74

78 GP • 35 W • 27 L • 16 T • 274 GF • 230 GA • 86 Pts • .551 Pct.

Division: East

Finish: 4th of 8 (6th of 16)

Playoffs: Lost quarter-final, 4–0, to Boston

Coach: Red Kelly

GM: Jim Gregory

Amidst much fanfare, the Leafs manage to get back into the play-offs. They promptly get swept by the Boston Bruins.

Swedish defenceman Börje Salming and winger Inge Hammarström make their debuts. Bernie Parent, who spent 1972–73 with the Philadelphia Blazers of the WHA, jumped that team when they breached his contract. He sought to return to the NHL—but not with the Leafs. His rights were traded to the Philadelphia Flyers for goalie Doug Favell and a first-round draft pick.

Out

Larry McIntyre, D—traded to Vancouver, May 29, 1973
Pierre Jarry, LW—traded to Detroit, November 29, 1973

In

Inge Hammarström, LW—signed as a free agent, May 12, 1973
Börje Salming, D—signed as a free agent, May 12, 1973
Eddie Johnston, G—traded from Boston, May 22, 1973
Eddie Shack, LW—traded from Pittsburgh, July 3, 1973
Tim Ecclestone, RW—traded from Detroit, November 29, 1973

Top Scorers

	GP	G	A	Pts	PIM
Darryl Sittler	78	38	46	84	55
Norm Ullman	78	22	47	69	12
Paul Henderson	69	24	31	55	40
Dave Keon	74	25	28	53	7
Ron Ellis	70	23	25	48	12

Goaltenders

	GP	MIN	GA	GAA	W–L–T	ShO
Doug Favell	32	1752	79	2.71	14–7–9	0
Ed Johnston	26	1516	78	3.09	12–9–4	1

Team Leaders

Games: Garry Monahan, Darryl Sittler, Ian Turnbull, Norm Ullman, 78
Goals: Darryl Sittler, 38

Assists: Norm Ullman, 47
Points: Darryl Sittler, 84
PIM: Brian Glennie, 100

Leafs Among League Leaders

Doug Favell, 3rd in GAA (2.71)
Darryl Sittler, 9th in goals (38), 8th in points (84), tied for 10th in
    power-play goals (11), tied for 10th in shots on goal (270)

Awards

None

Notable Draft Choices

Dave "Tiger" Williams (2nd round, 31st overall), LW,
    Swift Current Broncos
As a Leaf: 407 GP, 109 G, 132 A, 241 Pts, 1670 PIM
Career: 962 GP, 241 G, 272 A, 513 Pts, 3966 PIM

Mike Palmateer (5th round, 85th overall), goal, Toronto Marlboros
As a Leaf: 296 GP, 16868 MIN, 964 GA, 3.43 GAA, 129 W, 112 L,
    41 T, 15 ShO
Career: 356 GP, 20131 MIN, 1183 GA, 3.53 GAA, 149 W, 138 L,
    52 T, 17 ShO

1974–75

80 GP•31 W•33 L•16 T•280 GF•309 GA•78 Pts•.488 Pct.
Division: Adams
Finish: 3rd of 4 (13th of 18)
Playoffs: Lost quarter-final, 4–0, to Philadelphia

Coach: Red Kelly
GM: Jim Gregory

The National Hockey League institutes a new playoff system, under which twelve of eighteen teams qualify. The Leafs barely win a best-of-three series against the L.A. Kings, then are swept (and outscored 15–6, and manhandled) by the Philadelphia Flyers.

The Toronto Toros of the WHA, having stocked their lineup with ex-Leafs such as Carl Brewer and Frank Mahovlich, move their home games from Varsity Arena to Maple Leaf Gardens. Paul Henderson and Mike Pelyk sign WHA contracts this year.

At the end of the season, centres Dave Keon, whose leadership skills Harold Ballard has publicly questioned, and Norm Ullman are allowed to become free agents. They also jump to the WHA. Ballard describes the decision to let them go as one of the best he has ever made.

Out

Eddie Johnston, G—traded to St. Louis, May 27, 1974

Paul Henderson, LW—signed as a free agent with Toronto (WHA), June 10, 1974

Denis Dupere, LW—claimed by Washington in intra-league draft, June 12, 1974

Mike Pelyk, D—signed as a free agent with Cincinnati (WHA)

Rick Kehoe, RW—traded to Pittsburgh, September 13, 1974

Garry Monahan, C—traded to Vancouver, October 16, 1974

Tim Ecclestone, LW—traded to Washington, November 2, 1974

Dunc Wilson, G—claimed on waivers by N.Y. Rangers, February 15, 1975

In

Bill Flett, RW—traded from Philadelphia, May 27, 1974

Gary Sabourin, RW—traded from St. Louis, May 27, 1974

Blaine Stoughton, RW—traded from Pittsburgh, September 13, 1974

Dave Dunn, D—traded from Vancouver, October 16, 1974

Rod Seiling, D—traded from Washington, November 2, 1974

Top Scorers

	GP	G	A	Pts	PIM
Darryl Sittler	72	36	44	80	47
Ron Ellis	79	32	26	61	25
Dave Keon	78	16	43	59	4
George Ferguson	69	19	30	49	61
Lanny McDonald	64	17	27	44	86

Goaltenders

	GP	MIN	GA	GAA	W–L–T	ShO
Dunc Wilson	25	1393	86	3.70	8–11–4	0
Doug Favell	39	2149	145	4.05	12–17–6	1

Team Leaders

Games: Norm Ullman, 80

Goals: Darryl Sittler, 36

Assists: Darryl Sittler, 44

Points: Darryl Sittler, 80

PIM: Tiger Williams, 187

Leafs Among League Leaders

Bill Flett, tied for 9th in shorthanded goals (3)

Awards

Börje Salming, Second Team All-Star on defence

Notable Draft Choices
Doug Jarvis (2nd round, 24th overall), centre, Peterborough Petes
As a Leaf: 0 GP, 0 G, 0 A, 0 Pts, 0 PIM
Career: 964 GP, 139 G, 264 A, 403 Pts, 263 PIM; Stanley Cups
    with Montreal in 1976, 1977, 1978, 1979

1975–76
80 GP • 34 W • 31 L • 15 T • 294 GF • 276 GA • 83 Pts • .519 Pct.
Division: Adams
Finish: 3rd of 4 (7th of 18 overall)
Playoffs: Lost quarter-final, 4–3, to Philadelphia
Coach: Red Kelly
GM: Jim Gregory

The Montreal Canadiens win the first of what will be a string of four
consecutive Stanley Cups. When that string ends, they will have won
eight Stanley Cups since the Leafs last won. The Leafs are again eliminated in the quarter-finals by the Flyers, despite the installation of
pyramids—reputed, according to a current pop-culture craze, to have
mystical powers—in the team's dressing room and under the bench.

On the eve of the regular season, Ron Ellis, an eleven-year veteran, announces he has lost the desire to play and retires.

Dan Maloney of Detroit is charged with assault after he jumps
defenceman Brian Glennie from behind, then, after punching him
several times, twice picks Glennie up by the neck and drops his
head to the ice. He is ultimately acquitted. He becomes a Leaf in
1978.

On February 7, Darryl Sittler has a record-setting night against
the Boston Bruins: six goals and four assists for ten points as the

Leafs win 11–4. Bruins goaltender Dave Reece never plays another NHL game. The ever-magnanimous Ballard rewards Sittler with a silver tea service.

Sittler is the first Leaf to register 100 points in a season.

Out
Bill Flett, RW—claimed on waivers by Atlanta, May 20, 1975
Gary Sabourin, RW—traded to California, June 20, 1975
Dave Keon, C—signed as a free agent with Minnesota (WHA)
Norm Ullman, C—signed as a free agent with Edmonton (WHA)
Ron Ellis, RW—retired, October 4, 1975

In
Wayne Thomas, G—traded from Montreal, June 17, 1975
Stan Weir, C—traded from California, June 20, 1975

Top Scorers

	GP	G	A	Pts	PIM
Darryl Sittler	79	41	59	100	90
Lanny McDonald	75	37	56	93	70
Errol Thompson	75	43	37	80	26
Börje Salming	78	16	41	57	70
Ian Turnbull	76	20	36	56	90

Goaltenders

	GP	MIN	GA	GAA	W–L–T	ShO
Wayne Thomas	64	3684	196	3.19	28–24–12	2

Team Leaders
Games: George Ferguson, Darryl Sittler, 79
Goals: Errol Thompson, 43
Assists: Darryl Sittler, 59

Points: Darryl Sittler, 100
PIM: Tiger Williams, 299

Leafs Among League Leaders

Lanny McDonald, tied for 3rd in shorthanded goals (5)
Darryl Sittler, 9th in points (100), 3rd in shots on goal (346)
Errol Thompson, tied for 10th in goals (43), tied for 9th in
   game-winning goals (7), 6th in shooting percentage (20.5)
Stan Weir, 3rd in shooting percentage (21.1)
Wayne Thomas, tied for 3rd in games played in goal (64), 6th in
   wins (28), tied for 9th in shutouts (2), 10th in GAA (3.19)

Awards

Börje Salming, Second Team All-Star on defence

Notable Draft Choices

Randy Carlyle (2nd round, 30th overall), defenceman, Sudbury
   Wolves
As a Leaf: 94 GP, 2 G, 16 A, 18 Pts, 82 PIM
Career: 1055 GP, 148 G, 499 A, 647 Pts, 1400 PIM; Norris Trophy,
   1981

1976–77

80 GP 33 W 32 L 15 T 301 GF 285 GA 81 Pts .506 Pct.
Division: Adams
Finish: 3rd of 4 (tied for 7th of 18 overall)
Playoffs: Lose quarter-final, 4–2, to Philadelphia
Coach: Red Kelly
GM: Jim Gregory

Another year, another first-round defeat at the hands of the Flyers. Leafs coach Red Kelly, like so many who are to succeed him, falls from favour with Ballard and is axed. This is notable because Ballard did the firing in person rather than employing his usual tactic of removing the nameplate from the doomed employee's parking spot.

Out

Rod Seiling, D—signed as a free agent with St. Louis, September 9, 1976

Dave Dunn, D—signed as a free agent with Winnipeg (WHA)

Blaine Stoughton, RW—signed as a free agent with Cincinnati (WHA)

In

Tracy Pratt, D—traded from Colorado, March 8, 1977

Top Scorers

	GP	G	A	Pts	PIM
Lanny McDonald	80	46	44	90	77
Darryl Sittler	73	38	52	90	89
Ian Turnbull	80	22	57	79	84
Börje Salming	76	12	66	78	46
Jack Valiquette	66	15	30	45	7

Goaltenders

	GP	MIN	GA	GAA	W–L–T	ShO
Mike Palmateer	50	2877	154	3.21	23–18–8	4
Wayne Thomas	33	1803	116	3.86	10–13–6	1

Team Leaders

Games: Pat Boutette, Lanny McDonald, Ian Turnbull, 80
Goals: Lanny McDonald, 46
Assists: Börje Salming, 66
Points: Lanny McDonald, Darryl Sittler, 90
PIM: Tiger Williams, 338

Leafs Among League Leaders

Lanny McDonald, 5th in goals (46), tied for 8th in points (90), 1st
   in power-play goals (16), 5th in shorthanded goals (4), 6th in
   shots on goal (293)
Mike Palmateer, 8th in games played in goal (50), 8th in wins (33),
   tied for 5th in shutouts (4)
Börje Salming, tied for 3rd in assists (66)
Darryl Sittler, tied for 8th in goals (38), tied for 8th in points (90),
   tied for 7th in power-play goals (12), 4th in shots on goal (307)
Errol Thompson, 10th in shooting percentage (19.3)
Ian Turnbull, 8th in assists (57), tied for 9th in plus-minus (plus-47),
   3rd in shots on goal (316)
Jack Valiquette, tied for 6th in shorthanded goals (3)

Awards

Lanny McDonald, Second Team All-Star at right wing
Börje Salming, First Team All-Star on defence

Notable Draft Choices

John Anderson (1st round, 11th overall), left wing, Toronto Marlboros
As a Leaf: 534 GP, 189 G, 204 A, 393 Pts, 168 PIM
Career: 814 GP, 282 G, 349 A, 631 Pts, 263 PIM

1977–78

80 GP • 41 W • 29 L • 10 T • 271 GF • 237 GA • 92 Pts • .575 Pct.
Division: Adams
Finish: 3rd of 4 (6th of 18 overall)
Playoffs: Lost semifinal, 4–0, to Montreal
Coach: Roger Neilson
GM: Jim Gregory

Buoyed by all the success that his hockey team has exhibited, Ballard decides that he can leverage his sports-management expertise and buys the Hamilton Tiger-Cats of the Canadian Football League. Which doesn't completely distract him from making mischief in Toronto. He orders that the face of bearded backup goalie Gord McRae be removed from the team photo and replaced with a picture of a clean-shaven McRae taken several years before.

Lanny McDonald scores an overtime goal in game seven against the New York Islanders, propelling the Leafs into the semifinals against Montreal. The Habs outscore Toronto 16–6 in a four-game sweep. It will be fifteen years before the Leafs again reach the third round.

Darryl Sittler breaks his own team record, with 117 points, and Lanny McDonald again challenges, but falls short of, Frank Mahovlich's team record for goals.

Out

Wayne Thomas, G—claimed by N.Y. Rangers in waiver draft, October 10, 1977
Inge Hammarström, LW—traded to St. Louis, November 1, 1977
Bob Neely, D—traded to Colorado, January 9, 1978
Claire Alexander, D—traded to Vancouver, January 29, 1978
Errol Thompson, LW—traded to Detroit, March 13, 1978
Tracy Pratt, D—retired

In

Ron Ellis, RW—returned from retirement
Jimmy Jones, RW—signed as a free agent, October 25, 1977
Jerry Butler, RW—traded from St. Louis, November 1, 1977
Dan Maloney, LW—traded from Detroit, March 13, 1978

Top Scorers

	GP	G	A	Pts	PIM
Darryl Sittler	80	45	72	117	100
Lanny McDonald	74	47	40	87	54
Börje Salming	80	16	60	76	70
Ian Turnbull	77	14	47	61	77
Ron Ellis	80	26	24	50	17

Goaltenders

	GP	MIN	GA	GAA	W–L–T	ShO
Mike Palmateer	63	3760	172	2.74	34–19–9	5

Team Leaders

Games: Pat Boutette, Ron Ellis, Börje Salming, Darryl Sittler, 80
Goals: Lanny McDonald, 47
Assists: Darryl Sittler, 72
Points: Darryl Sittler, 117
PIM: Tiger Williams, 351

Leafs Among League Leaders

Ron Ellis, 9th in shooting percentage (20.3)
Jimmy Jones, tied for 9th in shorthanded goals (2)
Lanny McDonald, 4th in goals (47), tied for 10th in points (87)
Mike Palmateer, 4th in games played in goal (63), 3rd in wins (34),
    tied for 2nd in shutouts (5), 9th in GAA (2.74)
Börje Salming, 8th in assists (60)

Darryl Sittler, 6th in goals (45), tied for 2nd in assists (72), 3rd in points (117), tied for 5th in power-play goals (14), tied for 3rd in game-winning goals (8), 1st in shots on goal (311)

Awards
Börje Salming, Second Team All-Star on defence
Darryl Sittler, Second Team All-Star at centre

Notable Draft Choices
Joel Quenneville (2nd round, 21st overall), defence, Windsor Spitfires
As a Leaf: 93 GP, 3 G, 13 A, 16 Pts, 84 PIM
Career: 803 GP, 54 G, 136 A, 190 Pts, 705 PIM

1978–79
80 GP • 34 W • 33 L • 13 T • 267 GF • 252 GA • 81 Pts • .506 Pct.
Division: Adams
Finish: 3rd of 4 (9th of 17)
Playoffs: Lost quarter-final, 4–0, to Montreal
Coach: Roger Neilson
GM: Jim Gregory

The Leafs' credibility plumbs new depths after Ballard fires coach Roger Neilson on March 1. The team is struggling, with a record of 24–27–11. Columnists dutifully write Neilson's obituary, blaming his defence-first philosophy and a failure to develop the team's younger players.

When the Leafs take the ice two nights later at the Gardens, the new coach of the team is revealed to be—Roger Neilson. Ballard claims the whole thing was a hoax, but there are reports he tried and failed to secure the services of Eddie Johnston, coach of the Moncton farm team the Leafs share with the Chicago Blackhawks, who is under contract to Chicago.

At season's end, Ballard fires Neilson for good. GM Jim Gregory is also dismissed, to be replaced by Punch Imlach—laying waste to any progress the team may have been making, and setting the team back at least a decade.

Out

Mike Pelyk, D—retired

Stan Weir, C—signed as a free agent with Edmonton (WHA), June 1978

Randy Carlyle, D—traded to Pittsburgh, June 14, 1978

George Ferguson, C—traded to Pittsburgh, June 14, 1978

Brian Glennie, D—traded to Los Angeles, June 14, 1978

Kurt Walker, D—traded to Los Angeles, June 14, 1978

Jack Valiquette, C—traded to Colorado, October 19, 1978

Trevor Johansen, D—traded to Colorado, March 13, 1979

In

Dave Burrows, D—traded from Pittsburgh, June 14, 1978

Paul Harrison, G—traded from Minnesota, June 14, 1978

Dave Hutchison, D—traded from Los Angeles, June 14, 1978

Lorne Stamler, LW—traded from Los Angeles, June 14, 1978

Garry Monahan, C—traded from Vancouver, September 13, 1978

Walt McKechnie, C—traded from Minnesota, October 5, 1978

Paul Gardner, C—traded from Colorado, March 13, 1979

Top Scorers

	GP	G	A	Pts	PIM
Darryl Sittler	70	36	51	87	69
Lanny McDonald	79	43	42	85	32

Börje Salming	78	17	56	73	76
Ian Turnbull	80	12	51	63	80
Walt McKechnie	79	25	36	61	18

Goaltenders

	GP	MIN	GA	GAA	W–L–T	ShO
Mike Palmateer	58	3396	167	2.95	26–21–10	4
Paul Harrison	25	1403	82	3.51	8–12–3	1

Team Leaders

Games: Pat Boutette, Ian Turnbull, 80
Goals: Lanny McDonald, 43
Assists: Börje Salming, 56
Points: Darryl Sittler, 87
PIM: Tiger Williams, 298

Leafs Among League Leaders

Jerry Butler, tied for 9th in shorthanded goals (2)
Lanny McDonald, tied for 6th in goals (43), tied for 3rd in power-play goals (16), 3rd in shots on goal (314)
Garry Monahan, tied for 9th in shorthanded goals (2)
Mike Palmateer, 3rd in games played in goal (58), tied for 3rd in wins (26), tied for 2nd in shutouts (4), 6th in GAA (2.95)
Darryl Sittler, 4th in shots on goal (290)

Awards

Börje Salming, Second Team All-Star on defence

Notable Draft Choices

Laurie Boschman (1st round, 9th overall), left wing, Brandon Wheat Kings
As a Leaf: 187 GP, 39 G, 70 A, 109 Pts, 406 PIM
Career: 1009 GP, 229 G, 348 A, 577 Pts, 2260 PIM

1979–80

80 GP • 35 W • 40 L • 5 T • 304 GF • 327 GA • 75 Pts • .469 Pct.
Division: Adams
Finish: 4th of 5 (11th of 21)
Playoffs: Lose preliminary round, 3–0, to Minnesota
Coach: Floyd Smith (30–33–5), Dick Duff (0–2–0),
Punch Imlach (5–5–0)
GM: Punch Imlach

Major Conn Smythe, the last link with the era of sensible hockey management in Toronto, dies. Smythe ran the team for more than twenty-seven years, with a remarkable .547 winning percentage.

The Lanny McDonald trade prompts Sittler to remove the captain's C from his sweater.

Late in the season, coach Floyd Smith is injured in a car crash. Dick Duff takes his place for two games, both losses, before Imlach takes over for a ten-game stretch. They manage to win half those games.

Out

Garry Monahan, C—retired
Pierre Hamel, G—claimed by Winnipeg in expansion draft, June 13, 1979
Lorne Stamler, LW—claimed by Winnipeg in expansion draft, June 13, 1979
Pat Boutette, RW—traded to Hartford, December 27, 1979
Lanny McDonald, RW—traded to Colorado, December 29, 1979
Joel Quenneville, D—traded to Colorado, December 29, 1979
Dave Hutchison, D—traded to Chicago, January 10, 1980
Pat Ribble, D—traded to Washington, February 16, 1980
Jerry Butler, RW—traded to Vancouver, February 18, 1980
Tiger Williams, LW—traded to Vancouver, February 18, 1980
Walt McKechnie, C—traded to Colorado, March 3, 1980

In

Dave Farrish, D—traded from Quebec, December 13, 1979

Terry Martin, LW—traded from Quebec, December 13, 1979

Pat Hickey, LW—traded from Colorado, December 29, 1979

Wilf Paiement, RW—traded from Colorado, December 29, 1979

Carl Brewer, D—signed as a free agent, January 2, 1980

Pat Ribble, D—traded from Chicago, January 10, 1980

Richard Mulhern, D—claimed on waivers from Los Angeles, February 10, 1980

Mike Kaszycki, C—traded from Washington, February 16, 1980

Bill Derlago, C—traded from Vancouver, February 18, 1980

Rick Vaive, RW—traded from Vancouver, February 18, 1980

Top Scorers

	GP	G	A	Pts	PIM
Darryl Sittler	73	40	57	97	62
Börje Salming	74	19	52	71	94
John Anderson	74	25	28	53	22
Wilf Paiement	41	20	28	48	72
Laurie Boschman	80	16	32	48	78

Goaltenders

	GP	MIN	GA	GAA	W–L–T	ShO
Mike Palmateer	38	2039	125	3.68	16–14–3	2
Paul Harrison	30	1492	110	4.42	9–17–2	0

Team Leaders

Games: Laurie Boschman, Dave Burrows, 80

Goals: Darryl Sittler, 40

Assists: Darryl Sittler, 57

Points: Darryl Sittler, 97

PIM: Tiger Williams, 197

Leafs Among League Leaders

Lanny McDonald, 2nd in shots on goal (344—includes games with Colorado)

Wilf Paiement, tied for 9th in shorthanded goals (2), tied for 8th in shots on goal (270—includes games with Colorado)

Mike Palmateer, tied for 7th in shutouts (2)

Darryl Sittler, tied for 8th in assists (57), 9th in points (97), tied for 2nd in power-play goals (17), 5th in shots on goal (315)

Awards

Börje Salming, Second Team All-Star on defence

Notable Draft Choices

Craig Muni (2nd round, 25th overall), defence, Kingston Canadians
As a Leaf: 19 GP, 0 G, 2 A, 2 Pts, 6 PIM
Career: 819 GP, 28 G, 119 A, 147 Pts, 775 PIM; Stanley Cups with Edmonton in 1987, 1988, 1990

Bob McGill (2nd round, 26th overall), defence, Victoria Cougars
As a Leaf: 317 GP, 4 G, 25 A, 29 Pts, 988 PIM
Career: 705 GP, 17 G, 55 A, 72 Pts, 1766 PIM

1980–81

80 GP•28 W•37 L•15 T•322 GF•367 GA•71 Pts•.444 Pct.
Division: Adams
Finish: 5th of 5 (16th of 21)
Playoffs: Lost preliminary round, 3–0, to N.Y. Islanders
Coach: Joe Crozier (13–22–5), Mike Nykoluk (15–15–10)
GM: Punch Imlach

Imlach is hospitalized during the summer of 1980, and Ballard can't help getting involved in running the team. Against Imlach's wishes, he reinstates Sittler as captain.

Upon his return, Imlach replaces Floyd Smith with another crony, Joe Crozier. The team plays indifferently under him, so Imlach turns to the team's radio colour man, Mike Nykoluk. The Leafs finish one point ahead of Washington for the final playoff spot.

In January, Ron Ellis, who has scored two goals in twenty-seven games, is put on waivers. Before the season, the team tried and failed to buy out his contract. After Ellis clears waivers, Imlach tries to demote him to the Moncton farm team. He retires instead.

Out

Carl Brewer, D—retired
Mike Palmateer, G—traded to Washington, June 11, 1980
Dave Burrows, D—traded to Pittsburgh, November 18, 1980
Paul Gardner, C—traded to Pittsburgh, November 18, 1980
Mark Kirton, C—traded to Detroit, December 4, 1980
Ron Ellis, RW—retired January 1981
Robert Picard, D—traded to Montreal, March 10, 1981
Jim Rutherford, G—traded to Los Angeles, March 10, 1981

In

Dave Shand, D—traded from Atlanta, June 10, 1980
Robert Picard, D—traded from Washington, June 11, 1980
Vítezslav Duriš, D—signed as a free agent, September 25, 1980
Barry Melrose, D—claimed on waivers from Winnipeg, November 30, 1980
Jim Rutherford, G—traded from Detroit, December 4, 1980
René Robert, RW—traded from Colorado, January 30, 1981
Ron Sedlbauer, LW—traded from Chicago, February 18, 1981

Michel Larocque, G—traded from Montreal, March 10, 1981
Ron Zanussi, RW—traded from Minnesota, March 10, 1981

Top Scorers

	GP	G	A	Pts	PIM
Wilf Paiement	77	40	57	97	145
Darryl Sittler	80	43	53	96	77
Bill Derlago	80	35	39	74	26
Ian Turnbull	80	19	47	66	104
Börje Salming	72	5	61	66	154

Goaltenders

	GP	MIN	GA	GAA	W–L–T	ShO
Jiří Crha	54	3112	211	4.07	20–20–11	0

Team Leaders

Games: Bill Derlago, Darryl Sittler, Ian Turnbull, 80
Goals: Darryl Sittler, 43
Assists: Börje Salming, 61
Points: Wilf Paiement, 97
PIM: Rick Vaive, 229

Leafs Among League Leaders

Jiří Crha, tied for 5th in games played in goal (54)
Dan Maloney, 3rd in shooting percentage (25.0)
Wilf Paiement, 6th in shots on goal (302)

Awards

None

Notable Draft Choices

Jim Benning (1st round, 6th overall), defence, Portland Winter Hawks

As a Leaf: 364 GP, 37 G, 136 A, 173 Pts, 289 PIM

Career: 610 GP, 52 G, 191 A, 243 Pts, 461 PIM

1981–82

80 GP•20 W•44 L•16 T•298 GF•380 GA•56 Pts•.350 Pct.

Division: Norris

Finish: 5th of 6 (19th of 21)

Playoffs: Did not qualify

Coach: Mike Nykoluk

GM: Gerry McNamara

The McNamara era gets under way in typical fashion: the Leafs miss the playoffs. In an era that sees sixteen of the NHL's twenty-one teams qualify for the post-season, this is not as easy as it seems. It helps that the Leafs have the worst goals-against average in the league.

A demoralized Darryl Sittler informs Ballard that he is willing to waive his no-trade clause, and in January he is traded to Philadelphia. In October, Börje Salming scores his 500th point in the NHL. Rick Vaive becomes the first Leaf to score fifty goals in a season.

Out

Paul Harrison, G—traded to Pittsburgh, September 11, 1981

Pat Hickey, LW—traded to N.Y. Rangers, October 16, 1981

Ian Turnbull, D—traded to Los Angeles, November 11, 1981

Darryl Sittler, C—traded to Philadelphia, January 20, 1982

Laurie Boschman, C—traded to Edmonton, March 9, 1982

Wilf Paiement, RW—traded to Quebec, March 9, 1982

In

Don Luce, C—traded from Los Angeles, August 10, 1981

Bob Manno, D—signed as a free agent, September 30, 1981

Jim Korn, D—traded from Detroit, March 8, 1982

Miroslav Fryčer, RW—traded from Quebec, March 9, 1982

Walt Poddubny, LW—traded from Edmonton, March 9, 1982

Top Scorers

	GP	G	A	Pts	PIM
Rick Vaive	77	54	35	89	157
Bill Derlago	75	34	50	84	42
Wilf Paiement	69	18	40	58	203
John Anderson	69	31	26	57	30
Börje Salming	69	12	44	56	170

Goaltenders

	GP	MIN	GA	GAA	W–L–T	ShO
Vincent Tremblay	40	2033	153	4.52	10–18–8	1
Michel Larocque	50	2647	207	4.69	10–24–8	0

Team Leaders

Games: Rick Vaive, 77

Goals: Rick Vaive, 54

Assists: Bill Derlago, 50

Points: Rick Vaive, 89

PIM: Bob McGill, 263

Leafs Among League Leaders

Rick Vaive, 5th in goals (54), tied for 3rd in shorthanded goals (5), tied for 7th in game-winning goals (6)

Awards
None

Notable Draft Choices
Gary Nylund (1st round, 3rd overall), defence, Portland Winter
  Hawks
As a Leaf: 218 GP, 7 G, 50 A, 57 Pts, 398 PIM
Career: 608 GP, 32 G, 139 A, 171 Pts, 1235 PIM

Gary Leeman (2nd round, 24th overall), left wing, Regina Pats
As a Leaf: 545 GP, 176 G, 231 A, 407 Pts, 463 PIM
Career: 667 GP, 199 G, 267 A, 466 Pts, 531 PIM; Stanley Cup
with Montreal, 1993

Peter Ihnačák (2nd round, 25th overall), centre, Sparta Praha
As a Leaf: 417 GP, 102 G, 165 A, 267 Pts, 175 PIM
Career: 417 GP, 102 G, 165 A, 267 Pts, 175 PIM

1982–83
80 GP 28 W 40 L 12 T 293 GF 330 GA 68 Pts .425 Pct.
Division: Norris
Finish: 3rd of 5 (15th of 21)
Playoffs: Lost division semifinal, 3–1, to Minnesota
Coach: Mike Nykoluk
GM: Gerry McNamara

The Leafs draft Russ Courtnall, who goes on to play 1,029 games
and rack up 744 points in the regular season, and 83 playoff points
in 129 games. But most of those points are accumulated for teams

other than the Leafs. In 1988 he is traded for John Kordic, who registers a lifetime total of 12 points.

Out

Bob Manno, D—signed as a free agent with Merano (Italian Serie A)
Don Luce, C—retired
Dan Maloney, LW—retired
René Robert, RW—retired
Michel Larocque, G—traded to Philadelphia, January 11, 1983

In

Mike Palmateer, G—traded from Washington, September 9, 1982
Greg Terrion, LW—traded from Los Angeles, October 19, 1982
Dan Daoust, C—traded from Montreal, December 17, 1982
Gaston Gingras, D—traded from Montreal, December 17, 1982

Top Scorers

	GP	G	A	Pts	PIM
John Anderson	80	31	49	80	24
Rick Vaive	78	51	28	79	105
Peter Ihnačák	80	28	38	66	44
Walt Poddubny	72	28	31	59	71
Miroslav Fryčer	67	25	30	55	90

Goaltenders

	GP	MIN	GA	GAA	W–L–T	ShO
Mike Palmateer	53	2965	197	3.99	21–23–7	0

Team Leaders

Games: John Anderson, Peter Ihnačák, Jim Korn, 80
Goals: Rick Vaive, 51
Assists: John Anderson, 49

Points: John Anderson, 80
PIM: Jim Korn 236

Leafs Among League Leaders

Mike Palmateer, 7th in games played in goal (53), tied for 10th in
   wins (21)

Rick Vaive, 7th in goals (51), tied for 4th in power-play goals (18),
   tied for 6th in game-winning goals (8), 4th in shots on goal (296)

Awards

Dan Daoust, All-Rookie Team at centre

Notable Draft Choices

Russ Courtnall (1st round, 7th overall), Victoria Cougars
As a Leaf: 309 GP, 90 G, 128 A, 218 Pts, 243 PIM
Career: 1029 GP, 297 G, 447 A, 744 Pts, 557 PIM

1983–84

80 GP • 26 W • 45 L • 9 T • 303 GF • 387 GA • 61 Pts • .381 Pct.
Division: Norris
Finish: 5th of 5 (18th of 21)
Playoffs: Did not qualify
Coach: Mike Nykoluk
GM: Gerry McNamara

The Norris Division, in which the Leafs play, earns a well-deserved
reputation for the mediocrity of its teams. Not one of the five
teams manages to win half its games—and only one, Minnesota, at
39–31–10, wins more often than it loses. Among even this sorry lot,
the Leafs finish fifth.

Out

Barry Melrose, D—signed as a free agent with Detroit, July 5, 1983

Billy Harris, RW—traded to Los Angeles, February 15, 1984

In

Pat Graham, LW—traded from Pittsburgh, August 15, 1983

Bill Stewart, D—signed as a free agent, September 10, 1983

Dale McCourt, C—signed as a free agent, October 22, 1983

Dave Hutchison, D—signed as a free agent, November 15, 1983

Top Scorers

	GP	G	A	Pts	PIM
Rick Vaive	76	52	41	93	114
Dan Daoust	78	18	56	74	88
John Anderson	73	37	31	68	22
Bill Derlago	79	40	20	60	50
Jim Benning	79	12	39	51	66

Goaltenders

	GP	MIN	GA	GAA	W–L–T	ShO
Allan Bester	32	1848	134	4.35	11–16–4	0
Mike Palmateer	34	1831	149	4.88	9–17–4	0

Team Leaders

Games: Stewart Gavin, 80

Goals: Rick Vaive, 52

Assists: Dan Daoust, 56

Points: Rick Vaive, 93

PIM: Jim Korn 257

Leafs Among League Leaders

Rick Vaive, tied for 5th in goals (52), 6th in power-play goals (17)

Awards
None

Notable Draft Choices
Al Iafrate (1st round, 4th overall), defence, Belleville Bulls
As a Leaf: 472 GP, 81 G, 169 A, 250 Pts, 546 PIM
Career: 799 GP, 152 G, 311 A, 463 Pts, 1301 PIM

Todd Gill (2nd round, 25th overall), defence, Windsor Spitfires
As a Leaf: 639 GP, 59 G, 210 A, 269 Pts, 922 PIM
Career: 1007 GP, 82 G, 272 A, 354 Pts, 1214 PIM

1984–85

80 GP • 20 W • 52 L • 8 T • 253 GF • 358 GA • 48 Pts • .300 Pct.
Division: Norris
Finish: 5th of 5 (21st of 21)
Playoffs: Did not qualify
Coach: Dan Maloney
GM: Gerry McNamara

This year, the Leafs not only finish last in the Norris but twenty-first in the twenty-one-team league. They win just twenty of their eighty games, while losing a club record fifty-two. After four years, McNamara is still looking for his first .500 season. It never comes.

Out
Dave Hutchison, D—retired
Dale McCourt, C—signed as a free agent with Ambrì-Piotta (Switzerland)

Terry Martin, LW—claimed by Edmonton in waiver draft, October 9, 1984

Gaston Gingras, D—traded to Montreal, February 14, 1985

In

Jeff Brubaker, LW—claimed from Edmonton in waiver draft, October 9, 1984

Tim Bernhardt, G—signed as a free agent, December 5, 1984

Top Scorers

	GP	G	A	Pts	PIM
Rick Vaive	72	35	33	68	112
John Anderson	75	32	31	63	27
Bill Derlago	62	31	31	62	21
Miroslav Fry er	65	25	30	55	55
Dan Daoust	79	17	37	54	98

Goaltenders

	GP	MIN	GA	GAA	W–L–T	ShO
Tim Bernhardt	37	2182	136	3.74	13–19–4	0

Team Leaders

Games: Jim Benning, 80

Goals: Rick Vaive, 35

Assists: Dan Daoust, 37

Points: Rick Vaive, 68

PIM: Bob McGill, 250

Leafs Among League Leaders

John Anderson, tied for 9th in power-play goals (14)

Bill Derlago, tied for 3rd in shorthanded goals (5)

Greg Terrion, tied for 7th in shorthanded goals (4)

Awards

None

Notable Draft Choices

Wendel Clark (1st round, 1st overall), left wing, Saskatoon Blades
As a Leaf: 608 GP, 260 G, 181 A, 441 Pts, 1535 PIM
Career: 793 GP, 330 G, 234 A, 564 Pts, 1690 PIM

1985–86

80 GP • 25 W • 48 L • 7 T • 311 GF • 386 GA • 57 Pts • .356 Pct.
Division: Norris
Finish: 4th of 5 (19th of 21)
Playoffs: Lost division final, 4–3, to St. Louis
Coach: Dan Maloney
GM: Gerry McNamara

Molson Companies. Ltd., which owns the Montreal Canadiens, confirms that Ballard has given the brewery an option to buy a block of Maple Leaf Gardens stock. NHL president John Ziegler admits he was "very surprised" to learn of this. Dual ownership is in direct contravention of NHL rules.

First-overall draft pick Wendel Clark, almost instantly anointed as the franchise and the team's saviour, leads the team with thirty- four goals. His combination of an accurate wrist shot and aggressive style (he's also the most penalized Leaf) cements his status as a fan favourite.

Leafs show signs of competence in the second half of the season—sadly, about as much as you could ask of a Leaf team in this era—and win a playoff series for the first time since 1979, defeating Chicago in the first round.

After missing one too many practices, Rick Vaive is stripped of the captaincy. As if to reinforce the team's lack of direction or leadership, a successor is not named until 1989.

Out

John Anderson, RW—traded to Quebec, August 21, 1985
Stew Gavin, LW—traded to Hartford, October 7, 1985
Bill Derlago, C—traded to Boston, October 11, 1985
Jeff Brubaker, LW—claimed on waivers by Edmonton, December 5, 1985

In

Don Edwards, G—traded from Calgary, May 29, 1985
Brad Smith, RW—signed as a free agent, July 2, 1985
Marián Štastný, RW—signed as a free agent, August 12, 1985
Brad Maxwell, D—traded from Quebec, August 21, 1985
Chris Kotsopoulos, D—traded from Hartford, October 7, 1985
Tom Fergus, C—traded from Boston, October 11, 1985

Top Scorers

	GP	G	A	Pts	PIM
Miroslav Frycer	73	32	43	75	74
Tom Fergus	78	31	42	73	64
Rick Vaive	61	33	31	64	85
Russ Courtnall	73	22	38	60	52
Steve Thomas	65	20	37	57	36

Goaltenders

	GP	MIN	GA	GAA	W–L–T	ShO
Ken Wregget	30	1566	113	4.33	9–13–4	0
Don Edwards	38	2009	160	4.78	12–23–0	0

Team Leaders
Games: Dan Daoust, 80
Goals: Wendel Clark, 34
Assists: Miroslav Fryčer, 43
Points: Miroslav Fryčer, 75
PIM: Wendel Clark, 227

Leafs Among League Leaders
None

Awards
Wendel Clark, All-Rookie Team at left wing

Notable Draft Choices
Vincent Damphousse (1st round, 6th overall), centre, Laval Titan
As a Leaf: 394 GP, 118 G, 211 A, 329 Pts, 262 PIM
Career: 1378 GP, 432 G, 773 A, 1205 Pts, 1190 PIM; Stanley Cup
with Montreal in 1993

1986–87
80 GP • 32 W • 42 L • 6 T • 286 GF • 319 GA • 70 Pts • .438 Pct.
Division: Norris
Finish: 4th of 5 (16th of 21)
Playoffs: Lost division final, 4–3, to Detroit
Coach: John Brophy
GM: Gerry McNamara

The John Brophy era begins. Brophy was the most penalized
player in the history of the old Eastern Hockey League, and is

reputed to be the model for Paul Newman's character in the movie *Slap Shot*. Not surprisingly, he favours brawn over finesse. Which may explain the selection of defenceman Luke Richardson with the seventh-overall pick in the 1987 draft, rather than skilled players such as Joe Sakic, John LeClair, Éric Desjardins or Mathieu Schneider. What that latter group also has in common is that they all go on to play for Stanley Cup winners. Richardson never scores more than four goals in a season, but he's big and a punishing bodychecker, and during the Brophy era, that carries a lot of currency.

Such is the woeful state of the Norris Division—not one of the five teams post a .500 record—that Toronto is able to eliminate first-place St. Louis and take a 3–1 lead in their second-round series against third-place Detroit. In game four, Glen Hanlon posts the Wings' first playoff shutout since 1966. Four nights later, he repeats the feat to finish off the Leafs.

The Leafs continue to demonstrate their unique approach to developing prospects (throw them in the lineup and let them sink or swim) by pinning their goaltending hopes on a pair of twenty-two-year-olds, Ken Wregget and Allan Bester.

Out

Marián Šťastný, RW—signed as a free agent with Sierre (Switzerland)

Walt Poddubny, RW—traded to N.Y. Rangers, August 18, 1986

Gary Nylund, D—signed as a free agent with Chicago, August 27, 1986

Brad Maxwell, D—traded to Vancouver, October 3, 1986

Jim Benning, D—traded to Vancouver, December 2, 1986

Dan Hodgson, C—traded to Vancouver, December 2, 1986

Jeff Jackson, LW—traded to N.Y. Rangers, March 5, 1987

In

Daryl Evans, LW—signed as a free agent, August 1986

Mike Allison, LW—traded from N.Y. Rangers, August 18, 1986

Ken Yaremchuk, C—awarded to Leafs from Chicago as compensation for free-agent signing of Gary Nylund, September 6, 1986

Terry Johnson, D—traded from Calgary, October 3, 1986

Rick Lanz, D—traded from Vancouver, December 2, 1986

Mark Osborne, LW—traded from N.Y. Rangers, March 5, 1987

Top Scorers

	GP	G	A	Pts	PIM
Russ Courtnall	79	29	44	73	90
Rick Vaive	73	32	34	66	61
Steve Thomas	78	35	27	62	114
Wendel Clark	80	37	23	60	271
Gary Leeman	80	21	31	52	66

Goaltenders

	GP	MIN	GA	GAA	W–L–T	ShO
Allan Bester	36	1808	110	3.65	10–14–3	2
Ken Wregget	56	3026	200	3.97	22–28–3	0

Team Leaders

Games: Wendel Clark, Vincent Damphousse, Al Iafrate, Gary Leeman, 80

Goals: Wendel Clark, 37

Assists: Russ Courtnall, 44

Points: Russ Courtnall, 73

PIM: Wendel Clark, 271

Leafs Among League Leaders

Allan Bester, tied for 3rd in shutouts (2), 8th in save percentage (.889)

Russ Courtnall, tied for 2nd in shorthanded goals (6), 4th in shots
   on goal (282)
Steve Thomas, tied for 6th in game-winning goals (7)
Ken Wregget, 4th in games played in goal (56), tied for 6th in wins
   (22)

Awards
None

Notable Draft Choices
Luke Richardson (1st round, 7th overall), defence, Peterborough
   Petes
As a Leaf: 299 GP, 11 G, 39 A, 50 Pts, 597 PIM
Career: 1417 GP, 35 G, 166 A, 201 Pts, 2055 PIM

1987–88
80 GP•21 W•49 L•10 T•273 GF•345 GA•52 Pts•.325 Pct.
Division: Norris
Finish: 4th of 5 (20th of 21)
Playoffs: Lost division semifinal, 4–2, to Detroit
Coach: John Brophy
GM: Gerry McNamara (22–28–5); John Brophy, Dick Duff and
Gord Stellick (6–18–1)

After posting a winning percentage of .373 after almost seven seasons on the job, McNamara finally gets fired. Could it get worse?
Of course—these are the Leafs. A committee of Dick Duff, John
Brophy and Gord Stellick takes over. Their winning percentage
is .260.

Before he's gone, McNamara makes a trade that typifies his tenure, sending Rick Vaive, Bob McGill and Steve Thomas to Chicago for Ed Olczyk and Al Secord. Vaive, although on a downhill slope, scores 128 goals over the next four years. Thomas plays another seventeen years, during which he racks up 365 goals.

Secord, a power forward with several forty-goal seasons to his credit, proves to be in decline. He scores just twenty times in a year and a half and is dealt to Philadelphia. The trade isn't a complete bust: Olczyk is a skilled centre the Blackhawks drafted third overall in 1984, but who isn't meeting expectations, perhaps because of the added pressure of playing in his hometown. In Toronto, he becomes a consistent point-a-game player.

Out

Brad Smith, RW—retired
Bob McGill, D—traded to Chicago, September 3, 1987
Steve Thomas, LW—traded to Chicago, September 3, 1987
Rick Vaive, RW—traded to Chicago, September 3, 1987
Mike Allison, LW—traded to Los Angeles, December 14, 1987

In

Ed Olczyk, C—traded from Chicago, September 3, 1987
Al Secord, LW—traded from Chicago, September 3, 1987
Dave Semenko, LW—traded from Hartford, September 8, 1987
Dale DeGray, D—traded from Calgary, September 17, 1987
Sean McKenna, RW—traded from Los Angeles, December 14, 1987

Top Scorers

	GP	G	A	Pts	PIM
Ed Olczyk	80	42	33	75	55
Gary Leeman	80	30	31	61	62
Mark Osborne	79	23	37	60	102

Al Iafrate	77	22	30	52	80
Tom Fergus	63	19	31	50	81

Goaltenders

	GP	MIN	GA	GAA	W–L–T	ShO
Allan Bester	30	1607	102	3.81	8–12–5	2
Ken Wregget	56	3000	222	4.44	12–35–4	2

Team Leaders

Games: Gary Leeman, Ed Olczyk, 80
Goals: Ed Olczyk, 42
Assists: Mark Osborne, 37
Points: Ed Olczyk, 75
PIM: Al Secord, 221

Leafs Among League Leaders

Allan Bester, tied for 7th in shutouts (2)
Ken Wregget, tied for 5th in games played in goal (56), tied for 7th in shutouts (2)

Awards

None

Notable Draft Choice

Tie Domi (2nd round, 27th overall), Peterborough Petes
As a Leaf: 777 GP, 84 G, 112 A, 196 Pts, 2265 PIM
Career: 1020 GP, 104 G, 141 A, 145 Pts, 3515 PIM

1988–89

80 GP • 28 W • 46 L • 6 T • 259 GF • 342 GA • 62 Pts • .388 Pct.
Division: Norris
Finish: 5th of 5 (19th of 21)
Playoffs: Did not qualify
Coach: John Brophy (11–20–2), George Armstrong (17–26–4)
GM: Gord Stellick

The year is typified by a trade that, twenty years later, Gord
Stellick will still not have lived down: Courtnall for Kordic. A
team that is short on scoring gives up one of its few offensive
talents for a player who is just plain offensive. Adding insult
to the injury of Leafs fans, Kordic is assigned sweater number
27, the number worn by Darryl Sittler and, before him, Frank
Mahovlich.

At the trade deadline, Ken Wregget is sent to Philadelphia for
a pair of first-round draft picks, giving the Leafs three first-rounders in all. It's not the deepest of drafts, but that doesn't excuse the
Leafs for selecting Scott Thornton, Rob Pearson and Steve Bancroft, all from the Belleville Bulls of the Ontario Hockey League,
none of whom is an impact player. Fans are left to wonder if
there's a particularly good watering hole in Belleville, not to mention what was in the Leafs' scouting reports on Bill Guerin, Olaf
Kolzig or Adam Foote.

Stellick, who by his own admission was too inexperienced, is
fired after the season. In comes Floyd Smith. No one can say Smith
is inexperienced. He has had lots of experience. None of it was
coupled with success, but it was experience.

Out

Dave Semenko, LW—retired
Miroslav Fryčer, RW—traded to Detroit, June 10, 1988

Dale DeGray, D—claimed by Los Angeles in waiver draft, October 3, 1988

Russ Courtnall, RW—traded to Montreal, November 7, 1988

Al Secord, LW—traded to Philadelphia, February 7, 1989

Ken Wregget, G—traded to Philadelphia, March 6, 1989

In

Craig Laughlin, RW—signed as a free agent, June 10, 1988

Dave Reid, LW—signed as a free agent, June 23, 1988

Brad Marsh, D—claimed from Philadelphia in waiver draft, October 3, 1988

John Kordic, RW—traded from Montreal, November 7, 1988

Top Scorers

	GP	G	A	Pts	PIM
Ed Olczyk	80	38	52	90	75
Gary Leeman	61	32	43	75	66
Vincent Damphousse	80	26	42	68	75
Tom Fergus	80	22	45	67	48
Daniel Marois	76	31	23	54	76

Goaltenders

	GP	MIN	GA	GAA	W–L–T	ShO
Allan Bester	43	2460	156	3.80	17–20–3	2
Ken Wregget	32	1888	139	4.42	9–20–2	0

Team Leaders

Games: Vincent Damphousse, Tom Fergus, Brad Marsh, Ed Olczyk, 80

Goals: Ed Olczyk, 38

Assists: Ed Olczyk, 52

Points: Ed Olczyk, 90

PIM: Brian Curran, John Kordic, 185

Leafs Among League Leaders

Allan Bester, tied for 7th in shutouts (2), 9th in save percentage (.890)

Awards

None

Notable Draft Choices

Scott Thornton (1st round, 3rd overall), centre, Belleville Bulls
As a Leaf: 33 GP, 1 G, 3 A, 4 Pts, 30 PIM
Career: 941 GP, 144 G, 141 A, 285 Pts, 1459 PIM

1989–90

80 GP • 38 W • 38 L • 4 T • 337 GF • 358 GA • 80 Pts • .500 Pct.
Division: Norris
Finish: 3rd of 5 (12th of 21)
Playoffs: Lost division semifinal, 4–2, to St. Louis
Coach: Doug Carpenter
GM: Floyd Smith

Brophy's replacement as coach is Doug Carpenter, who had run the Leafs' farm teams in Moncton, Cincinnati and St. Catharines in the early 1980s before spending four years behind the bench with the New Jersey Devils. Concluding, wisely, that the "defence-first" strategies of Brophy and Dan Maloney hadn't helped the team at all, he unlocks the floodgates. For the first time since 1978–79, the team has a .500 season. Gary Leeman becomes the second Leaf to score fifty goals in a season.

Floyd Smith starts the new season by trading a first-round draft pick to New Jersey for defenceman Tom Kurvers. Kurvers is gone the next year. With the draft pick, the Devils take Scott Niedermayer.

In one of his final acts, Harold Ballard appoints defenceman Rob Ramage, acquired in a trade from the Cup-winning Calgary Flames, as captain. Meanwhile, sixteen-year veteran Börje Salming signs as a free agent with Detroit.

On April 11, 1990, Harold Ballard dies. His will stipulates that his assets be sold and the proceeds distributed to a group of charities. One of the executors of Ballard's estate, Steve Stavro, launches a bid for control of Maple Leaf Gardens, triggering a protracted series of legal battles. By the time the dust has settled, the charities are left with a relative pittance.

Out

Craig Laughlin, RW—signs as a free agent with Landshut (Germany)
Börje Salming, D—signs as a free agent with Detroit, June 12, 1989
Chris Kotsopoulos, D—signs as a free agent with Detroit, June 23, 1989
Derek Laxdal, RW—traded to N.Y. Islanders, December 20, 1989

In

Rob Ramage, D—traded from Calgary, June 16, 1989
Lou Franceschetti, RW—traded from Washington, June 29, 1989
Mark Laforest, G—traded from Philadelphia, September 8, 1989
Dave Hannan, LW—claimed from Pittsburgh in waiver draft, October 2, 1989
Tom Kurvers, D—traded from New Jersey, October 16, 1989
Gilles Thibaudeau, C—traded from N.Y. Islanders, December 20, 1989

Top Scorers

	GP	G	A	Pts	PIM
Gary Leeman	80	51	44	95	63
Vincent Damphousse	80	33	61	94	56

Ed Olczyk	79	32	56	88	78
Daniel Marois	68	39	37	76	82
Mark Osborne	78	23	50	73	91

Goaltenders

	GP	MIN	GA	GAA	W–L–T	ShO
Mark Laforest	27	1343	87	3.89	9–14–0	0
Allan Bester	42	2206	165	4.49	20–16–0	0

Team Leaders

Games: Vincent Damphousse, Lou Franceschetti, Gary Leeman, Rob Ramage, 80
Goals: Gary Leeman, 51
Assists: Vincent Damphousse, 61
Points: Gary Leeman, 95
PIM: Brian Curran, 301

Leafs Among League Leaders

Dan Daoust, tied for 5th in shorthanded goals (4)
Gary Leeman, tied for 7th in goals (51)
Dave Reid, tied for 5th in shorthanded goals (4)

Awards

None

Notable Draft Choices

Drake Berehowsky (1st round, 10th overall), defence, Kingston Frontenacs
As a Leaf: 133 GP, 7 G, 28 A, 35 Pts, 181 PIM
Career: 549 GP, 37 G, 112 A, 149 Pts, 848 PIM

Félix Potvin (2nd round, 31st overall), goal, Chicoutimi Saguenéens

As a Leaf: 369 GP, 21461 MIN, 1026 GA, 2.87 GAA, 160 W, 149 L, 49 T, 12 ShO

Career: 635 GP, 36767 MIN, 1727 GA, 2.76 GAA, 266 W, 260 L, 85 T, 32 ShO

1990–91

80 GP•23 W•46 L•11 T•241 GF•318 GA•57 Pts•.356 Pct.
Division: Norris
Finish: 5th of 5 (20th of 21)
Playoffs: Did not qualify
Coach: Doug Carpenter (1–9–1), Tom Watt (22–37–10)
GM: Floyd Smith

Whatever alchemy Carpenter worked last year has worn off. Leafs get off to a sorry start, and he is replaced by Tom Watt. Watt won the Jack Adams Award as best coach in 1981–82 for taking a very bad Winnipeg team and rendering them mediocre. He was less successful in his more recent NHL posting in Vancouver.

In June, Cliff Fletcher is named general manager—finally, the Leafs have a true professional at the helm. Four months later, Steve Stavro becomes chairman of the board of Maple Leaf Gardens Ltd. The second development negates all the positive value of the first.

Out

Dan Daoust, C—signed as a free agent with Ajoie (Switzerland)
Mark Osborne, LW—traded to Winnipeg, November 10, 1989
John McIntyre, C—traded to Los Angeles, November 9, 1990
Ed Olczyk, C—traded to Winnipeg, November 10, 1990

Scott Pearson, LW—traded to Quebec, November 17, 1990
Brian Curran, D—traded to Buffalo, December 17, 1990
Lou Franceschetti, RW—traded to Buffalo, December 17, 1990
Tom Kurvers, D—traded to Vancouver, January 12, 1991
Al Iafrate, D—traded to Washington, January 16, 1991
Paul Fenton, LW—traded to Washington, January 24, 1991
John Kordic, RW—traded to Washington, January 24, 1991
Brad Marsh, D—traded to Detroit, February 4, 1991
Allan Bester, G—traded to Detroit, March 5, 1991

In

Kevin Maguire, RW—traded from Philadelphia, June 16, 1990
Rob Cimetta, LW—traded from Boston, November 9, 1990
Mike Krushelnyski, C—traded from Los Angeles, November 9, 1990
Dave Ellett, D—traded from Winnipeg, November 10, 1990
Paul Fenton, LW—traded from Winnipeg, November 10, 1990
Aaron Broten, LW—traded from Quebec, November 17, 1990
Lucien DeBlois, C—traded from Quebec, November 17, 1990
Michel Petit, D—traded from Quebec, November 17, 1990
Mike Foligno, RW—traded from Buffalo, December 17, 1990
Brian Bradley, C—traded from Vancouver, January 12, 1991
Peter Zezel, C—traded from Washington, January 16, 1991

Top Scorers

	GP	G	A	Pts	PIM
Vincent Damphousse	79	26	47	73	65
Mike Krushelnyski	59	17	22	39	48
Dave Ellett	60	8	30	38	69
Rob Ramage	80	10	25	35	173
Wendel Clark	63	18	16	34	152

Goaltenders

	GP	MIN	GA	GAA	W–L–T	ShO
Peter Ing	56	3126	200	3.84	16–29–8	1
Jeff Reese	30	1430	92	3.86	6–13–3	1

Team Leaders

Games: Rob Ramage, 80
Goals: Vincent Damphousse, 26
Assists: Vincent Damphousse, 47
Points: Vincent Damphousse, 73
PIM: Luke Richardson, 238

Leafs Among League Leaders

Peter Ing, tied for 4th in games played in goal (56)
Dave Reid, 1st in shorthanded goals (8)
Peter Zezel, 2nd in shooting percentage (23.3 includes games played with Washington)

Awards

None

Notable Draft Choices

Yanic Perreault (3rd round, 47th overall), centre, Trois-Rivières Draveurs
As a Leaf: 176 GP, 54 G, 69 A, 123 Pts, 90 PIM
Career: 859 GP, 247 G, 269 A, 516 Pts, 402 PIM

Dmitri Mironov (8th round, 160th overall), defence, Krylja Sovetov
As a Leaf: 175 GP, 22 G, 63 A, 85 Pts, 146 PIM
Career: 556 GP, 54 G, 206 A, 260 Pts, 568 PIM

1991–92

80 GP • 30 W • 43 L • 7 T • 234 GF • 294 GA • 67 Pts • .419 Pct.
Division: Norris
Finish: 5th of 5 (19th of 22)
Playoffs: Did not qualify
Coach: Tom Watt
GM: Cliff Fletcher

Fletcher sends wingers Gary Leeman and Craig Berube, defence-men Michel Petit and Alexander Godynyuk and goalie Jeff Reese to Calgary for centre Doug Gilmour, defencemen Ric Nattress and Jamie Macoun, goalie Rick Wamsley and prospect Kent Manderville. It's the sort of fleecing the Leafs had often been involved in since 1967—but always, until now, on the receiving end.

Out

Rob Ramage, D—claimed by Minnesota in expansion draft, May 30, 1991

Vincent Damphousse, C—traded to Edmonton, September 19, 1991

Peter Ing, G—traded to Edmonton, September 19, 1991

Scott Thornton, C—traded to Edmonton, September 19, 1991

Luke Richardson, D—traded to Edmonton, September 19, 1991

Dave Reid, LW—signed as a free agent with Boston, December 1, 1991

Tom Fergus, C—traded to Vancouver, December 18, 1991

Craig Berube, LW—traded to Calgary, January 2, 1992

Alexander Godynyuk, D—traded to Calgary, January 2, 1992

Gary Leeman, RW—traded to Calgary, January 2, 1992

Michel Petit, D—traded to Calgary, January 2, 1992

Jeff Reese, G—traded to Calgary, January 2, 1992

Aaron Broten, LW—signed as a free agent with Winnipeg, January 21, 1992

Lucien DeBlois, C—traded to Winnipeg, March 10, 1992
Dave Hannan, C—traded to Buffalo, March 10, 1992
Claude Loiselle, C—traded to N.Y. Islanders, March 10, 1992
Daniel Marois, RW—traded to N.Y. Islanders, March 10, 1992

In

Bob Halkidis, D—signed as a free agent, July 24, 1991
Mike Bullard, C—NHL rights traded from Philadelphia, July 29, 1991
Glenn Anderson, RW—traded from Edmonton, September 19, 1991
Craig Berube, LW—traded from Edmonton, September 19, 1991
Grant Fuhr, G—traded from Edmonton, September 19, 1991
Guy Larose, C—traded from N.Y. Rangers, December 26, 1991
Doug Gilmour, C—traded from Calgary, January 2, 1992
Jamie Macoun, D—traded from Calgary, January 2, 1992
Ric Nattress, D—traded from Calgary, January 2, 1992
Ken Baumgartner, LW—traded from N.Y. Islanders, March 10, 1992
Dave McLlwain, C—traded from N.Y. Islanders, March 10, 1992
Mark Osborne, LW—traded from Winnipeg, March 10, 1992

Top Scorers

	GP	G	A	Pts	PIM
Glenn Anderson	72	24	33	57	100
Dave Ellett	79	18	33	51	95
Peter Zezel	64	16	33	49	26
Doug Gilmour	40	15	34	49	32
Wendel Clark	43	19	21	40	123

Goaltenders

	GP	MIN	GA	GAA	W–L–T	ShO
Grant Fuhr	65	3774	230	3.66	25–33–5	2

Team Leaders

Games: Dave Ellett, Bob Rouse, 79
Goals: Glenn Anderson, 24
Assists: Doug Gilmour, 34
Points: Glenn Anderson, 57
PIM: Bob Halkidis, 145

Leafs Among League Leaders

Grant Fuhr, 4th in games played in goal (66), tied for 10th in wins
(25), tied for 8th in shutouts (2)

Awards

None

Notable Draft Choices

Nikolai Borschevsky (4th round, 77th overall), right wing, Moscow
Spartak
As a Leaf: 142 GP, 48 G, 65 A, 113 Pts, 38 PIM
Career: 162 GP, 49 G, 73 A, 122 Pts, 44 PIM

1992–93

84 GP • 44 W • 29 L • 11 T • 288 GF • 241 GA • 99 Pts • .589 Pct.
Division: Norris
Finish: 3rd of 6 (8th of 24)
Playoffs: Lost conference final, 4–3, to Los Angeles
Coach: Pat Burns
GM: Cliff Fletcher

Pat Burns is named coach. Fletcher recognizes the need for discipline and structure on a team that has lacked both commodities for as long as anyone cares to remember. The Leafs finish over .500 for the first time since 1978–79. In the post-season, they beat Detroit in seven games, then beat St. Louis in seven games. But the grind takes its toll and in the conference final, they lose to the Los Angeles Kings in seven games.

Doug Gilmour sets club records with 95 assists and 127 points.

Out

Mike Bullard, C—signed as a free agent with Rapperswil-Jona (Switzerland)

Brian Bradley, C—claimed by Tampa Bay in expansion draft, June 18, 1992

Ric Nattress, D—signed as a free agent with Philadelphia, August 21, 1992

Grant Fuhr, G—traded to Buffalo, February 2, 1993

In

Sylvain Lefebvre, D—traded from Montreal, August 20, 1992

John Cullen, C—traded from Hartford, November 24, 1992

Bill Berg, LW—claimed on waivers from N.Y. Islanders, December 3, 1992

Dave Andreychuk, LW—traded from Buffalo, February 2, 1993

Top Scorers

	GP	G	A	Pts	PIM
Doug Gilmour	83	32	95	127	100
Nikolai Borschevsky	78	34	40	74	28
Glenn Anderson	76	22	43	65	117
Todd Gill	69	11	32	43	66
John Cullen	47	13	28	41	53

Goaltenders

	GP	MIN	GA	GAA	W–L–T	ShO
Félix Potvin	48	2781	116	2.50	25–15–7	2
Grant Fuhr	29	1665	87	3.14	13–9–4	1

Team Leaders

Games: Mike Krushelnyski, 84
Goals: Nikolai Borschevsky, 34
Assists: Doug Gilmour, 95
Points: Doug Gilmour, 127
PIM: Rob Pearson, 211

Leafs Among League Leaders

Dave Andreychuk, tied for 9th in goals (54), 1st in power-play
    goals (32), 10th in shots on goal (310—stats include games with
    Buffalo)
Nikolai Borschevsky, tied for 10th in plus-minus (plus-33)
Grant Fuhr, 9th in save percentage (.893—includes games with
    Buffalo)
Doug Gilmour, tied for 2nd in assists (95), tied for 7th in points (127)
Félix Potvin, tied for 9th in shutouts (2), 1st in GAA (2.50), 2nd in
    save percentage (.910)
Daren Puppa, 9th in GAA (3.23), 6th in save percentage (.898—
    stats include games with Buffalo)

Awards

Pat Burns, Jack Adams Award (best coach)
Doug Gilmour, Frank Selke Trophy (best defensive forward)
Félix Potvin, All-Rookie Team in goal

Notable Draft Choices

Kenny Jönsson (1st round, 12th overall), defence, Rögle Ängelholm

As a Leaf: 89 GP, 6 G, 29 A, 35 Pts, 38 PIM
Career: 686 GP, 63 G, 204 A, 267 Pts, 298 PIM

1993–94

84 GP•43 W•29 L•12 T•280 GF•243 GA•98 Pts•.583 Pct.
Division: Central
Finish: 2nd of 6 (5th of 26)
Playoffs: Lost conference final, 4–1, to Vancouver
Coach: Pat Burns
GM: Cliff Fletcher

The Leafs burst out of the gate, setting an NHL record by winning their first ten games, and fans continue to nurture serious Stanley Cup hopes. Once again the team reaches the conference finals, but the magic isn't there this time. After defeating Chicago and San Jose, they don't put up much of a fight against Vancouver and lose in five games.

Out

Bob McGill, D—signed as a free agent with N.Y. Islanders, September 7, 1993

Dave McLlwain, C—claimed by Ottawa in waiver draft, October 3, 1993

Mike Foligno, RW—traded to Florida, November 5, 1993

Greg Smyth, D—claimed on waivers by Chicago, January 8, 1994

Glenn Anderson, RW—traded to N.Y. Rangers, March 21, 1994

In

Greg Smyth, D—traded from Florida, December 7, 1993

Mark Greig, RW—traded from Hartford, January 25, 1994
Mike Gartner, RW—traded from N.Y. Rangers, March 21, 1994

Top Scorers

	GP	G	A	Pts	PIM
Doug Gilmour	83	27	84	111	105
Dave Andreychuk	83	53	46	99	98
Wendel Clark	64	46	30	76	115
Dave Ellett	68	7	36	43	42
Dmitri Mironov	76	9	27	36	78

Goaltenders

	GP	MIN	GA	GAA	W–L–T	ShO
Félix Potvin	66	3883	187	2.89	34–22–9	3

Team Leaders

Games: Sylvain Lefebvre, 84
Goals: Dave Andreychuk, 53
Assists: Doug Gilmour, 84
Points: Doug Gilmour, 111
PIM: Rob Pearson, 189

Leafs Among League Leaders

Dave Andreychuk, 4th in goals (53), 9th in points (99), tied for 6th
   in power-play goals (21), tied for 2nd in shorthanded goals (5),
   tied for 9th in game-winning goals (8), 6th in shots on goal (333)
Wendel Clark, tied for 10th in goals (46), tied for 6th in power-play
   goals (21), tied for 9th in game-winning goals (8)
Doug Gilmour, 2nd in assists (84), 4th in points (111)
Sylvain Lefebvre, 10th in plus-minus (plus-33)
Félix Potvin, 8th in games played in goal (66), 5th in wins (34), 8th
   in shutouts (3), 10th in save percentage (.907)

Awards
None

Notable Draft Choices
Fredrik Modin (3rd round, 64th overall), Sundsvall
As a Leaf: 217 GP, 38 G, 38 A, 76 Pts, 91 PIM
Career to date: 814 GP, 220 G, 221 A, 441 Pts, 413 PIM; won
    Stanley Cup with Tampa Bay in 2004

Sergei Berezin (10th round, 256th overall), Voskresensk Khimik
As a Leaf: 357 GP, 126 G, 94 A, 220 Pts, 34 PIM
Career: 502 GP, 160 G, 126 A, 286 Pts, 54 PIM

1994–95
48 GP • 21 W • 19 L • 8 T • 135 GF • 146 GA • 50 Pts • .521 Pct.
Division: Central
Finish: 4th of 6 (12th of 26)
Playoffs: Lost conference quarter-final, 4–3, to Chicago
Coach: Pat Burns
GM: Cliff Fletcher

A 103-day lockout delays the start of the 1994–95 season until late
January. An abbreviated schedule, with no inter-conference games,
is drawn up. Cliff Fletcher trades forty-six-goal scorer Wendel Clark
to Quebec, along with Sylvain Lefebvre and Landon Wilson. In
return, Toronto gets Mats Sundin, Garth Butcher and Todd Warriner. The teams also swap first-round picks.

Throughout the year, the saga of the Leafs' ownership unfolds.
The public trustee gets involved, as do battalions of lawyers, but

Steve Stavro lays the groundwork to privatize the company, a move that will hide his self-serving decisions from scrutiny by the fans. For perhaps the first time, the words "Ontario Teachers' Pension Plan" are heard in connection with the Toronto Maple Leafs.

Out

Wendel Clark, LW—traded to Quebec, June 28, 1994

Sylvain Lefebvre, D—traded to Quebec, June 28, 1994

Rob Pearson, RW—traded to Washington, June 28, 1994

Mike Krushelnyski, LW—signed as a free agent with Detroit, August 1, 1994

John Cullen, C—signed as a free agent with Pittsburgh, August 3, 1994

Bob Rouse, D—signed as a free agent with Detroit, August 5, 1994

Peter Zezel, C—awarded to Dallas as compensation for the signing of free agent Mike Craig, August 10, 1994

Mark Osborne, LW—signed as a free agent with N.Y. Rangers, January 25, 1995

Nikolai Borschevsky, RW—traded to Calgary, April 6, 1995

Drake Berehowsky, D—traded to Pittsburgh, April 7, 1995

Mike Eastwood, C—traded to Winnipeg, April 7, 1995

In

Garth Butcher, D—traded from Quebec, June 28, 1994

Mike Ridley, C—traded from Washington, June 28, 1994

Mats Sundin, C—traded from Quebec, June 28, 1994

Mike Craig, RW—signed as a free agent, July 29, 1994

Randy Wood, LW—claimed from Buffalo in waiver draft, January 18, 1995

Warren Rychel, LW—traded from Washington, February 10, 1995

Rich Sutter, RW—traded from Tampa Bay, March 13, 1995

Paul Di Pietro, C—traded from Montreal, April 6, 1995

Benoît Hogue, C—traded from N.Y. Islanders, April 6, 1995
Tie Domi, RW—traded from Winnipeg, April 7, 1995
Grant Jennings, D—traded from Pittsburgh, April 7, 1995

Top Scorers

	GP	G	A	Pts	PIM
Mats Sundin	47	23	24	47	14
Dave Andreychuk	48	22	16	38	34
Mike Ridley	48	10	27	37	14
Doug Gilmour	44	10	23	33	26
Todd Gill	47	7	25	32	64

Goaltenders

	GP	MIN	GA	GAA	W–L–T	ShO
Félix Potvin	36	2144	104	2.91	15–13–7	0

Team Leaders
Games: Dave Andreychuk, Mike Ridley, Randy Wood, 48
Goals: Mats Sundin, 23
Assists: Mike Ridley, 27
Points: Mats Sundin, 47
PIM: Warren Rychel, 101

Leafs Among League Leaders
Mats Sundin, tied for 10th in power-play goals (9), tied for 10th in
   shots on goal (173)

Awards
Kenny Jönsson, All-Rookie Team on defence

Notable Draft Choices
Daniil Markov (9th round, 223rd overall), defence, Moscow Spartak

As a Leaf: 200 GP, 9 G, 36 A, 45 Pts, 137 PIM
Career: 538 GP, 29 G, 118 A, 147 Pts, 456 PIM

1995–96

82 GP • 34 W • 36 L • 12 T • 247 GF • 252 GA • 80 Pts • .488 Pct.
Division: Central
Finish: 3rd of 6 (13th of 26)
Playoffs: Lost conference quarter-final, 4–2, to St. Louis
Coach: Pat Burns (25–30–10), Nick Beverley (9–6–2)
GM: Cliff Fletcher

With the Leafs caught in a second-half nosedive and in danger of missing the playoffs, Pat Burns is fired with seventeen games left to play. Nick Beverley comes in as interim coach to finish the season. Steve Stavro demands that Wendel Clark be reacquired, so Fletcher trades promising defenceman Kenny Jönsson and a first-round pick to the Islanders to get him. The Islanders use the draft pick to select goalie Roberto Luongo.

The Leafs meet St. Louis in the first round and are defeated in six games. In the summer, Mike Murphy is named coach.

Out

Garth Butcher, D—retired
Dmitri Mironov, D—traded to Pittsburgh, July 8, 1995
Mike Ridley, C—traded to Vancouver, July 8, 1995
Warren Rychel, LW—traded to Colorado, October 2, 1995
Kent Manderville, C—traded to Edmonton, December 4, 1995
Mike Hudson, C—claimed on waivers by St. Louis, January 4, 1996
Damian Rhodes, G—traded to N.Y. Islanders, January 23, 1996

Benoît Hogue, C—traded to Dallas, January 29, 1996
Randy Wood, LW—traded to Dallas, January 29, 1996
Bill Berg, LW—traded to N.Y. Rangers, February 29, 1996
Sergio Momesso, LW—traded to N.Y. Rangers, February 29, 1996
Dave Andreychuk, LW—traded to New Jersey, March 13, 1996
Darby Hendrickson, C—traded to N.Y. Islanders, March 13, 1996
Kenny Jönsson, D—traded to N.Y. Islanders, March 13, 1996
Ken Baumgartner, LW—traded to Anaheim, March 20, 1996

In

Sergio Momesso, LW—traded from Vancouver, July 8, 1995
Larry Murphy, D—traded from Pittsburgh, July 8, 1995
Dmitry Yushkevich, D—traded from Philadelphia, August 30, 1995
Don Beaupre, G—traded from N.Y. Islanders, January 29, 1996
Dave Gagner, C—traded from Dallas, January 29, 1996
Kirk Muller, LW—traded from N.Y. Islanders, January 29, 1996
Nick Kypreos, LW—traded from N.Y. Rangers, February 29, 1996
Wayne Presley, RW—traded from N.Y. Rangers, February 29, 1996
Wendel Clark, LW—traded from N.Y. Islanders, March 19, 1996
Mathieu Schneider, D—traded from N.Y. Islanders, March 19, 1996

Top Scorers

	GP	G	A	Pts	PIM
Mats Sundin	76	33	50	83	46
Doug Gilmour	81	32	40	72	77
Larry Murphy	82	12	49	61	34
Mike Gartner	82	35	19	54	52
Dave Andreychuk	61	20	24	44	54

Goaltenders

	GP	MIN	GA	GAA	W–L–T	ShO
Félix Potvin	69	4009	192	2.87	30–26–11	2

Team Leaders

Games: Mike Gartner, Jamie Macoun, Larry Murphy, 82
Goals: Mike Gartner, 35
Assists: Mats Sundin, 50
Points: Mats Sundin, 83
PIM: Tie Domi, 297

Leafs Among League Leaders

Mats Sundin, tied for 2nd in shorthanded goals (6), tied for 8th in
    game-winning goals (7)
Félix Potvin, 5th in games played in goal (69), tied for 7th in wins
    (30), 9th in save percentage (.910)

Awards

None

Notable Draft Choices

Tomáš Kaberle (8th round, 204th overall), defence, Kladno
As a Leaf: 738 GP, 73 G, 360 A, 433 Pts, 206 PIM
Career to date: 738 GP, 73 G, 360 A, 433 Pts, 206 PIM

1996–97

82 GP • 30 W • 44 L • 8 T • 230 GF • 273 GA • 68 Pts • .415 Pct.
Division: Central
Finish: 6th of 6 (23rd of 26)
Playoffs: Did not qualify
Coach: Mike Murphy
GM: Cliff Fletcher

Cliff Fletcher prepares an offer that will bring thirty-six-year-old Wayne Gretzky to Toronto—at less than market value. Grumbling that the signing wouldn't sell any more tickets, Steve Stavro refuses to authorize the deal. Gretzky signs with the New York Rangers, and collects more points in each of the next two years than the Leafs' best centre, Mats Sundin.

The Leafs take a giant step backward in the standings, and Fletcher begins unloading veterans, including captain Doug Gilmour. During the off-season, Fletcher is fired, while Ken Dryden is named president of the team. Unable to find anyone who meets his standards as GM, Dryden assumes the title himself. The actual duties of a GM are handled by Mike Smith, who is named associate GM.

Out

Todd Gill, D   traded to San Jose, June 14, 1996
Dave Gagner, C—traded to Calgary, June 22, 1996
Mike Gartner, RW—traded to Phoenix, June 22, 1996
Dave Ellett, D—traded to New Jersey, February 25, 1997
Doug Gilmour, C—traded to New Jersey, February 25, 1997
Kirk Muller, LW—traded to Florida, March 18, 1997
Larry Murphy, D—traded to Detroit, March 18, 1997

In

Jamie Baker, C—traded from San Jose, June 14, 1996
Craig Wolanin, D—traded from Tampa Bay, January 31, 1997
Jason Smith, D—traded from New Jersey, February 25, 1997
Steve Sullivan, C—traded from New Jersey, February, 25, 1997

Top Scorers

	GP	G	A	Pts	PIM
Mats Sundin	82	41	53	94	59
Doug Gilmour	61	15	45	60	46

Wendel Clark	65	30	19	49	75
Sergei Berezin	73	25	16	41	2
Larry Murphy	69	7	32	39	20

Goaltenders

	GP	MIN	GA	GAA	W–L–T	ShO
Félix Potvin	74	4271	224	3.15	27–36–7	0

Team Leaders

Games: Mats Sundin, 82
Goals: Mats Sundin, 41
Assists: Mats Sundin, 53
Points: Mats Sundin, 94
PIM: Tie Domi, 275

Leafs Among League Leaders

Doug Gilmour, tied for 6th in assists (60—includes games with New Jersey)
Félix Potvin, 1st in games played in goal (74)
Mats Sundin, 7th in points (94), tied for 5th in shorthanded goals (4), tied for 5th in game-winning goals (8)

Awards

Sergei Berezin, All-Rookie Team at forward

Notable Draft Choices

None of any consequence

1997–98

82 GP • 30 W • 43 L • 9 T • 194 GF • 237 GA • 69 Pts • .421 Pct.
Division: Central
Finish: 6th of 6 (20th of 26)
Playoffs: Did not qualify
Coach: Mike Murphy
GM: Ken Dryden

For the second year in succession, the Leafs miss the playoffs. Mike Murphy's record as a coach: 60–87–17, for a .418 winning percentage. He is replaced by Pat Quinn.

In February, Maple Leaf Gardens Ltd. buys the Toronto Raptors of the NBA. Both teams will play in the yet-to-be-completed Air Canada Centre, an arena conceived for basketball only. Gardens chairman Steve Stavro has spent most of the past two years deriding the ACC as inadequate and poorly located. However, he hasn't yet been able to begin work on a planned "shrine" to hockey on the site of Union Station—just around the corner from the inconveniently situated future home of the Raptors.

Out

Brandon Convery, C—traded to Vancouver, March 7, 1998
Jeff Brown, D—traded to Washington, March 24, 1998
Jamie Macoun, D—traded to Detroit, March 24, 1998

In

Derek King, LW—signed as a free agent, July 4, 1997
Kris King, LW—signed as a free agent, July 23, 1997
Glenn Healy, G—signed as a free agent, August 8, 1997
Igor Korolev, C—signed as a free agent, September 29, 1997
Jeff Brown, D—traded from Carolina, January 2, 1998
Sylvain Côté, D—traded from Washington, March 24, 1998

Top Scorers

	GP	G	A	Pts	PIM
Mats Sundin	82	33	41	74	49
Mike Johnson	82	15	32	47	24
Derek King	77	21	25	46	43
Igor Korolev	78	17	22	39	22
Mathieu Schneider	76	11	26	37	44

Goaltenders

	GP	MIN	GA	GAA	W–L–T	ShO
Félix Potvin	67	3864	176	2.73	26–33–7	5

Team Leaders

Games: Mike Johnson, Kris King, Mats Sundin, 82

Goals: Mats Sundin, 33

Assists: Mats Sundin, 41

Points: Mats Sundin, 74

PIM: Tie Domi, 365

Leafs Among League Leaders

Igor Korolev, 10th in shooting percentage (17.5)

Félix Potvin, 6th in games played in goal (67), tied for 9th in shutouts (5)

Mats Sundin, tied for 10th in goals (33)

Awards

Mike Johnson, All-Rookie Team at forward

Notable Draft Choices

Nikolai Antropov (1st round, 10th overall), right wing, Torpedo UST-Kamengorsk

As a Leaf: 509 GP, 125 G, 166 A, 291 Pts, 477 PIM

Career to date: 527 GP, 132 G, 172 A, 304 Pts, 483 PIM

Alexei Ponikarovsky (4th round, 87th overall) left wing, Dynamo-2
    Moscow
As a Leaf: 416 GP, 95 G, 121 A, 216 Pts, 274 PIM
Career to date: 416 GP, 95 G, 121 A, 216 Pts, 274 PIM

1998–99
82 GP • 45 W • 30 L • 7 T • 268 GF • 231 GA • 97 Pts • .591 Pct.
Division: Northeast
Finish: 2nd of 5 (5th of 27)
Playoffs: Lost conference final, 4–1, to Buffalo
Coach: Pat Quinn
GM: Ken Dryden

At Dryden's behest, Leafs move to the Eastern Conference. In another rare inspired move, he signs goaltender Curtis Joseph to replace Félix Potvin. Dryden is less adroit in his handling of the closing ceremonies at Maple Leaf Gardens in February. Several alumni stay home, feeling slighted by a form letter that begins "Dear former player," informs them they'll have to pay their own travel and hotel expenses, and makes no promise that they'll have a seat for the final game.

Whereas the Montreal Forum was closed with a passing of the torch (a reference to the famous quote from John McCrae's "In Flanders Fields" that was painted on the walls of the Canadiens' dressing room), the Gardens was sent off with the post-game passing of a . . . Maple Leafs flag, from Red Horner to Mats Sundin.

Even that bizarre gesture nearly falls through. During the first intermission, Horner, at age eighty-nine the oldest living captain, informs Ken Dryden that he's thinking of going home early to beat the traffic. Dryden talks him into staying through the lengthy ceremonies.

Meanwhile, Mike Smith makes one of the worst trades in the history of the Leafs, dealing Mathieu Schneider for Alexander Karpovtsev and a fourth-round draft pick. Ten seasons later, Schneider was still an effective NHL defenceman. Karpovtsev was long gone.

Still, in their first season under coach Quinn, the team improves tremendously and defeats Philadelphia and Pittsburgh before losing to Buffalo in the conference final.

Out

Rob Zettler, D—claimed by Nashville in expansion draft, June 26, 1998

Wendel Clark, LW—signed as a free agent with Tampa Bay, July 31, 1998

Mathieu Schneider, D—traded to N.Y. Rangers, October 14, 1998

Félix Potvin, G—traded to N.Y. Islanders, January 9, 1999

Darby Hendrickson, C—traded to Vancouver, February 16, 1999

Jason Smith, D—traded to Edmonton, March 23, 1999

In

Curtis Joseph, G—signed as a free agent, July 15, 1998

Steve Thomas, LW—signed as a free agent, July 30, 1998

Garry Valk, LW—signed as a free agent, October 8, 1998

Alexander Karpovtsev, D—traded from N.Y. Rangers, October 14, 1998

Bryan Berard, D—traded from N.Y. Islanders, January 9, 1999

Chris McAllister, D—traded from Vancouver, February 16, 1999

Yanic Perreault, C—traded from Los Angeles, March 23, 1999

Top Scorers

	GP	G	A	Pts	PIM
Mats Sundin	82	31	52	83	58
Steve Thomas	78	28	45	73	33

Sergei Berezin	76	37	22	59	12
Derek King	81	24	28	52	20
Igor Korolev	66	13	34	47	46

Goaltenders

	GP	MIN	GA	GAA	W–L–T	ShO
Curtis Joseph	67	4001	171	2.56	35–24–7	3

Team Leaders

Games: Mats Sundin, 82
Goals: Sergei Berezin, 37
Assists: Mats Sundin, 52
Points: Mats Sundin, 83
PIM: Tie Domi, 198

Leafs Among League Leaders

Curtis Joseph, 5th in games played in goal (67), 2nd in wins (35)
Steve Sullivan, 8th in shooting percentage (18.2)
Alexander Karpovtsev, 1st in plus-minus (plus-39—includes games
    with N.Y. Rangers)
Yanic Perreault, tied for 8th in shorthanded goals (3—includes
    games with Los Angeles)
Mats Sundin, tied for 10th in assists (52)
Steve Thomas, tied for 9th in game-winning goals (7)

Awards

None

Notable Draft Choices

None of any consequence

1999–2000

82 GP • 45 W • 27 L • 7 T • 3 OTL • 246 GF • 222 GA • 100 Pts • .597 Pct.
Division: Northeast
Finish: 1st of 5 (7th of 28)
Playoffs: Lost conference semifinal, 4–2, to New Jersey
Coach: Pat Quinn
GM: Pat Quinn

Prior to the season, Mike Smith tries to make a corporate end run around Ken Dryden's authority. It backfires, and Smith is dismissed. In what he calls an act of self-preservation, and with the backing of Steve Stavro, Pat Quinn manages to get himself named GM.

In October, Quinn makes a roster move worthy of his predecessor, trading a draft pick to Boston for winger Dmitri Khristich. To make room on the roster, he waives centre Steve Sullivan, who scored twenty goals last year but is deemed too small to be of value. Sullivan is picked up by Chicago and strings together seven more twenty-goal campaigns. Khristich scores twelve in 1999–2000, and only three more the following year before he is shipped off to Washington.

The fiftieth NHL All-Star Game is played at the Air Canada Centre in February. Pat Quinn coaches the North American team, which loses 9–4 to a team made up of players from the rest of the world. Defenceman Dmitry Yushkevich scores a goal and assists on another.

Late in the season, the Leafs lose one of their best defencemen— and a former first-overall pick—when Bryan Berard is accidentally hit in the eye by Marián Hossa's stick. It appears that Berard's career is over, and he is eventually released by the Leafs.

For the first time since 1963, the team finishes in first place. Toronto eliminates Ottawa in the playoffs, but loses the second round to New Jersey, which goes on to win the Stanley Cup.

Out

Fredrik Modin, LW—traded to Tampa Bay, October 1, 1999

Sylvain Côté, D—traded to Chicago, October 8, 1999
Derek King, LW—traded to St. Louis, October 20, 1999
Steve Sullivan, C—claimed on waivers by Chicago, October 23, 1999
Todd Warriner, LW—traded to Tampa Bay, November 29, 1999
Mike Johnson, RW—traded to Tampa Bay, February 9, 2000

In

Jonas Höglund, RW—signed as a free agent, July 13, 1999
Cory Cross, D—traded from Tampa Bay, October 1, 1999
Dmitri Khristich, RW—traded from Boston, October 20, 1999
Wendel Clark, LW—signed as a free agent, January 14, 2000
Darcy Tucker, LW—traded from Tampa Bay, February 9, 2000

Top Scorers

	GP	G	A	Pts	PIM
Mats Sundin	73	32	41	73	46
Steve Thomas	81	26	37	63	68
Jonas Höglund	82	29	27	56	10
Igor Korolev	80	20	26	46	22
Yanic Perreault	58	18	27	45	22

Goaltenders

	GP	MIN	GA	GAA	W–L–T	ShO
Curtis Joseph	63	3801	158	2.49	36–20–7	4

Team Leaders
Games: Jonas Höglund, Tomáš Kaberle, 82
Goals: Mats Sundin, 32
Assists: Mats Sundin, 41
Points: Mats Sundin, 73
PIM: Tie Domi, 198

Leafs Among League Leaders

Curtis Joseph, 8th in games played in goal (63), 4th in wins (36), tied for 9th in shutouts (4), 7th in save percentage (.915)

Igor Korolev, 6th in shooting percentage (19.8)

Mats Sundin, tied for 8th in game-winning goals (7)

Steve Thomas, tied for 3rd in game-winning goals (9)

Awards

Curtis Joseph, King Clancy Award (leadership on and off the ice)

Notable Draft Choices

Brad Boyes (1st round, 24th overall), centre, Erie Otters

As a Leaf: 0 GP, 0 G, 0 A, 0 Pts, 0 PIM

Career to date: 328 GP, 119 G, 133 A, 252 Pts, 107 PIM

Mikael Tellqvist (3rd round, 70th overall), goal, Djurgårdens IF Stockholm

As a Leaf: 40 GP, 2191 MIN, 110 GA, 3.01 GAA, 16 W, 16 L, 2 T, 2 OTL, 2 ShO

Career to date: 113 GP, 6034 MIN, 303 GA, 3.01 GAA, 45 W, 4L, 2 T, 8 OTL, 6 ShO

2000–01

82 GP • 37 W • 29 L • 11 T • 5 OTL • 232 GF • 207 GA 90 • Pts .518 Pct.

Division: Northeast

Finish: 3rd of 5 (14th of 30)

Playoffs: Lost conference semifinal, 4–3, to New Jersey

Coach: Pat Quinn

GM: Pat Quinn

The Leafs spend much of the year trying to get the disgruntled Eric Lindros out of Philadelphia. Lindros says he will play only for the Leafs. It would therefore appear that making a deal would not be difficult. Lindros winds up being traded to the New York Rangers.

On the plus side, Quinn takes advantage of Mike Smith's weakness for Russian players. He trades Alexander Karpovtsev to the Blackhawks, where Mike Smith is now GM, for defenceman Bryan McCabe. He also signs veteran forwards Gary Roberts and Shayne Corson.

Out

Kevyn Adams, C—claimed by Columbus in expansion draft, June 23, 2000

Alexander Karpovtsev, D—traded to Chicago, October 7, 2000

Kris King, LW—signed as a free agent with Chicago, October 9, 2000

Dimitri Khristich, RW—traded to Washington, December 11, 2000

In

Shayne Corson, LW—signed as a free agent, July 4, 2000

Gary Roberts, LW—signed as a free agent, July 4, 2000

Dave Manson, D—signed as a free agent, August 16, 2000

Bryan McCabe, D—traded from Chicago, October 7, 2000

Wade Belak, D—claimed on waivers from Calgary, February 16, 2001

Aki Berg, D—traded from Los Angeles, March 13, 2001

Top Scorers

	GP	G	A	Pts	PIM
Mats Sundin	82	28	46	74	76
Gary Roberts	82	29	24	53	109
Yanic Perreault	76	24	28	52	52
Sergei Berezin	79	22	28	50	8
Jonas Höglund	82	23	26	49	14

Goaltenders

	GP	MIN	GA	GAA	W–L–T	ShO
Curtis Joseph	68	4100	163	2.39	33–27–8	6

Team Leaders

Games: 7 players tied with 82
Goals: Gary Roberts, 29
Assists: Mats Sundin, 46
Points: Mats Sundin, 74
PIM: Tie Domi, 214

Leafs Among League Leaders

Curtis Joseph, 5th in games played in goal (68), 10th in wins (33),
    tied for 7th in shutouts (6)
Gary Roberts, 1st in shooting percentage (21.0)

Awards

None

Notable Draft Choices

Carlo Colaiacovo (1st round, 17th overall), defence, Erie Otters
As a Leaf: 111 GP, 12 G, 21 A, 33 Pts, 57 PIM
Career to date: 174 GP, 15 G, 47 A, 62 Pts, 86 PIM

Kyle Wellwood (5th round, 134th overall), centre, Belleville Bulls
As a Leaf: 189 GP, 31 G, 77 A, 108 Pts, 14 PIM
Career to date: 263 GP, 49 G, 86 A, 135 Pts, 18 PIM

2001–02

82 GP • 43 W • 25 L • 10 T • 4 OTL • 249 GF • 207 GA • 100 Pts • .585 Pct.
Division: Northeast
Finish: 2nd of 5 (3rd of 30)
Playoffs: Lost conference final, 4–2, to Carolina
Coach: Pat Quinn
GM: Pat Quinn

During the off-season, Quinn acquires European players Robert Reichel, Mikael Renberg, Alexander Mogilny and Anders Eriksson. It's a marked change of direction from his free-agent signings the previous summer.

Goaltender Curtis Joseph gets the start in Canada's first game at the 2002 Winter Olympics. After giving up five goals, he is benched for the rest of the tournament. Shortly afterwards, he breaks his left hand and misses two months, returning in time for the playoffs. The Leafs reach the Eastern Conference final but are defeated by the Carolina Hurricanes.

The Leafs have the twenty-fourth-overall pick in the 2002 draft and take forward Alexander Steen. After three inconsistent seasons, he is traded to St. Louis in 2008. With the next pick in the draft, Carolina takes goaltender Cam Ward—the Conn Smythe Trophy winner in 2006.

Out

Daniil Markov, D—traded to Phoenix, June 12, 2001
Sergei Berezin, LW—traded to Phoenix, June 23, 2001
Igor Korolev, C—traded to Chicago, June 23, 2001
Yanic Perreault, C—signed as a free agent with Montreal, July 4, 2001
Steve Thomas, LW—signed as a free agent with Chicago, July 17, 2001

Bryan Berard, D—signed as a free agent with N.Y. Rangers, October 5, 2001

Dave Manson, D—traded to Dallas, November 21, 2001

In

Travis Green, C—traded from Phoenix, June 12, 2001

Robert Reichel, C—traded from Phoenix, June 12, 2001

Mikael Renberg, RW—traded from Phoenix, June 23, 2001

Alexander Mogilny, RW—signed as a free agent, July 3, 2001

Anders Eriksson, D—signed as a free agent, July 9, 2001

Corey Schwab, G—signed as a free agent, October 1, 2001

Jyrki Lumme, D—traded from Dallas, November 21, 2001

Top Scorers

	GP	G	A	Pts	PIM
Mats Sundin	82	41	39	80	94
Darcy Tucker	77	24	35	59	92
Alexander Mogilny	66	24	33	57	8
Mikael Renberg	71	14	38	52	36
Robert Reichel	78	20	31	51	26

Goaltenders

	GP	MIN	GA	GAA	W–L–T	ShO
Curtis Joseph	51	3065	114	2.23	29–17–5	4
Corey Schwab	30	1646	75	2.73	12–10–5	1

Team Leaders

Games: 5 players tied with 82

Goals: Mats Sundin, 41

Assists: Mats Sundin, 39

Points: Mats Sundin, 80

PIM: Tie Domi, 157

Leafs Among League Leaders

Mats Sundin, 4th in points (80), tied for 2nd in goals (41), tied for 2nd in game-winning goals (9)

Darcy Tucker, 7th in shooting percentage (19.4)

Awards

Mats Sundin, Second Team All-Star at centre

Notable Draft Choices

Alexander Steen (1st round, 24th overall), centre, Västra Frölunda HC Göteborg
As a Leaf: 253 GP, 50 G, 76 A, 126 Pts, 106 PIM
Career to date: 314 GP, 56 G, 94 A, 150 Pts, 130 PIM

Matt Stajan (2nd round, 57th overall), centre, Belleville Bulls
As a Leaf: 390 GP, 71 G, 111 A, 182 Pts, 217 PIM
Career to date: 390 GP, 71 G, 111 A, 182 Pts, 217 PIM

Ian White (6th round, 191st overall), defence, Swift Current Broncos
As a Leaf: 240 GP, 19 G, 60 A, 79 Pts, 151 PIM
Career to date: 240 GP, 19 G, 60 A, 79 Pts, 151 PIM

2002–03

82 GP • 44 W • 28 L • 7 T • 3 OTL • 236 GF • 208 GA • 98 Pts • .579 Pct.
Division: Northeast
Finish: 2nd of 5 (9th of 30)
Playoffs: Lost conference quarter-final, 4–3, to Philadelphia
Coach: Pat Quinn
GM: Pat Quinn

Quinn and Curtis Joseph are unable to agree to terms on a new contract. Ultimately, Joseph signs with Detroit. To replace him, Ed Belfour is signed. Leafs made a flurry of trade-deadline deals, acquiring Glen Wesley, Owen Nolan, Phil Housley and Doug Gilmour. Gilmour dresses for one game, in which he suffers a career-ending injury. After being benched, Shayne Corson walks out on the team in April.

In July 2003, Steve Stavro is forced out as primary owner of the Leafs. The Ontario Teachers' Pension Plan assumes control of the team and Larry Tanenbaum is installed as chairman of the board. Dryden's position as team president is eliminated, and he is reassigned to the position of vice-chairman of Maple Leaf Sports and Entertainment.

Quinn is relieved of his duties as GM but remains as coach and sits on the search committee struck to appoint his replacement. John Ferguson Jr. is hired as GM in August.

Out

Garry Valk, LW—retired

Tie Domi, RW—rights traded to Nashville, June 30, 2002

Curtis Joseph, G—rights traded to Calgary, June 30, 2002

Corey Schwab, G—signed as a free agent with New Jersey, July 8, 2002

Dmitry Yushkevich, D—traded to Florida, July 18, 2002

Cory Cross, D—signed as a free agent by N.Y. Rangers, December 17, 2002

Alyn McCauley, C—traded to San Jose, March 5, 2003

In

Ed Belfour, G—signed as a free agent, July 2, 2002

Tie Domi, RW—signed as a free agent, July 14, 2002

Tom Fitzgerald, C—signed as a free agent, July 17, 2002

Róbert Švehla, D—traded from Florida, July 18, 2002
Trevor Kidd, G—signed as a free agent, August 26, 2002
Owen Nolan, RW—traded from San Jose, March 5, 2003
Glen Wesley, D—traded from Carolina, March 9, 2003
Doug Gilmour, C—traded from Montreal, March 11, 2003
Phil Housley, D—traded from Chicago, March 11, 2003

Top Scorers

	GP	G	A	Pts	PIM
Alexander Mogilny	73	33	46	79	12
Mats Sundin	75	37	35	72	58
Tomáš Kaberle	82	11	36	47	30
Nikolai Antropov	72	16	29	45	124
Róbert Švehla	82	7	38	45	46

Goaltenders

	GP	MIN	GA	GAA	W–L–T	ShO
Ed Belfour	62	3738	141	2.26	37–20–5	7

Team Leaders

Games: Tomáš Kaberle, Róbert Švehla, 82
Goals: Mats Sundin, 37
Assists: Alexander Mogilny, 46
Points: Alexander Mogilny, 79
PIM: Wade Belak, 196

Leafs Among League Leaders

Ed Belfour, 3rd in wins (37), tied for 5th in shutouts (7), 10th in
    GAA (2.26), 5th in save percentage (.922)
Alexander Mogilny, tied for 7th in shorthanded goals (3), tied for
    4th in game-winning goals (9), tied for 2nd in shooting percent-
    age (20.0)

Owen Nolan, tied for 7th in shorthanded goals (3—includes games
with San Jose)

Mats Sundin, tied for 8th in goals (37), 5th in power-play goals
(16), tied for 7th in shorthanded goals (3), tied for 7th in game-
winning goals (8)

Awards

Alexander Mogilny, Lady Byng Trophy (gentlemanly conduct)

Notable Draft Choices

John Mitchell (5th round, 158th overall), centre, Plymouth Whalers
As a Leaf: 76 GP, 12 G, 17 A, 29 Pts, 33 PIM
Career to date: 76 GP, 12 G, 17 A, 29 Pts, 33 PIM

2003–04

82 GP • 45 W • 24 L • 10 T • 6 OTL • 242 GF • 204 GA • 103 Pts • .610 Pct.
Division: Northeast
Finish: 2nd of 5 (5th of 30)
Playoffs: Lost conference semifinal, 4–2, to Philadelphia
Coach: Pat Quinn
GM: John Ferguson Jr.

The Leafs added free agents Joe Nieuwendyk and Ken Klee, and are
again busy at the trade deadline, but despite a solid regular season
are unable to get past Philadelphia in the second round.

Ken Dryden resigns. Having found a safe seat, he will run as a
Liberal candidate in the next federal election. The only surprise is
that a guy whose life is a series of five-year plans lasted seven years

on the job. But then again, he did nothing for his last two years with the Leafs.

Out

Jyrki Lumme, D—retired

Róbert Švehla, D—retired, May 8, 2003

Glen Wesley, D—signed as a free agent with Carolina, July 8, 2003

Paul Healey, RW—signed as a free agent with N.Y. Rangers, July 28, 2003

Jonas Höglund, LW—signed as a free agent with Florida, September 4, 2003

Doug Gilmour, C—retired, September 8, 2003

Travis Green, C—claimed by Columbus in waiver draft, October 3, 2003

Phil Housley, D—became a free agent, retired January 16, 2004

Ric Jackman, D—traded to Pittsburgh, February 11, 2004

Shayne Corson, LW—signed as free agent with Dallas, February 18, 2004

Craig Johnson, LW—claimed on waivers by Washington, March 5, 2004

In

Bryan Marchment, D—signed as a free agent, July 11, 2003

Joe Nieuwendyk, C—signed as a free agent, September 9, 2003

Ken Klee, D—signed as a free agent, September 27, 2003

Craig Johnson, LW—claimed on waivers from Anaheim, January 10, 2004

Brian Leetch, D—traded from N.Y. Rangers, March 3, 2004

Ron Francis, C—traded from Carolina, March 9, 2004

Calle Johansson, D—signed as a free agent, March 9, 2004

Chad Kilger, LW—claimed on waivers from Montreal, March 9, 2004

Top Scorers

	GP	G	A	Pts	PIM
Mats Sundin	81	31	44	75	52
Bryan McCabe	75	16	37	53	86
Joe Nieuwendyk	64	22	28	50	26
Gary Roberts	72	28	20	48	84
Owen Nolan	65	19	29	48	110

Goaltenders

	GP	MIN	GA	GAA	W–L–T	ShO
Ed Belfour	59	3444	122	2.13	34–19–6	10

Team Leaders

Games: Mats Sundin, 81
Goals: Mats Sundin, 31
Assists: Mats Sundin, 44
Points: Mats Sundin, 75
PIM: Tie Domi, 208

Leafs Among League Leaders

Ed Belfour, tied for 3rd in wins (34), 2nd in shutouts (10)
Gary Roberts, 2nd in shooting percentage (22.6)
Mats Sundin, tied for 1st in game-winning goals (10)

Awards

Bryan McCabe, Second Team All-Star on defence
Mats Sundin, Second Team All-Star at centre

Notable Draft Choices

None

2004–05

The NHL shuts down for the season and when it returns, it becomes clear that the Leafs didn't use the downtime profitably—in terms of hockey or business operations. John Ferguson signs aging goalie Ed Belfour to a last-minute contract extension. Before the lockout begins, Belfour undergoes back surgery—as a result of which the Leafs must pay his salary for the cancelled season.

Winger Owen Nolan's deal also becomes an issue, as it contains a clause extending the contract by a year if the 2004–05 season is shortened or cancelled by a labour dispute. Nolan claims a knee injury suffered late in 2003–04 was misdiagnosed by the team's medical staff and he was wrongly pronounced fit to play. He seeks to be paid his 2004–05 salary. Nolan sits out the 2005–06 season, then signs with Phoenix in the summer of 2006. During the summer of 2005, many of the Leafs' medical team are replaced.

Notable Draft Choices

Anton Strålman (7th round, 216th overall), defence, Skövde IK (Sweden)
As a Leaf: 88 GP, 4 G, 18 A, 22 Pts, 38 PIM
Career to date: 88 GP, 4 G, 18 A, 22 Pts, 38 PIM

2005–06

82 GP • 41 W • 33 L • 8 OTL • 257 GF • 270 GA • 90 Pts • .500 Pct.
Division: Northeast
Finish: 4th of 5 (18th of 30)
Playoffs: Did not qualify
Coach: Pat Quinn
GM: John Ferguson Jr.

Aging winger Tie Domi is signed to a two-year contract extension. He's bought out at the end of this season. The Leafs also take a chance on Jason Allison, who was a high-scoring forward with Boston in the late 1990s but hasn't played since suffering a concussion in January 2003. He is judged too slow for the "new" NHL. Ferguson lands Eric Lindros, who misses most of the second half with a wrist injury.

The team never looks as if it will make an impact, and misses the playoffs for the first time since 1998. In April, Pat Quinn is fired as coach. His replacement, Paul Maurice, has been running the Leafs' farm team and it has always been assumed that he was the coach-in-waiting. As is so often the case, Leafs' optimism is ill-founded. In his two seasons behind the bench, Maurice fails to get the team into the playoffs.

Ferguson makes a good deal, signing Tomáš Kaberle to a five-year extension at an average of just over $4 million a year, then buys out Ed Belfour, whose play has declined steeply. But he signs defenceman Bryan McCabe to a five-year deal that is richer than Kaberle's and includes a no-movement clause.

Out

Mikael Renberg, RW—signed as a free agent with Luleå HF (Sweden), May 26, 2004

Tom Fitzgerald, C—signed as a free agent with Boston, July 28, 2004

Karel Pila, D—signed as a free agent with HC Sparta Praha (Czech Republic), August 1, 2004

Robert Reichel, C—signed as a free agent with HC Chemopetrol Litvinov (Czech Republic), August 20, 2004

Trevor Kidd, G—signed as a free agent with HC Örebro 90 (Sweden), January 31, 2005

Joe Nieuwendyk, C—signed as a free agent with Florida, August 1, 2005

Owen Nolan, LW—released, August 1, 2005

Gary Roberts, LW—signed as a free agent with Florida, August 1, 2005

Brian Leetch, D—signed as a free agent with Boston, August 3, 2005

Alexander Mogilny, RW—signed as a free agent with New Jersey, August 16, 2005

Ron Francis, C—retired, September 14, 2005

Bryan Marchment, D—signed as a free agent with Calgary, October 11, 2005

Nathan Perrott, RW—traded to Dallas, November 6, 2005

Mariusz Czerkawski, RW—claimed on waivers by Boston, March 8, 2006

Ken Klee, D—traded to New Jersey, March 8, 2006

In

Jeff O'Neill, C—traded from Carolina, July 30, 2005

Jason Allison, C—signed as a free agent, August 5, 2005

Alexander Khavanov, D—signed as a free agent, August 10, 2005

Eric Lindros, C—signed as a free agent, August 11, 2005

Mariusz Czerkawski, RW—signed as a free agent, September 8, 2005

Luke Richardson, D—traded from Columbus, March 8, 2006

Top Scorers

	GP	G	A	Pts	PIM
Mats Sundin	70	31	47	78	58
Bryan McCabe	73	19	49	68	116
Tomáš Kaberle	82	9	58	67	46
Darcy Tucker	74	28	33	61	100
Jason Allison	66	17	43	60	76

Goaltenders

	GP	MIN	GA	GAA	W–L–OTL	ShO
Mikael Tellqvist	25	1399	73	3.13	10–11–2	2
Ed Belfour	49	2897	159	3.29	22–22–4	0

Team Leaders

Games: Tomáš Kaberle, 82
Goals: Mats Sundin, 31
Assists: Tomáš Kaberle, 58
Points: Mats Sundin, 78
PIM: Bryan McCabe, 116

Leafs Among League Leaders

Tomáš Kaberle, tied for 10th in assists (58)
Alexei Ponikarovsky, tied for 8th in shorthanded goals (4)
Matt Stajan, tied for 8th in shorthanded goals (4)

Awards

None

Notable Draft Choices

Jiří Tlustý (1st round, 13th overall), left wing, Kladno
As a Leaf: 72 GP, 10 G, 10 A, 20 Pts, 14 PIM
Career to date: 72 GP, 10 G, 10 A, 20 Pts, 14 PIM

Nikolai Kulemin (2nd round, 44th overall), left wing, Magnito-
  gorsk Mettallurg
As a Leaf: 73 GP, 15 G, 16 A, 31 Pts, 18 PIM
Career to date: 73 GP, 15 G, 16 A, 31 Pts, 18 PIM

2006–07

82 GP • 40 W • 31 L • 11 OTL • 258 GF • 269 GA • 91 Pts • .488 Pct.
Division: Northeast
Finish: 3rd of 5 (18th of 30)
Playoffs: Did not qualify
Coach: Paul Maurice
GM: John Ferguson Jr.

Ferguson trades goalie prospect Tuukka Rask to Boston for former Calder Trophy–winner Andrew Raycroft. He also signs defence-man Pavel Kubina to a contract many view as overly generous. The Leafs miss the playoffs on the final day of the regular season, when the Islanders defeat New Jersey and end up with ninety-two points. In May 2007, MLSE decides that what the inexperienced Ferguson needs is a mentor. In the end, no such person is hired.

Out

Jason Allison, C—became a free agent
Aki Berg, D—signed as a free agent with TPS Turku (Finland), April 26, 2006
Ed Belfour, G—became a free agent after Leafs declined to exercise their option for 2006–07 season, June 30, 2006
Tie Domi, RW—contract bought out, June 30, 2006
Luke Richardson, D—signed as a free agent with Tampa Bay, July 11, 2006.
Eric Lindros, C—signed as a free agent with Dallas, July 17, 2006
Alexander Khavanov, D—signed as a free agent with HC Davos (Switzerland), September 17, 2006
Clarke Wilm, LW—signed as a free agent with Jokerit Helsinki (Finland), October 27, 2006
Mikael Tellqvist, G—traded to Phoenix, November 28, 2006
Brendan Bell, D—traded to Phoenix, February 27, 2007

In

Andrew Raycroft, G—traded from Boston, June 24, 2006
Hal Gill, D—signed as a free agent, July 1, 2006
Pavel Kubina, D—signed as a free agent, July 1, 2006
Mike Peca, C—signed as a free agent, July 18, 2006
Boyd Devereaux, C—signed as a free agent, October 7, 2006
Travis Green, C—claimed on waivers from Anaheim, January 10, 2007
Yanic Perreault, C—traded from Phoenix, February 27, 2007

Top Scorers

	GP	G	A	Pts	PIM
Mats Sundin	75	27	49	76	62
Tomáš Kaberle	74	11	47	58	20
Bryan McCabe	82	15	42	57	115
Alexei Ponikarovsky	71	21	24	45	63
Darcy Tucker	56	24	19	43	81

Goaltenders

	GP	MIN	GA	GAA	W–L–OTL	ShO
Andrew Raycroft	72	4108	205	2.99	37–25–9	2

Team Leaders

Games: 6 players tied with 82
Goals: Mats Sundin, 27
Assists: Mats Sundin, 49
Points: Mats Sundin, 76
PIM: Bryan McCabe, 115

Leafs Among League Leaders

Andrew Raycroft, 4th in games played in goal (72), tied for 8th in wins (37)
Mats Sundin, 7th in shots on goal (321)

Awards
None

Notable Draft Choices
Too early to tell, but none immediately apparent

2007–08
82 GP • 36 W • 35 L • 11 OTL • 231 GF • 260 GA • 83 Pts • .439 Pct.
Division: Northeast
Finish: 5th of 5 (23rd of 30)
Playoffs: Did not qualify
Coach: Paul Maurice
GM: John Ferguson Jr. (19–22–8), Cliff Fletcher (17–13–3)

John Ferguson makes what should be a good deal, acquiring goalie Vesa Toskala and forward Mark Bell from San Jose. But Toskala doesn't play as well as he did in San Jose, while Bell, who sits out a suspension for violating the league's substance-abuse program and faces a jail term for a drunk-driving offence, simply can no longer play at the NHL level.

In November, MLSE president Richard Peddie is quoted as saying it was a mistake to hire Ferguson. In January, Ferguson is sent packing and replaced by Cliff Fletcher on an interim basis. After the season, Fletcher fires Maurice and brings in Ron Wilson as coach.

Early in the season, Jason Blake—signed after a career year with the Islanders in which he scored forty goals—reveals he suffers from a rare but treatable form of leukemia. Although his offensive output slumps, he appears in all eighty-two games and is awarded the Bill Masterton Trophy at year's end.

Out

Jeff O'Neill, C—retired

Yanic Perreault, C—signed as a free agent with Chicago, July 1, 2007

Mike Peca, C—signed as a free agent with Columbus, August 22, 2007

Travis Green, C—signed as a free agent with EV Zug (Switzerland), November 5, 2007

Wade Belak, D—traded to Florida, February 26, 2008

Hal Gill, D—traded to Pittsburgh, February 26, 2008

Chad Kilger, LW—traded to Florida, February 26, 2008

In

Mark Bell, LW—traded from San Jose, June 22, 2007

Vesa Toskala, G—traded from San Jose, June 22, 2007

Jason Blake, LW—signed as a free agent, July 1, 2007

Dominic Moore, C—claimed on waivers from Minnesota, January 11, 2008

Top Scorers

	GP	G	A	Pts	PIM
Mats Sundin	74	32	46	78	76
Nikolai Antropov	72	26	30	56	92
Tomáš Kaberle	82	8	45	53	22
Jason Blake	32	15	37	52	28
Alexander Steen	76	15	27	42	32

Goaltenders

	GP	MIN	GA	GAA	W–L–OTL	ShO
Vesa Toskala	66	3837	175	2.74	33–25–6	3

Team Leaders

Games: Jason Blake, Tomáš Kaberle, Matt Stajan, 82

Goals: Mats Sundin, 32
Assists: Mats Sundin, 46
Points: Mats Sundin, 78
PIM: Bryan McCabe, 116

Leafs Among League Leaders
Jason Blake, 5th in shots on goal (332)
Vesa Toskala, tied for 9th in games played in goal (66), tied for 9th in wins (33)

Awards
Jason Blake, Bill Masterton Trophy (perseverance and sportsman-
  ship)

Notable Draft Choices
None immediately apparent

2008–09
82 GP • 34 W • 35 L • 13 OTL • 250 GF • 293 GA • 81 Pts • .415 Pct.
Division: Northeast
Finish: 5th of 5 (24th of 30)
Playoffs: Did not qualify
Coach: Ron Wilson
GM: Cliff Fletcher (7–9–6), Brian Burke (27–26–7)

Another Leaf captain departs under a cloud, amidst chaos in the front office. There is talk that Mats Sundin, the franchise's all-time leader in goals and points, may be moved at the trade deadline. Protesting that he does not believe in being a "rental player," and that he would rather win a Cup with a team he's been part of for the whole season, he refuses to waive the no-trade clause in his contract. A disgruntled segment of Leafs Nation, believing a Sundin trade could yield significant players or draft choices, brand him a "traitor."

The season ends, and Fletcher gives the Montreal Canadiens permission to try to work out a deal with Sundin. The problem is, Sundin can't decide *if* he wants to play in 2008–09, let alone where, and becomes a free agent on July 1. Summer passes, then autumn, without a decision. Finally, on December 18, he signs with the Vancouver Canucks, with whom he does not win the Stanley Cup.

Sundin is not the only member of the "Muskoka Five"—a quintet of players with no-trade, no-movement clauses in their contracts—to depart the scene. Darcy Tucker becomes a free agent and signs with Colorado, while Bryan McCabe is traded for the less-expensive Mike Van Ryn.

After insisting strenuously that he is not interested in the job, Brian Burke—widely assumed to be the team's saviour—is hired as the team's permanent GM. The Stanley Cup drought continues unabated.

Out

Johnny Pohl, C—signed as a free agent with HC Lugano (Switzerland), May 27, 2008

Andrew Raycroft, G—placed on waivers, June 24, 2008

Kyle Wellwood, C—claimed on waivers by Vancouver, June 25, 2008

Darcy Tucker, LW—signed as a free agent with Colorado, July 1, 2008

Andy Wozniewski, D—signed as a free agent with St. Louis, July 17, 2008

Bryan McCabe, D—traded to Florida, September 2, 2008

Carlo Colaiacovo, D—traded to St. Louis, November 24, 2008

Alexander Steen, LW—traded to St. Louis, November 24, 2008

Mats Sundin, C—signed as a free agent with Vancouver, December 18, 2008

Mark Bell, LW—claimed on waivers by N.Y. Rangers, February 25, 2009

Nikolai Antropov, RW—traded to N.Y. Rangers, March 4, 2009

Dominic Moore, C—traded to Buffalo, March 4, 2009

In

Jamal Mayers, RW—traded from St. Louis, June 19, 2008

Jeff Finger, D—signed as a free agent, July 1, 2008

Niklas Hagman, LW—signed as a free agent, July 1, 2008

Curtis Joseph, G—signed as a free agent, July 1, 2008

Mikhail Grabovski, C—traded from Montreal, July 3, 2008

Jonas Frögren, D—signed as a free agent, July 4, 2008

Ryan Hollweg, LW—traded from N.Y. Rangers, July 14, 2008

Mike Van Ryn, D—traded from Florida, September 2, 2008

Lee Stempniak, LW—traded from St. Louis, November 24, 2008

Brad May, LW—traded from Anaheim, January 7, 2009

Martin Gerber, G—claimed on waivers from Ottawa, March 4, 2009

Top Scorers

	GP	G	A	Pts	PIM
Jason Blake	78	25	38	63	40
Alexei Ponikarovsky	82	23	38	61	38
Matt Stajan	76	15	40	55	54
Mikhail Grabovski	78	20	28	48	92
Nikolai Antropov	63	21	25	46	24

Goaltenders

	GP	MIN	GA	GAA	W–L–OTL	ShO
Vesa Toskala	53	3056	166	3.26	22–17–11	1

Team Leaders

Games: Pavel Kubina, Alexei Ponikarovsky, 82
Goals: Jason Blake, 25
Assists: Matt Stajan, 40
Points: Jason Blake, 63
PIM: Pavel Kubina, 94

Leafs Among League Leaders

Jason Blake, 7th in shots on goal (302)

Awards

None

Notable Draft Choices

Luke Schenn (1st round, 5th overall), defence, Kelowna Rockets
As a Leaf: 70 GP, 2 G, 12 A, 14 Pts, 71 PIM
Career to date: 70 GP, 2 G, 12 A, 14 Pts, 71 PIM

18

Unsteady Hands at the Tiller: The Coaches Who Contributed to the Leafs' Stanley Cup Drought

George Armstrong (1988–89; record: 17 W, 26 L, 4 T, .404 Pct.)
During the Leafs' darkest days, after Gerry McNamara was bounced as general manager in favour of Gord Stellick, Ballard fired John Brophy and told Armstrong to take over the coaching reins for the rest of the 1988–89 season. Being the loyal Leaf that he was, Armstrong did it, explaining to the team that it wasn't his idea. The Leafs missed the playoffs.

Nick Beverley (1995–96; record: 9 W, 6 L, 2 T, .588 Pct.)
When Pat Burns was sent packing near the end of the 1995–96 season, Nick Beverley was called out of the front office to go behind the bench for the last seventeen games. Beverley was efficient and did a reasonable job, but he couldn't get the Leafs past the first round of the 1996 playoffs. They lost to the St. Louis Blues in six games.

John Brophy (1986–88; record: 64 W, 111 L, 18 T, .378 Pct.)
One of the legendary tough guys of minor-league hockey, Brophy insisted on a hard-nosed approach to the game. Since GM Gerry McNamara had a penchant for bringing in soft Czechoslovaks, the mix was not a good one. Brophy took over the team in 1986 and lasted almost halfway through the 1988–89 season, his brightest moment being an opening-round defeat of the St. Louis Blues in the 1987 playoffs. It was the only round he ever won.

Pat Burns (1992–96; record: 133 W, 107 L, 41 T, .546 Pct.)
Burns was a true taskmaster who insisted on putting defence first. His centres, he liked to say, were "busier than a one-legged man in an ass-kicking contest." On offence, he seemed more interested in getting the puck behind the net rather than in it. He arrived in 1992 and left in 1996, having twice taken the team to the conference final and giving Leafs fans of the era more hope than they had enjoyed in decades.

Doug Carpenter (1989–90; record: 39 W, 47 L, 5 T, .456 Pct.)
Carpenter spent almost four years with the New Jersey Devils, missing the playoffs three times and getting fired in the fourth. At that point, Jim Schoenfeld took over and got the team to the conference final. Based on that stellar record, Carpenter was clearly Leafs material. In his one full season with the Leafs, 1989–90, he scraped

into the playoffs and was gone in five games. He was fired eleven games into the next season.

King Clancy (1966–67, 1971–72; record: 16 W, 4 L, 5 T, .740 Pct.)
The Hall of Fame defenceman whom everybody loved stepped into the breach a couple of times to help out. The first time, in the Stanley Cup season of 1966–67, he filled in for Punch Imlach and lost only twice in ten games, winning seven. In 1971–72, he replaced John McLellan for fifteen games, guiding the Leafs to a 9–3–3 record. Perhaps they should have hired him full time.

Joe Crozier (1980–81; record: 13 W, 22 L, 5 T, .388 Pct.)
Although Punch Imlach was the coach of record for the last ten games of the 1979–80 season, it was his crony Joe Crozier who stood behind the bench. The Leafs won five of the ten games and made the playoffs, but they were promptly swept by the Minnesota North Stars. Next season, with the Crow officially installed as coach, the Leafs managed to win only 13 of their first 40, and he was axed.

Dick Duff (1979–80; record: 0 W, 2 L, 0 T, .000 Pct.)
Another one of the disasters of that fateful 1979–80 season was Imlach's attempt to put Dick Duff behind the bench. Duff was an old-time Maple Leaf who, to put it charitably, was not widely revered for his work ethic. The players were at war with Imlach and weren't about to put forth their best effort for one of his friends.

Punch Imlach (1959–69, 1979–80; record: 365 W, 270 L, 125 T, .563 Pct.)
More than anyone else, Imlach was responsible for the devastation that followed the Leafs' last Stanley Cup win in 1967. He was behind the bench for that Cup, but he was also a major reason why they haven't won one since. In an earlier era, Imlach's hardline approach had been successful, but when the world changed, Imlach didn't.

Red Kelly (1973–77; record: 133 W, 123 L, 62 T, .516 Pct.)
There was little chance for the Leafs to win any Stanley Cups during the Kelly era. At that time, the Montreal Canadiens were one of the best teams in NHL history. Kelly tried his best, even resorting to the mysticism of "pyramid power," which was supposed to elevate the players' skills, but he suffered the usual fate of Leafs coaches.

Dan Maloney (1984–86; record: 45 W, 100 L, 15 T, .328 Pct.)
Given the kind of mentality that governed the Leafs in those days, there was a very good reason for Maloney to be named as coach: he couldn't play at the NHL level anymore, but his contract had not expired. Rather than pay Maloney to do nothing, Ballard put him behind the bench—another example of profits taking precedence. The results were predictable.

Paul Maurice (2006–08; record: 76 W, 66 L, 22 OTL, .463 Pct.)
Before arriving in Toronto, Maurice was a good coach, having taken the Carolina Hurricanes to the Stanley Cup final. When he left Toronto, he was a good coach again, taking the undermanned Hurricanes to the 2009 conference final. In between, he spent two mediocre years in Toronto, sealing his own fate when he said his 2007–08 team was playoff material.

John McLellan (1969–73; record: 126 W, 139 L, 45 T, .479 Pct.)
When Imlach was fired as Leafs coach for the first time, in 1969, McLellan came in to replace him. Unlike many who were to follow, McLellan was a good coach and was even voted coach of the year in 1971. He resigned in 1973 to become assistant general manager and was a stabilizing force in the front office, but he died from a heart attack in 1979 when he was only fifty one.

Mike Murphy (1996–98; record: 60 W, 87 L, 17 T, .418 Pct.)
Because the New Jersey Devils had won the 1995 Stanley Cup with a skill-killing trap, the concept was being copied leaguewide. When Murphy became Leafs coach in 1996, he quickly decided that his team was short on offensive skill and would therefore have to play a game predicated almost totally on defence. After missing the playoffs in both his seasons, Murphy was fired.

Roger Neilson (1977–79; record: 75 W, 62 L, 23 T, .541 Pct.)
It was typical of Ballard that his response to a thoughtful and innovative coach was to ridicule him. Neilson arrived in 1977 and was fired in 1979, but Ballard hadn't bothered to arrange a replacement. Furthermore, public outrage was widespread, so Ballard brought him back. He wanted Neilson to emerge from the dressing room with a bag over his head, but Neilson refused. After the season, he was fired again, this time permanently.

Mike Nykoluk (1981–84; record: 89 W, 144 L, 47 T, .402 Pct.)
Following an extensive search—all the way to the radio booth, where Nykoluk was working as a colour man on Leafs broadcasts—Ballard found a coach to take over his sad-sack team in 1980. In three and a half seasons, Nykoluk finished last in his division three times. The Leafs qualified for the playoffs twice and went out in the first round both times.

Pat Quinn (1998–2006; record: 300 W, 186 L, 52 T, 26 OTL, .568 Pct.)
When Quinn replaced Murphy, he immediately ditched the defence-first approach and got the Leafs playing exciting hockey. Quinn had been one of the best coaches in the league, and although some of the game had passed him by, he was still forceful and competent enough to make the Leafs respectable for most of his tenure. But he never got the team to the Stanley Cup final.

Floyd Smith (1979–80; 30 W, 33 L, 5 T, .478 Pct.)
The coaching career of Floyd Smith is probably best encapsulated by his famous statement (following yet another loss), "I've got nothing to say and I'm only going to say it once." At that time, he was coaching the Buffalo Sabres—a job he had been awarded by his old buddy Imlach. He got his Leafs job the same way, but in neither case did he excel.

Tom Watt (1990–92; 52 W, 80 L, 17 T, .406 Pct.)
Having established losing records with both the Winnipeg Jets and the Vancouver Canucks, Watt had the perfect background for a Leafs coach of that era. He was brought in for the 1990–91 season and lasted two years, both of which saw the Leafs finish last in their division. Even in that era, that wasn't good enough to qualify for the playoffs.

Ron Wilson (2008–09; 34 W, 35 L, 13 OTL, .415 Pct.)
After being unable to win the Stanley Cup with the highly talented San Jose Sharks, Wilson was released and quickly snapped up by interim general manager Cliff Fletcher. Despite Wilson's credentials as a strong special-teams coach, the Leafs did not excel in those areas, to put it mildly, and once again missed the playoffs.

19

The Ones That Got Away: Looking Back at Leaf Drafts

In March 1996, when general manager Cliff Fletcher sent a first-round pick to Long Island to reacquire popular winger Wendel Clark, he responded to critics by saying, "Draft, shmaft. This is show business." The words came back to haunt him when he returned as GM in January 2008 and pronounced, "Today, if you want to compete, you have to draft well and develop your own core of players."

The fact is, the Leafs have taken a rather cavalier approach to the draft over the years. During the Ballard era, money spent on scouting was considered to be money wasted. The nadir was reached in 1989, when Toronto stumbled into a trio of first-round picks, and used all of them to take players—none particularly distinguished—from the Belleville Bulls.

Not to be overlooked are the years when they did draft quality players (such as Rick Kehoe in 1971, Randy Carlyle in '76, or Doug Jarvis in '75) and traded them to teams that were quicker to spot their true value.

In fairness, the Leafs did draft a pair of Hall of Famers in 1970 (Darryl Sittler) and 1973 (Lanny McDonald). And it must be said that every team, no matter how talented its scouting staff might be, misses out on some quality players. But the Leafs seemed to have a knack for missing out on more prospects than most.

What follows is a look at the annual drafts, along with some of the players the Leafs might have landed if they had drafted more judiciously. The list runs from 1969, when the amateur draft in its current format was established, to 2004. Players drafted after that year haven't had a reasonable chance to develop.

1969

With the ninth-overall pick, Leafs take Ernie Moser, a right wing from the Estevan Bruins. He never played a single NHL game. Still available: Bobby Clarke, a centre from the Flin Flon Bombers who scored 358 goals and 852 assists for 1,210 points in 1,144 NHL games. He won two Stanley Cups and was inducted into the Hockey Hall of Fame in 1987.

1970

Having chosen one Hall of Famer in Darryl Sittler and a prolific scorer in Errol Thompson, the Leafs chose Gerry O'Flaherty, a right wing from the Kitchener Rangers, 36th overall. He scored 99 goals and 95 assists in 438 games, most of them with Vancouver.

But there was still a Hall of Famer to be had: goaltender Billy Smith (taken 59th overall by Los Angeles), who played 680 NHL games, all with the New York Islanders, won four Stanley Cups and was inducted in 1993.

1971

The Leafs had sent their first-round pick to Philadelphia in exchange for Bernie Parent. A fair deal—especially if they'd been able to hold onto the future Hall of Fame goalie. In the second round, 20th overall, the Canadiens drafted defenceman Larry Robinson—another future Hall of Famer with six Stanley Cup championships, two Norris Trophies and a Conn Smythe Trophy to his credit.

1972

The Leafs kicked things off by claiming a Toronto Marlboro, centre George Ferguson, 11th overall. With the 33rd-overall pick, the Islanders landed Bob Nystrom, a 200-goal scorer who was a key part of their four championship teams. In the sixth round, Buffalo took a flier on a University of Denver alum, Peter McNab (363 career goals). To their credit, Toronto found Pat Boutette, a small (five foot eight) but gritty forward in the ninth round. He would have his best years with Hartford and Pittsburgh.

1973

Toronto had three first-round selections this year, and hit home runs with two of them: future Hall of Famer Lanny McDonald (4th overall) and defenceman Ian Turnbull (15th), who contributed greatly to the Leafs' offence throughout the 1970s. In between, they chose defenceman Bob Neely 10th overall. Imagine what the Leafs might have looked like had they grabbed 400-goal scorer Rick Middleton from the Oshawa Generals (drafted 14th overall by the Rangers).

1974

Picking 13th overall, the Leafs chose centre Jack Valiquette (84 goals and 218 points in 350 NHL games). Nine slots later, the Islanders drafted centre Bryan Trottier, a 500-goal scorer and six-time Cup winner who entered the Hall of Fame in 1997.

1975

With the sixth-overall pick, the Leafs took centre Don Ashby (188 games, 40 goals). They followed that up with Doug Jarvis, an excellent player whom they foolishly dealt to the Montreal Canadiens. Next came career minor leaguer Bruce Boudreau and three players who never saw any NHL action. Along the way, they managed to draft a future coach (Ron Wilson) and a future GM (Ken Holland), but still no legitimate NHL prospects. After the 13th round, they stopped picking. In the 15th round, 210th overall, the Los Angeles Kings drafted Dave Taylor—431 goals and 1,069 points in 1,111 NHL games.

1976

Lacking a first-rounder, the Leafs picked Randy Carlyle in the second round. With their next two choices, they took the immortal Alain Bélanger and Gary McFadyen, both times overlooking Swedish centre Kent Nilsson (drafted 64th overall by Atlanta), who scored 264 goals in 553 NHL games and won a Stanley Cup with Edmonton in 1987. He also won back-to-back Avco Cups with Winnipeg in the WHA, where he put together successive 100-point seasons. Ironically, the Toronto Toros chose Nilsson in the first round, 11th overall, in the 1976 WHA draft.

1977

With consecutive picks (11th and 12th overall) in the first round, Toronto took left winger John Anderson and defenceman Trevor

Johansen. With one of those picks, they might have taken Mike Bossy, one of the most prolific scorers in NHL history (573 goals in just 752 games), a four-time Cup champion and a Hall of Fame inductee in 1991.

1978

Defenceman Joel Quenneville (second round, 21st overall) was a sound choice, though he was dealt to Colorado along with Lanny McDonald midway through his second season. But they followed that up with the likes of Mark Kirton, Jordy Douglas, Mel Hewitt, John Scammell and Kevin Reinhart. All the while, Darryl Sutter was waiting to be taken, 179th overall, by Chicago.

1979

Going by the Leafs' picks, you'd never know this was considered the greatest draft class in NHL history. In the first round, Toronto chose Laurie Boschman—who, stop me if you've heard this one, developed into a decent NHL player only after he was traded away. His linemate in Brandon, Brian Propp, had the good fortune to be drafted five slots later by Philadelphia, for whom he scored the bulk of his 425 career goals. The Leafs went on to select Normand Aubin, Vincent Tremblay and Frank Nigro, apparently not noticing Thomas Steen. Winnipeg did, and grabbed him 103rd overall. He played fourteen seasons for the Jets, racking up more than 800 points.

1980

Back in 1977–78, Harold Ballard wanted so badly to acquire Detroit winger Dan Maloney that he traded the team's first-round pick in this draft to acquire him. If he'd invested in scouting, he'd have held onto the pick (11th overall) and perhaps even taken a better player in Brent Sutter. With a pair of second-round picks and a third-rounder, they took defencemen Craig Muni, Bob McGill and Fred Boimistruck.

Still available in the fourth round: future Hall of Famer Jari Kurri. And if the xenophobic Ballard couldn't bring himself to sign off on that choice, Bernie Nicholls was chosen even later in the fourth.

1981

It's often said in hockey: "Build from the net out." We must conclude that Harold Ballard never got that memo, or else he'd have used the 6th-overall pick on Hall of Fame netminder Grant Fuhr (who went two spots later to Edmonton). The Leafs clearly believed the solution was to keep stockpiling young defencemen and rushing them into the lineup with a minimum of seasoning. This year's victim: Jim Benning (sparing Al MacInnis, Calgary's 15th-overall choice, who was inducted into the Hall of Fame in 2007).

1982

Defenceman Scott Stevens, taken fifth overall, entered the Hall of Fame the same year as MacInnis. So you know he wasn't drafted by Toronto—he went to Washington. The Leafs took Gary Nylund, a big, physical defenceman who could move the puck a little. Who knows how his career might have panned out had he not injured a knee during a pre-season game in 1982, forcing him to miss a good chunk of the next two seasons. Or if the Leafs had had a clue of how to develop a defenceman. Or if they hadn't given up on him in 1986. Or if they hadn't drafted him in the first place . . .

1983

The Leafs found a decent player in the first round in Russ Courtnall. If only they'd recognized that fact, rather than trading him for John Kordic five years later. Beyond that, a thin gruel. Somehow, they managed not to see anything in Toronto Marlboros centre Peter Zezel (taken 41st overall by Philadelphia, 200 goals in more than 800 games), Esa Tikkanen (80th overall by Edmonton, five

Stanley Cups) or Rick Tocchet (Flyers again, 121st overall, more than 400 NHL goals). Given Gerry McNamara's weakness for Czech players, you'd think they'd have taken a flier on Petr Klíma (Detroit, 86th overall) or Dominik Hašek (Chicago, 199th overall). We can only conclude the difference is that these were *good* players.

1984

Al Iafrate, whom the Leafs drafted fourth overall, tied Ian Turnbull's team record for goals by a defenceman (22). He was a fast skater and his powerful shot from the point rivalled MacInnis's. But he was a high-risk, high-reward player. Todd Gill, taken in the second round, was a steadier presence, albeit nowhere near as likely to appear on the nightly highlight package. In the sixth round, they went with centre Fabian Joseph, who never played in the NHL, bypassing Brett Hull (117th overall). In the ninth round, Los Angeles found 600-goal scorer Luc Robitaille, while the Flames landed high-scoring defenceman Gary Suter.

1985

Leafs had the first pick overall, and Craig Simpson of Michigan State University warned that he wouldn't sign with them if they drafted him. So they took Wendel Clark, who history suggests was the better choice anyway. But they followed that up by taking defenceman Ken Spangler—who never played a shift in the NHL—22nd overall. Picking five spots later, Calgary came up with Joe Nieuwendyk, who scored 500 goals and helped three different teams to win the Stanley Cup. The Leafs finally landed him, via free agency, in 2003–04. After the lockout, he signed with Florida.

1986

Drafting sixth overall, the Leafs selected a major scoring threat in Vincent Damphousse (432 goals over seventeen years). However, he was dealt to Edmonton after just five years and went on to win the Stanley Cup with Montreal in 1993. In the third round, 48th overall, they took defenceman Sean Boland, who never turned pro. Pittsburgh's fourth-round choice, winger Rob Brown, racked up 49 goals and 115 points in just his second season. Granted, those numbers were easier to achieve with Mario Lemieux passing him the puck. But he might've been a nice complement to a player of Damphousse's calibre.

1987

The Leafs' seventh-overall selection, Luke Richardson, is emblematic of the John Brophy era in Toronto, when brawn trumped brains at every opportunity. While Richardson hung on for twenty-one years and more than 1,400 NHL games, it must be pointed out that the Quebec Nordiques' 15th-overall pick, Joe Sakic, is the eighth-highest scorer in NHL history with 1,641 points and has won the Stanley Cup twice.

1988

Maybe if Jeremy Roenick, Rod Brind'Amour or Teemu Selanne had been playing in eastern Ontario, the Leafs would have drafted them. Instead, they chose Scott Pearson (292 games, 56 goals) from the Kingston Canadians.

1989

By the Chinese calendar, 1989 was the year of the snake. By all accounts, the Leafs' scouting department thought it was the year of the Bull. With three first-round picks at their disposal, they spent them all on members of the Belleville Bulls, who finished next to last in their division in the Ontario Hockey League. They chose Scott Thornton third overall, leaving Bill Guerin available for the New Jersey Devils. He was part of the Penguins' Stanley

Cup win in 2009. They took Rob Pearson 12th, leaving Olaf Kolzig to the Washington Capitals. And 21st, they took Steve Bancroft. With the very next pick, Quebec selected Adam Foote, who won two Stanley Cups and an Olympic gold medal.

1990

Going back to Kingston this year, the Leafs drafted defenceman Drake Berehowsky 10th overall. Nine spots later, Winnipeg took future 500-goal scorer Keith Tkachuk. With the next pick, New Jersey claimed goaltender Martin Brodeur, the NHL's all-time leader in wins, with 557, and a three-time Stanley Cup champion.

1991

Leafs would have had the third pick overall, except they traded it to New Jersey for defenceman Tom Kurvers. Kurvers lasted eighty nine games in Toronto, while the Devils chose defenceman Scott Niedermayer with the pick. Niedermayer, who announced he would return to play in 2009–10, is still a productive offensive defenceman who has played on four Stanley Cup winners. The Leafs finally got a chance to draft in the third round and took Yanic Perreault, a player with an uncanny ability to win faceoffs, but not much else to commend him. In the fourth, they chose forward Terry Chitaroni from the Sudbury Wolves. They must have had a lot of faith in Kurvers; otherwise, they might have drafted defenceman Alexei Zhitnik, who was still available at 81st overall.

1992

Brandon Convery scored 40 goals in 44 games for the Sudbury Wolves in 1991–92, and the Leafs couldn't help but notice. They took him eighth overall. With the 14th pick, Washington selected Russian defenceman (and rushing defenceman) Sergei Gonchar.

Still one of the league's highest-scoring blueliners, he was a vital part of Pittsburgh's Stanley Cup victory in 2009.

1993

With a pair of first-rounders, the Leafs acquired defenceman Kenny Jönsson and winger Landon Wilson. Jönsson made the All-Rookie Team and showed some potential before being traded for Wendel Clark. Wilson never played a game in Toronto. After those two were off the board, Montreal picked their future captain, Saku Koivu, while the Islanders claimed Todd Bertuzzi.

1994

This wasn't a particularly deep draft, but history suggests that, instead of goaltender Éric Fichaud, netminder Evgeni Nabokov would have been the better choice.

1995

From the Oshawa Generals, the Leafs chose defenceman Jeff Ware 15th overall. He played twenty-one NHL games, recording a single assist. With the next pick, Buffalo took goalie Martin Biron. Another good netminder, Miikka Kiprusoff, was still around in the fifth round.

1996

The Leafs didn't have a pick until the second round, 36th overall, and they chose Czech defenceman Marek Posmyk. Twenty spots later, the Islanders selected Slovak defenceman Zdeno Chára, who won the Norris Trophy in 2009.

1997

This year, Toronto had to wait until the third round, 57th overall. Their pick was Boston College centre Jeff Farkas, who appeared in

eleven games and assisted on two goals. With the 156th pick, Buffalo chose Brian Campbell, a defenceman with some offensive skill.

1998

Tenth overall, the Leafs chose lanky Kazakh forward Nikolai
Antropov. Over the next decade, fans would be both tantalized and
frustrated as his flashes of talent were interspersed with frequent
injuries. In 2007 he finally broke through, scoring 26 goals, but he
was traded to the Rangers at the deadline in 2009. Similarly, it took
their fourth-round selection, Alexei Ponikarovsky, a few years to
establish himself as a consistent 20-goal scorer. In the sixth round,
154th overall, they took Kitchener defenceman Allan Rourke. With
selection number 171, Detroit came up with Pavel Datsyuk.

1999

It's a hard luck story: Swiss centre Luca Cereda, whom the Leafs
drafted 24th overall, had a heart defect that required surgery, effec-
tively ending his hopes of becoming an NHL player. Two spots later,
Ottawa was more fortunate with its choice of Martin Havlát.

2000

In the first round, the Leafs took centre Brad Boyes from the Erie
Otters. For any other team, he would have gone on to play a prominent role, anchoring one of the top two lines. And Boyes certainly
would do that—for other teams, of course. In March 2003, in the
midst of a supposed youth movement, Boyes was sent to San Jose
as part of the deal that brought thirty-one-year-old winger Owen
Nolan to Toronto. (In the same "youth movement," Curtis Joseph
was replaced with Ed Belfour, two years his senior.) Boyes scored 26
goals for Boston in 2005–06, then put together seasons of 43 and 33
goals for St. Louis. The rest of the draft failed to yield a player of any
concern for the Leafs, while Los Angeles found rushing defenceman

Lubomir Visnovsky in the fourth round and Buffalo chose a good two-way forward, Paul Gaustad, in the seventh.

2001

Seventeenth overall, the Leafs drafted defenceman Carlo Colaia-covo. While he showed some potential, he was frequently injured and in one of Cliff Fletcher's last moves was traded to St. Louis. In the second round they took Karel Pilař, a big defenceman who had a hard shot and some skill in his own end. But he was twice stricken with viral myopathy in his heart, and since 2004 has shuttled between Europe and the AHL. Later in the second round, Los Angeles drafted centre Mike Cammaleri, a native of the Toronto suburb of Richmond Hill, who has scored 30 goals in two of his four full NHL seasons.

2002

Alexander Steen goes to the Leafs 24th overall. He scores 18 goals in his rookie season of 2005–06, but proves to be inconsistent and falls out of favour with coach Ron Wilson in 2008–09. He's traded to St. Louis. In the second round, 57th overall, they choose Matt Stajan, a forward with an abundance of smarts, if not a natural scorer's touch. He becomes a regular right away, but struggles to establish himself as more than a third-line forward on a team that is infamous for accumulating third-line forwards. In the later rounds, they select Swedish defenceman Staffan Kronwall 285th overall. He has size and is capable defensively, but is injury-prone. The Leafs waive him in February 2009, and he's claimed by Washington. Meanwhile, with the 291st and final pick, Detroit takes another Swede, Jonathan Ericsson, who has the potential to play on the Wings' top defence pair.

2003

The Leafs don't draft until the second round, 57th overall. They pick John Doherty, a big (six foot four, 235 pound) defenceman from a Massachusetts prep school who struggles to crack the lineup at the University of New Hampshire. He plays 34 games in the low minors. Five spots later, St. Louis takes right winger David Backes, who also goes the college route but makes his team, reaches the NHL in 2006–07, and breaks through with 31 goals and 165 penalty minutes in 2008–09.

2004

Another year where the Leafs spend a lot of time waiting. This time, their first pick is in the third round, 90th overall. They choose goalie Justin Pogge. He wins the MVP award in the Western Hockey League in 2006 and is named goaltender of the year in all of Canadian junior hockey. He makes his NHL debut during the 2008–09 season. Was there a better pick? Well, how about Johan Franzen, claimed by Detroit with the 97th pick? At this writing, the winger is coming off seasons in which he scored 27 and 34 goals, along with 25 more in the playoffs during the Wings' two runs to the Stanley Cup final.

Acknowledgments

When Brian Wood suggested the idea for this book, my first reaction was laughter. "Why the Leafs suck? How many volumes do you want?" And as it happened, one of the biggest difficulties with writing a book faithful to this concept was keeping it down to a suitable length. The Ballard years alone could have been turned into an almost endless recitation of one lunacy after another.

For those of us who lived through that era, the stories are innumerable and unforgettable. But the majority of Ballard's travesties were perpetrated more than a quarter-century ago, and most of today's Leafs fans are too young to care. So instead of writing a history of the Leafs, I have attempted to provide a series of glimpses into their distant past before focusing on the team's more recent failures and the people responsible for them.

A lot of good friends helped me arrive at this decision and contributed sage advice in other areas. Pierre LeBrun was wonderful, as he always is. Scott Morrison, who was in the front lines for many of the Leafs' worst debacles, was an ally as well. Steve Kouleas, a walking compendium of Leafs lore, was good enough to read some of the chapters and point out some oversights.

Steve Buffery, who provided invaluable assistance in a manner that should best be kept confidential, has my eternal gratitude, and so does Roy MacGregor, as insightful a hockey writer as the sport has ever seen. Every hockey parent should read his collection of stories, *The Seven A.M. Practice.*

Dave Carter and Gail MacDonald were always there for support. Gillian Goddard at the *Toronto Sun* went far beyond the call of duty in helping select and procure the photographs for the book. Thanks also to Don Meehan, Wayne Gretzky and Lawrence Martin for their time and cooperation, as well as to the above-mentioned Brian Wood.

Marian Strachan provided the initial editing, a job she performed uncommonly well, having had a lot of practice cleaning up my mistakes over the years. Brad Wilson of HarperCollins and freelance editor Lloyd Davis's valuable editorial work made the final product complete.

Lucie Leduc provided her usual support, and if her optimism is any indication of the reading public's enthusiasm, the book will be well received indeed.

And of course there's Christie Blatchford, my landlady when I'm in Toronto, who likes to say that having me around the house provides all the misery of a marriage without the compensation of sex. She was involved in every aspect of the book's development. Having read her own excellent work, *Fifteen Days*, I was willing to pay some attention when she offered advice (not a course of action that should be followed indiscriminately).

As is always the case in these matters, despite the help of these contributors, there is bound to be a mistake or two. If this is so, the fault is mine.